WITHDRAWN FROM
THE LIBRARY

Literature and Society in Medieval France
The Mirror and the Image 1100–1500

D1440486

Literature and Society in Medieval France

The Mirror and the Image 1100–1500

Lynette R. Muir

MACMILLAN

© Lynette R. Muir 1985

All rights reserved. No reproduction, copy or transmission
of this publication may be made without written permission.

No paragraph of this publication may be reproduced, copied
or transmitted save with written permission or in accordance
with the provisions of the Copyright Act 1956 (as amended).

Any person who does any unauthorised act in relation to
this publication may be liable to criminal prosecution and
civil claims for damages.

First published 1985

Published by
Higher and Further Education Division
MACMILLAN PUBLISHERS LTD
Houndmills, Basingstoke, Hampshire RG21 2XS
and London
Companies and representatives
throughout the world

Typeset by
Wessex Typesetters
Frome, Somerset

Printed in Hong Kong

British Library Cataloguing in Publication Data
Muir, Lynette R.
Literature and society in medieval France: the mirror
and the image 1100–1500.—(New studies
in medieval history)
1. French literature – to 1500
2. Literature and society
I. Title   II. Series
840'.1   PQ151
ISBN 0–333–32557–5
ISBN 0–333–32558–3 (Pbk)

KING ALFRED'S COLLEGE
WINCHESTER

840.9
MU| 0218939

Contents

List of Plates

1. William prepares to capture Nîmes with barrel-loads of armed knights. © British Library.
2. Lancelot forces his way into Guinevere's bed-chamber – with her permission. © British Library.
3. The secular clergy were often on very friendly terms with their parishioners. © Bibliothèque de l'Arsenal, Paris.
4. The world is round, like an apple, with all matter falling towards the centre. © Bibliothèque de la Ville de Rennes.
5. Even at the bottom of the sea, Alexander discovers the strong preying on the weak. © British Library.
6. Alexander is raised to new heights by a team of gryphons. © British Library.
7. This mirror offers the ladies a warning image of what they will one day become. © Herzog August Bibliothek, Wolfenbüttel, Germany.
8. The Pilgrim nearly falls into the clutches of Avarice. © British Library.
9. The *sots* construct their ideal world on very insecure foundations. © Helen Taylor. Based on photographs of the Liège production.
10. With his wife's help, Pathelin makes delirious fun of his creditor, the gullible draper. © The Medieval Players.

Acknowledgements

This book grew out of a discussion with the late Denis Bethell on the relationship between literature and history and the benefits that might accrue from more wide-ranging and general exchanges of ideas and information between scholars working in the two disciplines.

The preparation of such a book would have been impossible without the help and advice of many people. First and foremost I would like to recall with gratitude the contribution of Denis Bethell himself; his breadth of interest, love of literature and ability to cite the most recondite texts was a constant stimulus and joy to his friends in other fields of study.

I would also like to express my sincere gratitude to his successor as General Editor of the series, Dr Maurice Keen, who has been most helpful in presenting the historian's view-point and most patient with my many questions; and to Sarah Mahaffy, Vanessa Peerless and Valery Rose of Macmillan for their assistance and interest.

Many of my colleagues at Leeds and elsewhere have made suggestions, answered questions or provided references; Elizabeth Williams and Gwilym Rees have been most helpful in checking the typescript and the proofs; Barbara Gill typed the Genealogical Tables, Jenifer Fairpo compiled the Bibliographical Index. The Medieval Players provided me with the photograph of the *Farce of Pathelin* and Madame Jeanne Wathelet-Willem of the University of Liège went to considerable trouble to make available to me photographs of the *sottie*; I am most grateful to all of them.

But for the help of so many people, there would be many more errors of omission and commission in this book. For those that remain the fault and the responsibility are mine. *Mea culpa.*

Guide to the Presentation of the Texts

All the works referred to in this volume are identified by English titles with the original French given, once only, in parentheses. Quotations have a reference title in parentheses after them, either the author or, where appropriate, a short form of the title, normally the English one. Sometimes, however, the French version is used to avoid confusion between, for example, the many *Mirrors*, or to facilitate reference to the entries in Appendix IV.

No secondary literature is quoted but suggestions for further reading are given with the notes to each chapter (Appendix II). Appendix III is a list of modern English translations of medieval French texts and Appendix IV comprises an alphabetically arranged Bibliographical Index of all the medieval French texts cited, with a selection of other topics and references. Bibliographical sources for the editions used are also included.

As many of the works discussed in the book are not available in English, all quotations have been translated direct from the original French and the volume, page and line references are to the French editions. With very few exceptions the translations are in prose. In addition to the normal abbreviations, the letter 'S' indicates a paragraph, section, *laisse* or chapter. Verse references are given without any preceding letter, for example (567–8). Biblical quotations are translated from the Vulgate.

1. Introduction: the Mirror and the Image

> A queer thing is a mirror; a picture-frame that holds
> hundreds of different pictures, all vivid and all vanished
> for ever.
>
> (G. K. Chesterton)

'IN THE beginning was the Word . . . and the Word was God',
'And God formed Man from the dust of the ground and
breathed into his nostrils the breath of life' (John 1:1; Genesis
2:7). We can recreate the body of medieval man from the dust of
archaeology and archive but only the words of the poets can
breathe life into the historian's clay.

In this survey of the French literature of the Middle Ages
I have tried to give a picture of medieval society in France as it
saw itself, mirrored in its own literature, with all the truth and
also the subjective distortion of such a reflection. The choice of
what to include from the immense mass of available material –
more than a million lines of religious drama alone – has
generally been made on grounds of content and relevance to
contemporary society rather than literary merit. The masterpieces of the period rub shoulders with more modest works and
authors of few literary pretensions, for the popular literature of
an age can tell us as much about the public that enjoyed it as the
more esoteric or highbrow winners of literary prizes; indeed,
the great masterpieces often have a universality that transcends
contextual reality. Yet this reality of detail, revealed in the
throw-away remark, the trite phrase, the half-line that completes a rhyming couplet, can be a rich mine of information-
bearing rock.

It is axiomatic that a man may be known by his friends, and
that books are silent friends; *ergo* (as the scholastics would say)
it must be possible to know a man by his books, and if a man
then a whole society; for the prejudices of a character reveal the
problems of a period and its social conditions shape its songs
and stories. The Middle Ages had no concept of 'literature' in
the limited, modern, examination-syllabus sense; just as a

'romance' at first simply meant a work written in French and not in Latin, so literature was all that was written, embracing the whole cultural experience of society – in modern terms not merely the highbrow novels, plays and poems of the élite but also whodunits, soap-opera, magazine stories and Marvel comics. Until recently, this literature has been at best neglected, at worst rejected scornfully by the historian as partial, subjective, biased and unreliable, in every way unworthy of a place in serious historical study.

Medieval literature is fundamentally and continually didactic. Not only, as in later ages, in its desire to give pleasure and instruction at one and the same time, but in its commitment to educating man for his role in the society of his time, whether it be by examples of Christian heroism in the *chansons de geste*, or advice to the courtly lover; a reminder of the cunning of women and the verbal dexterity of lawyers in the *fabliaux* and farces, or the pedantic exposition of the encyclopaedists; the castigation of the sins of this world by the moralists, or the religious writers' counsel to the pilgrim on his way to the next. In its efforts to teach contemporary man, such literature can also be very informative to his twentieth-century successor. Obviously, many details of daily life and manners may be gleaned from narratives, in the same way that we see tiny pictures in the margins of the illuminated manuscripts, but more useful still, I think, is what these texts tell us about the people themselves, their likes and dislikes, fears and joys, heroes and ideals. The outward forms can be easily detected in art as well as in literature but the poets who are bound to please their audience or starve can best give a really clear indication of the sentiments and tastes of the age.

As we shall see in the examples quoted, especially in chapters 5 and 6, the social and moral pressures of the Middle Ages are often the same as our own, even if we may call 'anti-social behaviour' what they called 'sin'. Both then and now the stress, reflected in literature, is on the tension between man's individual needs and his social obligations. The pressure of the group, be it castle or court, city or religious community, forced man to conform to a rigid social code of behaviour or face the consequences. At the beginning of the period, in the twelfth century, the community was pre-eminent and man sought to know and understand himself by his reactions and interplay with other members of his peer group. By the fifteenth century, at the end of the Middle Ages, the emphasis in literature has shifted markedly, reflecting almost certainly a comparable social development. Society and the individual are now the two poles, and the need to maintain a tenuous balance between them is the main preoccupation of the authors and their creations: as the Creation is the mirror of God so, too, is literature the mirror of its creator: society.

The French Reflection

WITH only minimal written records of its linguistic evolution, and virtually no literature before 1100, French was a late starter compared to the Germanic language group. However, the great explosion of learning, art and technology sometimes called the twelfth-century renaissance acted as a forcing-house for the new literature, which blossomed and spread at a phenomenal rate and dominated European vernacular culture for the next two and a half centuries. Then a number of factors, including internal anarchy and the pressures of the new humanism spreading from Italy produced a marked change in France in the mid-fourteenth century: linguistically, Old French gives way to Middle French and in literature, with the exception of drama, writers rather than genres become the distinguishing feature of the late Middle Ages: we talk of Chartier or Villon rather than Arthurian romance. This distinction is reflected in the present study where five chapters include almost exclusively works from the spring and summer of the twelfth and thirteenth centuries while the last two chapters are devoted respectively to drama and to some of the most significant writers of the mellow autumn and bitter winter of medieval France.

The status of French as a European language second only to Latin meant that it played a decisive role in the evolution of culture throughout the medieval world. When the first French texts appeared, in the twelfth century, the French-speaking public included: Norman England; present-day France, with the sister-language of Provençal dominating the Languedoc; parts of northern Spain, especially Catalonia; the Low Countries; and many parts of Italy. In addition, the use of Latin as the standard language of communication for the whole of Christendom meant that a very large number of people from the Germanic and Slavonic language-areas had some knowledge of Romance; furthermore, French became the principal language of the newly set-up Kingdom of Jerusalem and a major component of the lingua franca of the crusades.

French literature was, therefore, appealing to a public that in size and geographical distribution rivalled that of Latin and soon even surpassed it.[1] At the beginning, only certain kinds of literature were composed in French, those genres like romance, drama or epic, designed to entertain and inspire the members of the second and third estates – the nobility and the commons – whose ignorance of Latin condemned them as illiterate even when they could read and write vernacular. But French did not remain a second-class language. The new urban society's thirst for knowledge led, in the thirteenth century, to a growing demand for vernacularisation of Latin works and a veritable avalanche of treatises, encyclopaedias and compendia, as well as translations of the Bible and of authors of Classical antiquity. It is, perhaps, significant that the first of Aristotle's works to be translated into French was a scientific treatise, the *Meteorologica*, which Matthieu le Vilain rendered into French as the *Livre des Méthéores* around 1260–70, a full hundred years before the philosophical works, the *Ethics* and *Politics*, whose translation was commissioned by King Charles V from Nicholas of Oresme in the latter part of the fourteenth century.

In this study of the vernacular literature of France, I have concentrated on the works composed in standard French – in so far as such a term may be used – with only occasional indications of the other literary groups such as Anglo-Norman or Provençal. The material is presented in two quite distinct and separate ways. Each chapter treats a number of related texts or authors grouped by subject matter or genre and described in a roughly chronological order. This diachronic approach provides as it were the warp of the tapestry. At the end of each chapter, however, there is a weft, a synchronic section which gathers together a number of incidents or ideas

from works of different genres or centuries but relating to a
common theme or an aspect of general significance: the use of
the marvellous, for example, or the relationship of words and
pictures. These excursuses are inevitably selective and limited,
an indication only of possible areas of further investigation.
Hopefully, they will also counteract a little the suggestion of
each genre being in a watertight compartment, written and
read by a quite separate group of people.

All selection is inevitably a judgement and a limitation, so, as
I have had to select the works to be mentioned or quoted out of
the enormous number of possible texts I have tried to avoid
confusing unnecessarily the image of French literature that
they present and I have therefore used no quotations at all in
the body of the text from secondary literature, either historical
or critical. The medieval writers are left to speak for themselves. A wide variety of works are cited but not very much lyric
poetry except at the end of the period. The reasons for this are
two-fold: first, lyrics more than any other type of literature
depend heavily on form and language, which loses a great deal
in translation; and secondly, the lyric poem is often such a
personal medium of expression that it may tell us less about the
social context than the more communal genres like epic and
romance, satire or drama. The difficulty of form and the limited
appeal of the subject matter may also account for the relatively
small proportion of lyric poetry translated in the Middle Ages
compared to the narrative genres, which were widely available
in translation. Several major literary themes first developed in
the twelfth century in France subsequently swept Europe,
among them the doctrines of courtly love; the Arthurian
romances including the Grail; and the epic tales of Renart the
fox. In later centuries these originally French stories formed a
major element of the literary legacy not only of England,
Germany, Italy and Spain but also of regions as diverse as the
Balkans, Norway and the Netherlands.

Despite the dominance of story in these internationally
popular works, form was not entirely neglected. The development of prose as an alternative mode for narrative fiction in the
thirteenth century did not preclude the use of verse for serious
historical or critical works. In the fifteenth century the *ballade*
was considered an appropriate vehicle for elevated and serious

subjects, as the ode was to be in the sixteenth; while verse remained the only acceptable medium for tragic drama until the eighteenth century.

Such artificial literary forms encouraged authors to use elaborate imagery and figures, allegory, symbolism and personification, while the increasing number of translations of Latin works in elevated language-registers encouraged the development of a French capable of expressing the same ideas and concepts. By the end of the Middle Ages, Latin had been ousted from its pre-eminent place in the cultural hierarchy, and French had taken over all three literary Estates and was catering for clergy, nobility and commons alike in a rich, flexible and vital language that moved easily between bawdy innuendo and sublime rhetoric, from tavern-slums to the courts of Heaven.

Nurtured at the twin breasts of Holy Scripture and Classical myth, guided by writers skilled in the grammar and rhetoric inherited from antiquity, the infant literature throve mightily, expanding in stature and increasing in accomplishment. The number, length and variety of texts in medieval French is awe-inspiring: love-lyrics, drinking songs, romantic adventures and noble deeds, satires and saints' lives, tracts and treatises, they form a vast tapestry of medieval life and thought, creating, in La Fontaine's words,

> An ample comedy, its scenes many and diverse,
> Its stage, the universe.
> God, men and beasts all play their role therein.
> (*Fables*, Bk V, 1)

Rose-tinted Spectacles and Burning-glass

THE use of figurative language is a characteristic of literature but, like verse, it is not nowadays usually found in works of information or instruction. Nor does the more elaborate imagery often occur in works of scholarship, treatises or textbooks. The Middle Ages, however, was accustomed to symbolism and figural interpretation in every field, from the multiple levels of biblical exegesis – literal, allegorical, spiritual and moral – to the semiotic use of image and picture in heraldry, fable or art. Since the present study is concerned to indicate the way in which popular creative literature of all kinds, fiction and history, verse and prose tales, songs and drama, can reveal the spirit and feeling of the age in which they were written, I have made extensive use of imagery in the presentation of the texts, especially the metaphor of a mirror with its multiple reflections.

The mirror was one of the commonest symbols in medieval writing. Not only do many works, both in Latin and vernacular have the word 'mirror' (*speculum, miroir*) in their title – from the *Mirror of Marriage* to the *Mirror of Simple Souls* – but the image of the vision in the glass is used by author after author, right through the Middle Ages. The reflection is different, however, from that put forward by Hamlet in his charge to the players to 'hold as 'twere the mirror up to Nature' (*Hamlet*, III.ii). It is not simply a mirror 'that is used to reflect the whole length of the highway', as Stendhal suggested of the novel; for medieval writers, the mirror was rather a blend of oracle and example, reflecting not so much what was as what ought to be, combining the tactless honesty of the Queen's looking-glass in *Snow White* with the inchoate and potentially deceptive pictures revealed by the mirror of Tolkien's Galadriel.

The images in this medieval looking-glass are obscured now by time and changing values, linguistic evolution and scribal corruption. But even if we can clear the glass of this accumulation of centuries we are still left with the problem of the fidelity of the reflection. All mirrors distort to some extent and some are intended to distort in a particular way and for a specific purpose. Nor is an apparently realistic reflection necessarily accurate: a photograph may be more misleading than a painting because it appears to be more natural. Before the historian can judge the image he is seeking he must have some idea of the intention of the mirror's maker and the context within which it was created.

The two commonest distortions in medieval or any other literature are idealisation and criticism: the world is viewed through the rose-tinted spectacles of optimistic adoration or incinerated with the burning-glass of pessimistic satire. The epic heroes of the *chansons de geste* glorified the fighting Christian virtues, courage and perseverance, loyalty and patriotism – it was a literature of propaganda, a Land of Hope and Glory where society was presented in black and white with few shades of grey; but even if such a society was very seldom realised it was certainly considered a most desirable goal by many people then and in later centuries too. The romance, the other lens of the rose-tinted spectacles, presented a world whose setting was even more unreal, though its characters were often remarkably human. Nor was the world of chivalry as fairy-tale a setting for medieval readers as for modern: castles and forests, chargers and tournaments were as much a part of medieval life as fast cars, jet-planes and Mediterranean villas are today.

The idealised societies have their own veracity; the exaggerations are those of the lover whose adulation, if taken with a pinch of salt, need not mislead the wary spectator. More deceptive, because apparently more true to life, is the world of laughter, of *fabliau* and farce, satirist and critic. A caricature must be lifelike to be recognised and appreciated but it is by definition an exaggeration. Unfortunately, satire quickly loses its topicality and effect and the reader is left without the guidance of contemporary comparison and knowledge to enable him to identify the critical stereotype.

Opposites create balance: satire and ideal, *Renart* and the *Rose* held the scales in the early centuries, creating a precarious accuracy of vision. In later times, the increasingly personal tone of the authors who denounced their deteriorating society created a one-sided and dangerously distorted world vision. Their works showed not only the warts of reality but often, like the Mirror of Conscience, also stressed the spiritual distortions of sin:

> But right anon, my hap it was
> To look into another glass. . . .
> I saw myself, foul and unclean
> And to behold right hideous,
> Abominable and vicious.
> This mirror and this glass
> Showed to me what I was.
> (*Pilgrimage of Human Life*,
> trans. Lydgate, p. 600)[2]

Like an infinite number of mirrors set within frames of elaborate allegory or gilded rhetoric, ornamental verse forms or plain prose, medieval literature reflects the society which wrote and read and retold it, a society diverse and real and vital as our own. The present book is an attempt to portray a small part of this vast output of four centuries, a mosaic of images, fragments of that whole distorting hall of mirrors where in a glass darkly we can see reflected the whirling world of medieval France.

2. The Fighting Community

> . . . a mirror hither straight,
> That it may show me what a face I have.
> (Shakespeare)

WITH the exception of a few incomplete saints' lives, there is no vernacular literature extant from France before the beginning of the twelfth century. Nor is there evidence that such texts ever existed. But from the twelfth century itself a very considerable number of works survive, many of which, including the earliest, belong to the epic narrative genre known as *chansons de geste* from the Latin *gesta*, 'deeds'.

The deeds in question are mainly those of the emperor Charlemagne and his warriors,[1] especially the twelve peers, and although they have survived in written form they were clearly intended for oral narration. Nevertheless, despite the fact that normally epic poems are the earliest and most primitive form of literature that a society produces, it would be a mistake to look on twelfth-century France as being culturally primitive or naïve. However simple the audiences may have been, and that is by no means certain, the composers of these epics are cultivated men of letters educated in the rich Latin heritage of medieval Europe and making extensive use of rhetorical devices and stylistic refinements.

One purpose of the early *chansons de geste* seems to have been propaganda, and, in order to unite warring Christendom and stir up public opinion in favour of the crusades, they had to appeal to the listening warriors and spur them on to imitate the heroes whose deeds are not beyond the efforts of fighting-men as those of more peaceable saints might be. Above all, these heroes are real men performing real deeds, for the historicity of these epics was never doubted: 'It must be true, I read it in the papers, didn't you?' The words are from a modern song but the concept of the authority of the written words was as true in the Middle Ages as it is today, especially if that written source were in Latin; the medieval chronicles carried all the conviction of a leading article in the Sunday 'heavies' or a television documentary.

In historical works the *chanson* most often cited (indeed often the only one quoted at all) is the *Song of Roland* (*Chanson de Roland*). This is a pity, for despite (or perhaps because of) the obvious and undisputed excellence of this masterpiece it cannot be considered a typical example of the genre of which over sixty poems have survived, several of them being more or less contemporary with their illustrious prototype. If we are looking for the reflection of the tastes and ideals of a society in its literature, we shall discover them in the typical products of a period, not the literary masterpieces.

The society which produced the *chansons de geste* was a society under pressure. The community was threatened from without by the menace of other creeds, particularly Islam, and from within by the tensions between ties of blood and of feudal loyalty. It is these tensions which form the mainspring of the Carolingian epics.

Christendom vs The Rest

THE oldest surviving *chanson de geste*, the Oxford manuscript version of the *Song of Roland*, belongs to the *Cycle du Roi* or King's Cycle, whose poems are centred on Charlemagne and his immediate circle, especially his nephew Roland, and deal most often with the emperor's wars against the Saracens – a general medieval term for pagans of all kinds but especially Muslims – in Spain and southern France.

The historical basis of the *Song of Roland* is an incident in AD 778 when the Basques ambushed the Franks in the pass at Roncevaux in the Pyrenees and wiped them out. The leader of the defeated French rearguard was not Roland but a certain Eggihardus. Numerous theories have been set forward to account for the immense change that took place in the story between the Latin chronicle of the event and the vernacular versions which were first written down three hundred and more years later. The interesting factor from the point of view of the present study is that these changes made a rather ignominious historical defeat into a patriotic block-buster: the defeat of the rearguard under Eggihardus is transformed into a successful though costly holding operation of 10,000 French against 400,000 Saracens who are finally put to flight leaving the French dead on the field of victory. A further innovation is the introduction of the Judas-figure of Ganelon, the traitor, but for whom it seems the Saracens would not have thought of attacking the rearguard.

Although the Saracens are necessarily shown to be inferior to the French, they are by no means contemptible as foes. The French win because of the supremely heroic and epic stature of their leaders, Archbishop Turpin, Oliver and Roland, a stature largely the result of the divine help and inspiration of their Christian belief and their role as Defenders of the Faith. But they are not supermen. They quarrel and they bleed. Roland especially, who is often held up as the ideal hero of the period, is shown in the poem to be aggressive, hot-headed and quick-tempered. Against his well-known rallying of the French forces to fight because 'a man should endure hardship for his lord, and suffer both extremes of heat and cold and sacrifice for him both skin and hide' (*Roland*, S. LXXIX), must be set Oliver's outspoken condemnation of his friend and leader for his folly and *hubris* in refusing to summon help when they know the odds are impossibly heavy. The Middle Ages venerated *mesure*, the reasonable mean, personified in this poem by Oliver who is wise (*sage*)[2] but by no means less valiant than the bold Roland whose *desmesure* is severely condemned by the author through the words of both Oliver and Turpin. Nevertheless, since Roland is the primary hero of the poem he must ultimately show the ability to accept his human condition and admit his faults. He dies only after being reconciled with Oliver and, more importantly, with God.

The prototype for the hero who triumphs despite his faults because of his ultimate faith and humility is probably St Peter, who is portrayed in the gospels as being frequently rebuked by Christ for his impetuosity and other faults and eventually denies his Master but repents as quickly as he sins. It is worth remembering here that there are clearly drawn parallels in the poems between Charlemagne with his twelve peers, one of whom is a traitor, and Christ with the Twelve Apostles, one of whom 'also betrayed him'. A medieval audience would have had no difficulty in seeing the proud, hot-headed, valiant and ultimately humble Roland as a warrior-saint, an ideal to be followed the more readily in that he was also a fallible human being. Charlemagne, in contrast, especially in his final confrontation with Baligant, is shown as a more remote and hieratic figure. His white beard flowing freely over his breastplate, the 200-year-old Emperor defeats the Saracen champion in a single combat of truly epic stature. But even Charlemagne, after his victory, when the divine strength and inspiration are withdrawn, is shown as a weary, grieving old man who, when the angel comes to tell him of his next task, can only sigh. 'The emperor did not wish to go at all. "God," said the king, "My life is weary toil." He wept and tore at his white beard' (*Roland*, S. CCXCVIII).

The picture of Roland, immune to fear and pain despite the thirty wounds any one of which would have slain an emir, rallying his forces and exhorting them to serve their lord at whatever cost, is by no means the only one presented to twelfth-century audiences by the *jongleurs* – the minstrels who performed these epics though they probably did not compose them. Almost contemporary with the *Song of Roland* is the *Song of William (Chanson de Guillaume)* which offers in the first and older part of the poem a very different and much more harrowing portrayal of a hero who seems designed almost as a direct antithesis of the rumbustious nephew of Charlemagne. Vivien, the nephew of William, Count of Orange – one of Charlemagne's principal vassals – is shown at the beginning of the poem in the company of the drunken, cowardly Tedbald of Bourges, and Esturmi, his equally unheroic nephew. (The uncle/nephew pair is one of the commonest couplings to be found in the *chansons de geste*.) News of a Saracen landing on the coast at Archamp interrupts the feasting. Vivien urges Tedbald to send for William but, full of drunken bravado, Esturmi rejects the idea because William will then get all the credit: 'If there are twenty thousand of your men and William comes with only five of his followers, or three or four or any small number, you may fight and conquer the Arabs but everyone will say that Lord William did it. Whoever earns it he always gets the credit'

(*William*, S. vi). Tedbald accepts his nephew's bad advice, summons his men and sets off for Archamp where they find the Saracens have landed in force and set up camp on the salt marshes. Now sober and apparently very hung-over, Tedbald is terrified and urgently inquires if he sent for William. Learning that on his own specific orders no messenger was despatched to summon help, Tedbald compounds his crimes by declaring his intention of fleeing the battlefield. He breaks the shaft of the banner and tramples it in the mud lest the Saracens should attack them. Then, so terrified that, in a scene of typically outspoken medieval humour, he fouls his breeches, he flees towards Bourges followed by Esturmi and some of the French: 'As gold divides itself from silver, so all the good men set themselves apart: the cowards fled away with Tedbald, all the valiant knights remained with Vivien' (*William*, S. xxviii). This kind of reduction by selection may have been suggested by the biblical story of Gideon (Judges 7). A similar principle is applied by Shakespeare's Henry V before the Battle of Agincourt (*Henry V*, iv.iii).

Vivien remains on the battlefield because when he was knighted he swore never to retreat before the pagans. Like Roland he lacks *mesure* but his heroism is personal and has more of the fervour of the saint. He does not expect others to remain with him and indeed specifically tells the remaining knights that they are not 'his men' and owe him no loyalty. (The feudal bond between a lord and his warriors was direct and personal: if he were killed on the battlefield they had no obligation to remain.) The French beg Vivien to lead them and swear to follow him. 'We will have sworn to you by the laws God gave to men, to his Apostles when he dwelt among them, that we will never fail you while you still live' (*William*, S. xxviii).

Vivien accepts their oath and with casual aplomb produces a white pennon and three gold nails out of his crimson hose – the loose roll-tops of riding-boots were used as pockets right through to the nineteenth century – and proceeds to manufacture a new banner with his lance as the shaft. Thus equipped he attacks the Saracens but eventually his men are all killed and Vivien himself is severely wounded. While he awaits the arrival of William for whom he had sent – unlike Roland he has no false pride about asking for help – he wanders over the battlefield in agony: 'Vivien wandered over the plain, his helmet falling over the nosepiece and his entrails dropping at his feet. With his left arm he held them up while in his right hand was a steel sword, crimson-stained from pommel to point. The scabbard was filled with liver and blood. He leant upon it with the point to the ground' (*William*, S. LXXI).

Vivien's martyrdom, for such it is evidently intended to be, finally terminates with his death in William's arms, a death which in contrast to the vividly described physical horrors of his prolonged agonising, is calm, dignified and fit for a hero. The remainder of the poem describes William's revenge for his nephew and his final victory over the invaders.

The contrast between the two heroes, Roland and Vivien, and their two very different uncles also, indicates that already at the very beginning of the twelfth century, the *chansons de geste* were far from being stereotyped purveyors of chauvinistic propaganda; and their range can be seen to be even wider if we consider the third of the early poems, the fragmentary *Gormont and Isambard* which, like the *Song of Roland* and the *Song of William*, deals with a society fighting pagan enemies, though these come from England led by Gormont, King of Cirencester who, helped by a renegade Christian Frenchman, Isambard, invades France and confronts the French army led by Louis, son of Charlemagne. Isambard is the main character, even the hero of the poem, despite his apostasy, and eventually, when all his men have been killed or fled, he is left virtually alone, like Roland or Vivien, on the field of battle. Now, at the moment of his death he calls on the Virgin Mary, recalls the death and resurrection of Christ and 'sees an olive tree in full leaf. He makes his way to it with difficulty and seats himself on the cool grass, turning his face towards the east. He prostrates himself and cries *mea culpa* then raises himself a little.' Here the poem ends abruptly but it is obvious he will die reconciled to Christianity (*Gormont*, S. XXIII).

The use of the *chansons de geste* as propaganda for the crusades by emphasising the rewards that waited in Heaven for those who died fighting for Christendom, would have been less effective if they had not been good stories in their own right; in creating them the authors depicted a wide range of heroes and villains – traitors, cowards, renegades – within the community itself. The ethics of these poems are not simplistic. Roland may say and believe that 'Pagans are wrong and Christians are right' (*Roland*, S. LXXIX), but that does not make the Christians good: in a war situation, each side commonly believes its cause. Archbishop Turpin reminds the French to 'confess your sins and ask God for mercy. I will absolve you to save your souls. If you die you will be holy martyrs' (*Roland*, S. LXXXIX). Valour alone was not enough; there must be repentance and contrition as well.

Nevertheless, although in fiction the fighting Christian community presented a more or less united front to the attacks of Saracen, Saxon or Sassenach, the society that provided the audience for these tales was only too conscious of the worm in the apple, the serpent in the garden. The conflict between right and wrong, good and evil, was clearly seen by twelfth-century theologians and creative artists alike as an integral part of the human condition, not a remote philosophical concept. Nowhere is this more clearly portrayed than in the mid twelfth-century play of *Adam*, written like the Oxford *Roland* and the *Song of William* in Anglo-Norman, and portraying the protoplasts, Adam and Eve, in their relationship with God, in terms of feudal duties and loyalties. The Saviour begins by explaining to Adam and Eve their relationship to each other in terms of a marriage contract – 'let this be the law of marriage' – and then gives them Paradise as a fief, warning Adam against daring to choose to disobey his rightful lord:

> Take my advice and still be true to me.
> Reject all evil, hold to what is good;
> Love your liege-lord and keep yourself with him,
> Nor leave my counsel for another's words.
> If truly you do this you shall not sin.
>
> (*Adam*, 67–71)

Adam accepts the fief and the bond:

> If for one fruit I lose a fief like this
> It would be right to cast me forth to die. . . .
> He must be held a traitor and abhorred,
> Who by such treachery betrays his Lord.
>
> (*Adam*, 106–7, 110–11)

Despite his protestations, however, Adam of course does commit the act of disobedience which breaks his bond with his overlord. Only after a long period of repentance will that same lord redeem him from the bonds of Satan. As in the *chansons de geste*, the concept of the cosmic struggle of the community is expressed in personal, individual terms, by the creation of the representative personality on whom the reader or listener can focus.

But even this reduction of scale cannot provide an endless variety of possibilities for literature that is based on a fight. All action/adventure stories from the *Iliad* to *Star Wars* rely heavily on the context, the imaginative reality of the setting. If a *chanson de geste* or an episode in a TV thriller series is analysed it will almost invariably divide into exposition, development and denouement; or, in the vernacular of the genre, build-up, punch-up and clear-up. What is more, the fight itself will need a variety of gimmicks to make it different, original and interesting, and these must lay stress on the individual rather than the group. A common technique in the *chansons de geste* is to wipe out the bulk of the fighting men in anonymous blocks: 'The battle is impressive and great; the French strike out with their gleaming swords. There you would have seen great suffering and loss, so many men dead and wounded and bleeding' (*Roland*, S. cxxva). In the *Song of William*, when William's wife greets her defeated lord on his return she first asks after the army: 'What have you done with the men, my lord", she said, "The four thousand seven hundred you took with you?" ' (*William*, S. cxliii).

Then, having been told they are dead, she asks after the principal characters by name, individually. Only after the pawns have been removed from the board does the author get down to the end-game and describe the death of the main characters in strict hierarchical order, culminating in the *Song of Roland*, for example, with Roland's own extended and heroic death scene.

Limiting the number of detailed descriptions of battles does not entirely solve the problem of variety, however. Nor of realism. An important difference between a medieval story and a modern one is that the audience for the former were almost all fighting men themselves, whereas the average reader or spectator of a James Bond epic today has little experience of combat. In addition, the director of a film or television episode can use a great variety of exotic locations; he can change the levels by falling, climbing or swinging or by abrupt shifts of camera angle. The medieval story-teller has only words to rely on but they can be used to great effect. It is no use describing a fight, it must be narrated in such a way that the reader or listener experiences the excitement.[3] Adjectives and adverbs are useless unless the reader is involved. On the whole, epics have survived because they do just this. The oral nature of the work, allowing the narrator's voice to add colour, also helped, as did the familiarity of the audience with the weapons and techniques employed. They knew exactly what a lance-thrust or a sword-blow could achieve. Above all, in the pre-gunpowder era the writer had no problem in getting his heroes to come to grips with each other, literally. A long-range battle is difficult to narrate convincingly and it is noteworthy that even Robin Hood never uses his bow to dispose of a major villain: he tackles him with sword, quarterstaff or his bare hands.

But however skilful the narration and however close the clinch there is still a limit to the variety of effective battle descriptions between enemies. Probably the most moving fight sequence in the *Song of Roland* is not one between Christian and pagan but between the hero and his friend and companion Oliver. The latter has received so many wounds he can barely see and he strikes his friend with whom he has quarrelled over Roland's refusal to send for help:

> Oliver has received a mortal wound; he has bled so much that his sight is distorted and he cannot see clearly, near to or at a distance, nor recognise, anyone at all. When he encounters his companion he strikes him on the jewelled helm, cleaving it as far as the nosepiece but without actually penetrating the head. At this blow, Roland looked at him and then he asked him gently and quietly: 'Noble companion, did you do that deliberately? I am Roland who always loved you dearly. You did not challenge me at all.'   (*Roland*, S. CXLIX)

The significance of the reference to challenge would not have been lost on the audience, familiar with the rules for lawful challenge before battle.[4]

The crusading fervour of the twelfth and thirteenth centuries cast a particularly rosy glow over the principal characters in these epics of war against the pagans: Roland for all his faults dies not merely as a hero but a martyr, his soul being taken to Heaven by the archangel Michael himself; other angels attend and encourage the weary emperor, whose white hair and beard, constantly referred to in battle-scenes and councils, emphasise his patriarchal, almost prophetic status as a latter-day Moses leading the Chosen People. Indeed his role as a defender of the faith brought him canonisation in 1165 and popular devotion to Blessed Charlemagne was widespread in the Middle Ages though nowadays his cult has practically disappeared in France except in Paris: he is the patron saint of the Sorbonne University.

Both uncle and nephew were given places in Dante's Paradise of the Warriors (*Paradiso*, Canto xviii, 43), an honour not bestowed, however, on the equally saintly but less well-known William of Orange and his nephew Vivien. Yet the Latin *Vita* of St Guilhem-le-désert (canonised in 1066) made use of material from the poems of the William of Orange cycle which in turn drew on the Latin texts. William's relics, including a fragment of the True Cross given him by Charlemagne when he left the emperor's service, were the subject of a prolonged battle of charters in the twelfth century between the monks of Aniane and those of Gellone; each side claimed they had the true relics and therefore could attract the lucrative pilgrim trade. The two monasteries are a few miles apart and not far from Montpellier through which passed the southern French stretch of the trans-European route to the third-greatest pilgrim shrine of the Middle Ages, the tomb of St James at Compostella in north-west Spain. Even today, Santiago attracts many thousands of pilgrims every year, those coming from France mostly crossing the Pyrenees through the very pass of Roncevaux where Roland had fought and died. The exact link between the *chansons de geste* and the pilgrim-routes is still a matter for scholarly debate but there is certainly some connection, and it was to become more clear-cut in the course of the fourteenth century when the story of Roncevaux became part of the legend of St James, in both literature and art.[5]

Lord and Vassal

As effective as the battle between opposing ideologies is the device, used by Homer onwards, of conflict of loyalties, and a very high proportion of the *chansons de geste* from the twelfth century or later have as their subject not the struggle between Christian and pagan but between lord and vassal, emperor and subject, family and family. From these stories emerges a picture of violence, clashing loyalties, heroism and villainy that makes most modern television drama look like 'Children's Hour'; by far the most important single element in the creation of these stories is the feudal bond between the lord and the vassal and the problems of divided allegiance that may arise from it.

The cycle of poems centred on the figure of William, Count of Orange – including the *Song of William* discussed in the previous section – derives most of its inspiration not from the fights against the pagan invaders (though there are many such battles in the cycle) but from the clash between William and his overlord, Louis, son of Charlemagne. The four poems that form the core of the cycle were already considered a coherent unit by the mid-twelfth century and were copied together in the so-called cyclic manuscripts. In the chronologically earliest of the four, the *Crowning of Louis*, Charlemagne quarrels with his young son who is afraid to take the crown his father offers him on stringent conditions: 'If you are going to take bribes, fair son, or encourage and promote excess or commit lechery or glorify evil or deprive any young orphan of his fief or any widow of as much as fourpence then in Jesus' name I forbid you, Louis my son, to accept this crown' (*Crowning*, S. ix). Furious at his son's hesitation, Charlemagne threatens to have Louis put into a monastery. William steps in and urges the youth to accept, promising him loyalty and service if he becomes king: 'Seeing the crown sitting there on the altar, the count seized it without delay, came up to the youth and set it on his head. "Receive this, fair lord, in the name of the king of Heaven: may he give you the strength to be a just ruler" ' (*Crowning*, S. ix).

The remainder of the poem shows how William keeps his oath, fighting against rebellious barons and invading pagans until the crown is finally secured to the young king, who is not at all grateful: 'Then Louis had become very powerful but when he was great he gave William no thanks for it' (*Crowning*, S. LXIII). This theme of the loyal vassal of an ungrateful overlord is continued and developed in the next poem, the *Waggon-Train of Nîmes*, which opens with a scene of the now securely established king rewarding his followers with fiefs. None is offered to William whose nephew, Bertrand, bitterly comments: 'You and I, uncle, are quite forgotten' (*Waggon-Train*, S. I). Angry and hurt, William confronts the king and there is a long scene which is probably the finest analysis of feudal relationships in the whole corpus of *chansons de geste*. It is also a consummate piece of character analysis, with Louis moving from bluster to mock humility to scorn. He first tells William he has no fief to offer him at the moment; then, driven out of that position, he offers William various fiefs to which others have prior, valid claims, culminating in the fief belonging to Count Berangier. At this point William loses his temper, reminding the king that Berangier was killed saving Louis' life and has the right to expect his son to inherit his lands: 'Anyone who wishes to harm the child's interests is an arrant fool and, so help me God, a traitor and a renegade' (*Waggon-Train*, S. xv).

Then the king plays his trump card. In a grandiloquent and blatantly insincere speech he offers William a quarter of his kingdom:

> I will give you one quarter of France, a quarter of the abbeys and a quarter of the markets, a quarter of the towns and a quarter of the archdioceses, a quarter of the men-at-arms and a quarter of the knights, a quarter of the estate holders and a quarter of the footmen, a quarter of the girls and a quarter of the women, a quarter of the priests and a quarter of the churches; I give you a quarter of the horses in my stables; I give you a quarter of the ready money in my treasury; I willingly bestow on you a quarter of the empire that is mine to govern. (*Waggon-Train*, S. xv)

Bitter and disgusted, William throws the offer back in the king's face and stamps out of the hall followed by his faithful nephew. Soon, however, with one of the changes of mood typical of the fiery count, he returns to Louis and asks permission to win a fief for himself from the pagans who are occupying large areas of southwestern France. In a speech that reminds us of the very real danger such large, independent fiefs could represent to the crown, not only in Carolingian times but in the twelfth century when the Plantagenet kings of England were, in respect of their French possessions, vassals of the French king, William promises he will hold his fief under Louis but without asking for any help from his lord.

The rest of the poem describes how William carried out his plan and won himself the town of Nîmes by a stratagem of the wooden horse variety, which provides a particularly original and amusing context for the battle between Christians and pagans. This mixture of serious clashes between William and his lord alternating with scenes of high comedy is typical of this cycle. It is found, for example, in the second part of the *Song of William*, after Vivien's tragic and painful death, with the introduction of the character of Rainouart, the kitchen boy, who defeats the most powerful of opponents with the aid of a large *tinel* (or club) so heavy he has difficulty in controlling his blows so that he kills the horses as well as the riders:

> Then said Bertrand: 'Did you ever think that you might kill them with a thrusting blow?' 'That is true', said Rainouart, 'I had not thought of that.' He looked ahead and saw king Corduel who was riding a swift warhorse. Then Rainouart charged at him with his cudgel and thrust at his chest and broke him in pieces so that the blood flowed from his mouth and nose. As soon as he had fallen Bertrand mounted the charger. (*William*, S. CLXXI)

The cohesive nature of the poems makes the cycle of William, Count of Orange, particularly effective as a serial and contrasts with the more loosely organised King's cycle, centred on Charlemagne and Roland, or the cycle of Doon de Mayence, rechristened by a modern critic the cycle of revolt, for in it the mixture of feudal loyalty and Christian crusading spirit typical of the other cycles is replaced by bitter and tragic histories of treachery and vengeance, with the heroic emperor Charlemagne now the villain of the piece.

The Feud and the Family

THE epic of revolt comprises a number of poems linked together by subject matter rather than by characters; a series of variations on the theme of conflict between feudal duty to one's lord and the claims of kinship. Two *chansons de geste, Raoul de Cambrai* and *Renaud de Montauban*, present particularly effective and well-contrasted variations.

(a) *'Raoul de Cambrai'*

This is probably the blackest and bitterest of all the epics, a powerful and tragic story of injustice breeding hatred and revenge, corrupting the principal characters and ensnaring them in an endless insoluble vendetta that drags on through three generations. In this poem Charlemagne is the catalyst not the protagonist. He sets up the situation by doing exactly what William stopped Louis from doing in the *Waggon-Train of Nîmes*: he gives away to one of his vassals the fief belonging to his defunct brother-in-law although the widow has a young son, Raoul. When Raoul is fifteen he takes as squire Bernier, bastard son of Ybert de Ribemont. Some years after, spurred on by his uncle, Guerri, Raoul demands his fief from King Louis who declares he cannot dispossess the present incumbent of Cambrai. Raoul declares his intention of taking it by force for 'the honour [a feudal term for an estate] of the father should pass by right to the child as all men know' (*Raoul*, S. XXXIII). Louis tries to calm Raoul and instead compounds his folly by promising the next fief to fall vacant: 'for if there should die one of the counts anywhere from here to the Vermandois . . . you shall have the honours and the land' (*Raoul*, S. XXXIV). The pact is sealed by Louis giving Raoul a glove, a symbol of the bargain, and also forty hostages; furthermore, Raoul makes him swear an oath on the relics of St Firmin, St Peter and St Augustine, 'that he will give him in time the honours of whatever count may die between the Loire and the Rhine' (*Raoul*, S. XXXV). In due course a fief falls vacant, that of Herbert of Vermandois, and Louis tries to renege on the deal because the count has left four sons and he is reluctant to sacrifice four for one. By threatening the hostages, Raoul forces him to grant him the fief but the king will give no help to the new lord to hold it. All present realise that war is inevitable. Bernier, Raoul's squire, is kin to the Vermandois and tries to hold Raoul back but he is deaf to the entreaties of both the squire and his own mother. The Vermandois is invaded and the war is on.

One of the most vivid scenes in the long campaign described is that of the burning of the nunnery at Origny on the Loire. Misled by the tales of three thieves who seek refuge in his camp and claim the citizens of Origny are planning to attack him, Raoul orders his men into battle although only the previous day he had promised the abbess of the convent not to harm them. Having slaughtered the innocent inhabitants of the town, Raoul sets fire to it:

> Count Raoul the proud-hearted had fire set to the streets. The dwellings burn and the ceilings fall, the wine is spilt flooding the cellars. The hams are burning and the sides of bacon melt, the lard giving added fuel to the flames which leap up to the towers and the main belfry so the roofs have to fall. Between the walls there is such a blaze that the nuns are burned, so great is the fire. The whole hundred are burned in this great disaster; burned is Marseus, mother of Bernier, and Clamados, duke Renier's daughter. You could smell them in the holocaust.   (*Raoul*, S. LXXI)

Bernier sees his mother lying on a marble floor, her psalter smouldering on her breast. In rage and grief he laments her death, curses Raoul and renounces his homage to him, swearing vengeance. Inevitably, the grim process of revenge continues. Bernier refuses all Raoul's offers of recompense and eventually slays his former liege lord and is in turn slain by Raoul's uncle, Guerri, an indomitable old warrior who more than any one else keeps the vendetta alive. Finally, many years later, besieged and overcome by the sons of Bernier, Guerri contrives to escape from the city at night and go into exile, 'but no one knows for sure what became of him' (*Raoul*, S. CCCXLIV).

The historical background of this story is more substantial though less Carolingian than is the case for many of the *chansons de geste* though most have at least a kernel of fact hidden inside them. The *Annales Flodoardi* refer to the battle between Raoul and the sons of Herbert of Vermandois, who died in 943. There are a number of references to the characters in other chronicles, and a comparison of Latin and vernacular texts makes it clear that in some cases the chronicler has borrowed from the poet as well as vice versa (cf. the Latin *Vita* and the William of Orange cycle, p. 19 above).

(b) *'Renaud de Montauban'*

Renaud and his three brothers, the *Four Sons of Aymon*, with their wonder horse, Bayard, and their half-brother the enchanter Maugis, became in later centuries some of the best-known figures in medieval literature, but in their earliest appearances in the *chansons de geste*, the elements of magic and picaresque adventure were played down in favour of the clash between feudal and family loyalties. As in *Raoul de Cambrai*, it is the ineptitude of Charlemagne that sparks off the potentially tragic series of events. The very day that Charlemagne has knighted him, Renaud defeats the emperor's nephew, Bertholais, at chess, and Bertholais strikes him. When Renaud complains to the emperor, Charlemagne refuses to discipline his nephew. Renaud then asks for justice for the death of his uncle killed by traitors on the emperor's orders. This time it is Charlemagne who strikes Renaud who in turn goes back to Bertholais, kills him with the chess-board and escapes with his brothers after a furious battle. It is now open war between them and the emperor, a war in which their father, Aymon, bound by fealty to Charlemagne is forced to denounce his own sons, swearing to do nothing to help them and to hand them over to the emperor if he has the chance. Aymon's dilemma contributes much tension and excitement to the story but it also serves another purpose: by stressing his father's total loyalty to his feudal lord, the author motivates and explains Renaud's own refusal to take direct action against the emperor and his repeated and persistent attempts to make peace with him. But Charles, like Guerri in *Raoul de Cambrai*, is obstinate and vengeful. At one moment in the tale, Maugis magically transports the emperor into the midst of Renaud's forces who have already captured four of the twelve peers: Roland, Ogier the Dane, Duke Naime and Archbishop Turpin. Despite the threats of Richard, the most violent of the four brothers, Renaud tries again to make peace with the emperor, supported by the pleas of the peers: 'Let us for God's sake be reconciled and make peace. I will do anything at all that you ask me except renounce Christ but otherwise anything' (*Renaud*, p. 336).

Charlemagne will only agree on condition Maugis is handed over to him for execution, and this Renaud absolutely refuses to do. Although he is their prisoner the emperor remains inflexible and Renaud lets him go free: 'for you are my true lord, that I know well. When it pleases God and you, without any conditions we will be friends again as we were before' (*Renaud*, pp. 338–9). The war breaks out again but eventually peace is made. Renaud as he had promised goes to Jerusalem as a penitent pilgrim – a not uncommon form of legal penalty in the Middle Ages – and returns to work and die as a simple labourer on the building of Cologne cathedral where he comes up against the wrath of the local labour force who murder him and throw his body in the Rhine – a story that perhaps symbolises the workers' hostility towards the unpaid labour of the zealously faithful.[6]

(c) *The Romantic Epic: 'Ogier the Dane' and 'Huon of Bordeaux'*

Many of the same themes are found in the *chanson de geste* which treats of Ogier the Dane and his struggle against Charlemagne. There is a fight over a game of chess with, in this case, Charlemagne's son killing Ogier's son; exile and war and eventually reconciliation between the hero and the emperor, so that Ogier can aid Charlemagne in the war against the pagans. More original is the story of Huon of Bordeaux who is befriended by Auberon, king of the elves. As a result of 'the great power that Jesus has given me, I do what I will in the land of Faerie' (*Huon*, 3674–5). Auberon's parentage is as mixed as his power sources: his father was Julius Caesar and his mother was the beautiful Morgan le Fay (*Huon*, 3513–5). As in the story of Ogier, once more the quarrel between Charlemagne and Huon results from the behaviour of the emperor's son, called here Karlot. Huon is befriended by Auberon who gives him a magic horn and other treasures. In these stories as in the later versions of *Renaud de Montauban* we see the change that took place in the centuries that followed the great era of crusading fervour. What had been a semi-documentary, reasonably realistic propaganda literature had mutated into folk-tale and legend. An idea of the depths of the change can be seen in the prologue to *Huon of Bordeaux* – written later, of course – the *Romance of Auberon* (*Roman d'Auberon*) in which the fabulous parentage of Auberon has been developed to give him Saint George as a twin brother and Judas Maccabeus for an ancestor; the mongrel nature of this work, which draws on romance, legend and apocryphya and has nothing of epic except the use of assonanced *laisses* for its structure, is evident in the episode in which George, having seduced and eloped with the king of Persia's daughter, is wounded in a fight with a dragon at a fountain in the desert, which brings on the labour-pains of the princess. But God sends them help in the form of the Virgin Mary, who with Joseph and the Child is fleeing from Herod's soldiers. George repays her help by winning back from some robbers Joseph's moustaches which they had taken (along with the new-born infant). The Virgin puts them back on Joseph's face 'and immediately they were firmly rooted'. This miracle inspired George 'to serve God and do his will' (*Auberon*, 1996, 2000).

Non-combatants in the Fighting Community

INEVITABLY, in a literature based on war the warriors take the lion's share of the limelight and the women, priests and peasants are relegated to minor roles. In epic literature, even the ordinary man-at-arms is rarely individualised and when he is, it is invariably a prelude to the discovery that he is in fact of high birth as in the story of the porter whom William meets in the *Crowning of Louis*:

> He called Bertrand: 'Listen to this, nephew. Did you ever hear a porter speak so nobly? Give him the armour suited to a knight.' 'Willingly, lord,' answered Bertrand. He looked at

him, his hands and his feet and saw he was well and
nobly built and handsome and so he armed him as a knight
with a strong coat of mail and a steel helmet, a good sword
and a cutting spear, with horse and sumpter, squire and
palfrey, mule and pack-horse; for his service he gave him
good reward.   (*Crowning*, S. xxxix)

Under these circumstances it is scarcely surprising that the
townsman and the peasant are virtually ignored. A rare,
humorous exception in the *Waggon-Train of Nîmes* proves the
rule: William meets a peasant with a barrel of salt on his cart
and questions him about the town of Nîmes which William
wishes to attack. The dialogue is written with a nice understanding of the different interests of warrior and trader, for
when William asks about the town's occupants the peasant can
only talk about the price of bread: ' "Fool," said William, "I am
not asking about that but about the pagan knights in the town,
king Otran and his fellows." "I know nothing of them," said
the peasant, "and I would not tell you a lie" ' (*Waggon-Train*, S.
xxxiii). There is further humour of this kind when William
takes over the local peasants' carts and barrels to get his men
into Nîmes and disguises himself and his nephews as merchants. Bertrand, trying in vain to goad the oxen and get the
cart moving, is the subject of much raillery from his fellow
knights: 'Sir Bertrand, pay attention to your driving, we don't
like the idea of being upset' (*Waggon-Train*, S. xlix). William,
on the contrary, revels in his disguise and in the role-playing,
making up elaborate stories to account for the scar on his nose,
saying it was a punishment for being a cut-purse as a youth.
Throughout this sequence, William behaves more like a Robin
Hood or Renart the Fox than a crusading paladin and saint in
the making.

The clergy, with the exception of the fighting Archbishop,
Turpin, are rarely mentioned except in very uncomplimentary
terms. When Louis is afraid to take the crown, Charlemagne
threatens to have him tonsured and put in a monastery to toll
the bell (*Crowning*, S. ix). But the most extreme attitude to
monks is that of Aymon, father of Renaud de Montauban.
When the four brothers, outlawed and hunted, visit their home
and their mother, Aalis, in secret, they are ragged and hungry

and she prepares them a good meal. Aymon comes in on them and curses his sons, reminding them he has sworn an oath not to succour them. Noting their tattered, famished appearance, he suggests they attack religious houses:

> For you are not knights but rather rascals. You can find many men in religion, clerics and priests and monks in great comfort, who have white flesh on their sides and white throats, their liver and lungs set in white lard and their flesh is tender and they have fat kidneys; they make better eating than swan or peacock. Break down the abbeys, destroy them freely. If anyone will give you supplies, then you can pardon him but whoever does not want to shall have no hope of ransom. Cook them on a fire of coals and eat them – they will no more harm you than venison. God curse me, who died on the cross, if I would not rather eat them than die of hunger. A monk roasts better than any mutton. Get out of my hall, leave my castle for from me you shall have nothing worth as much as a spur. (*Renaud*, p. 93)

Though Aymon's tone here is bitter and sarcastic it is by no means certain that he is entirely joking. The whole scene is a sort of echo of the burning of the nunnery in *Raoul de Cambrai*, with Aymon's comments suggesting the depths to which he believes his sons have sunk.

That the churchmen, except those of high birth, were looked down on by the warrior caste is emphasised in the last poem of the cycle of William of Orange, *William the Monk* (*Le Moniage Guillaume*), which tells how the hero renounced the world after the death of his wife and entered religion. The basis of the story is as usual historical and William's tomb can still be seen today in the church at Gellone (near Montpellier) now called after him, St Guilhem-le-désert. As we have come to expect with this cycle, the story is extremely humorous and the fiery, hard-hitting count quickly becomes a very unpopular member of the community. This leads to a series of hilarious episodes in which his fellow monks try, in vain, to rid themselves of their unwanted brother. Finally William leaves the abbey, retires to the desert as a hermit, fights and defeats the devil and ends his days in the odour of sanctity.

The attitude of the *chansons de geste* to religion is thus

ambivalent. Even in the *Song of Roland* which is clearly influenced by the crusades with the hero attended on his death-bed by the archangel Michael, it is evident that only a very militant Christianity is acceptable. This emphasises the problems that beset feudal Europe whose fierce warriors, Franks and Saxons, English and Normans were virtually uncontrollable unless their fighting powers and energies were channelled into some useful venture, such as the capture of Jerusalem.

Although a fundamental change in the attitude to women took place in European literature in the eleventh and twelfth centuries, with the introduction of the concept usually called courtly love (see below, p. 47), the role of women in the *chansons de geste* as in most epic literature is strictly limited. The amazon is unknown. The valkyrie of Germanic and Norse literature has no parallel in French even in the later romances. The woman's typical role is described in *Renaud de Montauban* when the wife of Bueve d'Aigremont ventures to raise her voice in a council:

> When the duke heard her he began to get angry. 'Lady,' said Bueve to her, 'go and hide yourself in your rooms which are painted in gold: there you can criticise with your maidens. Pay attention to the dyeing of silk – that is your business. Mine is to fight with a steel sword and joust against a knight. A curse on the beard of noble or prince who seeks advice in a woman's chamber.' (*Renaud*, p. 14; see also pp. 227–35 below)

Nevertheless, a few female characters do emerge with a touch of individuality, all of them wives or mothers of the heroes. Bernier's mother, who is burned to death in the fire at Origny, has a scene with Raoul in which she is briefly but effectively characterised. Raoul's own mother plays a considerable role, as does the mother of Renaud de Montauban. Charlemagne's queen appears in more than one poem and so does his mother, Bertha Bigfoot (*Berthe au grand pied*), but it is William of Orange's wife, Guibourg, who is the most fully developed, original and delightful female character in the cycles, playing an extensive role even in the early *Song of William*. One of the scenes which best portrays her is that of William's final return

from the Archamp whither he has gone to the help of his
nephew, Vivien. For the second time his men have been killed
or taken prisoner and William himself has been forced to
change his broken battered armour for Saracen arms. Thus
equipped he approaches his fortress of Orange not far ahead of
the pursuing pagans – a classic adventure-situation except that
in these tales the hero does not always escape in the nick of time
to reappear in the next episode: medieval writers had more
sense of realism than they are often given credit for. In this
instance, as William reaches the castle-gate he demands
admission but the porter refers the matter to Guibourg who, in
the absence of all the men, has taken command of the castle.
Even when William identifies himself by name she refuses to
open the gate until he has taken off his helmet so she can see for
herself who it is:

> 'No, by God,' she said, 'not unless you show me on your nose
> the scar that William the hook-nosed marquis received in
> battle from King Tedbalt the Slav.' . . . He undid the laces on
> his jewelled helmet and let it fall back on his shoulders so that
> his whole face was visible to her. When the lady saw him she
> knew him well.   (*William*, S. cxlii)

Once William is inside she looks after his horse, and only then
does she question him about the lost army and lament with
him the death and imprisonment of his kinsmen.

She is also a very practical woman. On his first return, she
sits him down to a good meal – at the lower end of the hall, for
they are both too sad to sit at the high table in the empty room.
Only when he has eaten and drunk does she rally him,
half-jokingly: 'Anyone who eats a loaf of fine bread and yet does
not leave the two baked bread-cakes, and eats the whole of a
great leg of pork and after that a great roasted peacock and in
two draughts swallows a gallon of wine, should certainly give
his neighbour a hard fight' (*William*, S. ciii). Like many of the
characters in this undeservedly neglected cycle, Guibourg is
splendidly drawn, believable and human; a true warrior's
helpmate, she embodies the advice that God gives to Eve in the
play of *Adam*:

Love and cherish Adam always:
He is your husband, you his wife.
Be to him always obedient
And do not contravene his laws.
Serve him and love him from your heart,
For this is the law of marriage.
If you will be his true helpmeet
You shall dwell with him in glory.

(Adam, 32–9)

Fact and Fantasy in the Epics: Charlemagne's Visit to Jerusalem

THE fifty-plus poems that make up the three main cycles of the Carolingian epic, known from the twelfth century onwards as the 'Matter of France', are essentially historical novels. Their roots are firmly fixed in the world of Charlemagne and his son, Louis, as preserved in Latin chronicle, annal and charter. But they are historical in the way the medieval audiences understood history: a reflection of their own times in the mirror of the past. This indifference to modern standards of historical accuracy is a hall-mark of medieval culture; in art as in literature the creative artist scorned the pettifogging details of period clothes and weapons as much as he rejected the idea of an objective re-creation of past events. Instead, he used the time-gap to provide the necessary distance between the story and the hearer for the spell to work. Moreover, the Carolingian epic was written for an audience of warriors who could understand and appreciate the quality of weapons and armour, the dilemma of conflicting feudal and family loyalties and the niceties of combat. They enjoyed the stories of the heroes of the past because they were true and also because the life of these fighting men resembled the life they themselves knew, in all the things that mattered.

Because there was this distance in time, they could afford to laugh with and sometimes at these heroic figures whose weaknesses emphasised their common humanity. If a hero can be weak then a weak man may be heroic: Superman offers an unattainable ideal but William Shortnose, Renaud, even Roland – of them a man could say: there with the grace of God go I.

But these are not merely saints' lives with exciting bits put in to sugar the pill. The heroes are often shown, as we have seen, in a less than heroic light, and nowhere is this more true than in that exotic oddity among crusading poems, the *Voyage of Charlemagne to Jerusalem* (*Pèlerinage de Charlemagne*) which is based loosely on the chronicle accounts of the emperor's subduing Constantinople and collecting from that city many precious relics for the churches of France. Surprisingly, this poem was first composed early in the twelfth century and like the *Song of Roland* apparently in England. The concept of pilgrimage, so integral to medieval Christianity and so often reflected in the *chansons de geste*, is here given a new and unexpected twist.

Angered at his wife's imprudent remark that the king of Jerusalem is a more imposing figure in his crown and regalia than her own husband, Charlemagne set off to test the veracity of the statement, taking with him the twelve peers and an impressive retinue. They eventually meet King Hugh and find themselves at a considerable disadvantage with his collection of automata, including a castle that spins round very fast when the wind blows and makes them all ill. Hugh welcomes them with feasting and, after a heavy evening's drinking, the Franks indulge in a favourite sport – boasting of what they will do to their unwitting host. Each peer strives to outdo his fellows with outrageous *gabs*, unaware that a spy is hidden in a hollow pillar in the sleeping chamber. Next day they are confronted by an incensed king who threatens to have them all killed unless they make good their boasts. However, in this almost-parody of the folk motif of the contest of strength, the Franks have an unexpected ally. An angel appears to Charlemagne and rebukes him severely for allowing such an incident to occur, but then promises that they will be assisted to achieve their *gabs*. After three or four have been carried out the king, with his city flooded and his palace in ruins around him, concedes defeat and offers to become Charlemagne's vassal. He suggests they seal the bargain by the marriage of his daughter, Jacqueline, to Oliver whose boast – that he would lie with her a hundred times in one night – was surprisingly the first one King Hugh ordered to be fulfilled. (Incidentally, Oliver was successful not through angelic assistance but rather because his performance in achieving thirty times in one night so impressed the princess that she swore he had reached the target figure.)

Eventually Charlemagne reaches home again, loaded with treasure and precious relics and prepared even to forgive his wife her foolish remarks; especially as at the crown-wearing in Jerusalem it was unanimously declared that the emperor of the Franks was a more impressive figure than the king of Jerusalem.

The broad humour and fantastic detail of the poem stand out in sharp contrast to the more realistic pseudo-historical adventures narrated in the other early *chansons de geste*, but as the centuries passed the heroic adventures of Charlemagne and his peers maintained their popularity at the cost of adapting to the changing tastes of the times, till in the fifteenth century *Charlemagne's Merry Pilgrimage* (as the modern English adaptation calls it) becomes more typical than exceptional. The stories were also translated and retold in many different languages from Icelandic to Italian, and it is in Italy that the final degradation of the genre can be found in the comic masterpieces of Ariosto and Boiardo. Roland the *preux*, the proud Christian warrior fighting for God and fair France (*dulce France*) is transmogrified into Orlando, enamoured (*innamorato*) of the heartless Angelica and driven mad (*furioso*) by her disdain, so that his friend Astolfo has to travel to the moon to recover the lost wits of his lunatic friend. A brief quotation from each poem will illustrate the changes that have taken place between the twelfth and the sixteenth centuries even in such a basic detail as the description of a battle:

When Roland heard this by God he was much distressed. He spurred his horse and let it gallop on and struck the count as hard as he could. He broke the shield and smashed the hauberk, pierced the chest and broke the bones, splitting his spine away from his back, and with his lance drove forth his soul. He spiked him nicely flinging down his body; with lance outstretched he struck him down dead from his horse, breaking his neck in two.   (*Roland*, S. xciii)

But Orlando was not willing to let himself be taken at the first try. As soon as they formed their circle around him he broke it. He lowered his lance, aimed where he saw the thickest crowd of soldiers and rode; and he caught one, then another and another on the lance like pastry on a spit. He speared six of them. The lance was not long enough to hold a seventh. The seventh man, nevertheless, was so severely wounded by the blow that he died too. (*Orlando Furioso*, trans. R. Hodgens, p. 138)

Truly between the *Chanson de Roland* and the *Orlando Furioso* there is a great gulf fixed.

The Flawed Ideal: the Matter of Britain

'THERE are only three subjects [*matieres*] for any man of sense: those of France, of Britain and of Rome the great.' Jean Bodel, author of a *chanson de geste*, a miracle play and other poems wrote these words early in the thirteenth century, by which time the 'Matter of Britain' – or Celtic tales – and the 'Matter of Rome' – the legends of Classical antiquity – had come to rival and even surpass the Carolingian stories in popularity. By the mid-thirteenth century, the 'Matter of Britain' had spread throughout Christendom and achieved the pre-eminent position in European culture that it still holds even today.

Although the term 'Arthurian Romance' suggests to most people the love stories of Lancelot and Guinevere, Tristan and Iseult, which were such an important and novel feature of the 'Matter of Britain' (see p. 49 below), it should not be forgotten that the earliest texts presented King Arthur as a historical figure, ruling a vast pan-European empire. Geoffrey of Monmouth created Arthur the king (as distinct from the historical Arthur, leader and war lord) in his Latin *History of the Kings of Britain* in 1135, and by the end of the century writers such as Wace or Chrétien de Troyes in French, and Lawman in English, had developed Geoffrey's comparatively brief narrative of battles and politics into a cohesive and rich historical tapestry whose reality was widely accepted even though this compellingly believable Golden Age of British history had never in fact existed.

The Middle Ages believed in the Arthurian world as it believed in the legends of Greece and Rome, because they provided a necessary imaginative focus for the ideas and beliefs of the community, with the added advantage that Arthur as a Christian, heroic figure was even more satisfactory a subject for stories than the pagans of Classical antiquity. With his court and Round Table, he formed a social group as coherent and inter-reliant as that of Charlemagne and his peers but not limited, as they were, by the known facts of history.

Arthur's wars against the Saxons or against the other kings of Britain, which loom so large in Geoffrey's *History*, give way in the romances to the endless tales of individual knights in quest of adventure. Love and personal psychology are important in some tales, pre-eminent in others, but all take place against this strongly defined community background: the Knights of the Round Table are the first genuinely international peace-keeping force in a Europe just beginning to emerge from a state of constant warfare.

Arthur's role as arbitrator is already established in the twelfth century. In Beroul's *Tristan*, Queen Iseult sends to Arthur asking him to come and act as judge in her trial by ordeal, to which she has submitted in order to clear herself and Tristan of the accusations against them. However, it is in the great prose romances of the first half of the thirteenth century, especially the *Vulgate* or *Prose Lancelot*, that we find the ultimate development of the concept of the Arthurian kingdom as an ideal state brought to a tragic end through the actions of its founder, Arthur, and his principal supporter, Lancelot.

In the final branch of the *Vulgate Cycle*, the *Mort Artu* or *Arthur's Death*, Geoffrey's brief account of the treachery of Arthur's nephew, Mordred, and the adulterous queen has developed into a narrative of exceptional impact and power. As soon as Lancelot and Guinevere renew the adulterous liaison that had been renounced during the *Quest of the Holy Grail*, the tragic outcome is as inevitable as in a Greek play. The romantic, pathetic tale of the Maid of Astolat is followed by the drama of Lancelot's discovery in the queen's room, the rescue of Guinevere from the stake and the siege of the lovers in Lancelot's castle of Joyous Garde.

At this point in the narrative, the author's skill becomes clear, for it is in the heat of the discovery of the affair between his queen and his friend that Arthur renounces the principles of a lifetime and refuses to take counsel with his barons. ' "And I command you," he said, "first and foremost because you are a king, and the other barons also who are present that you make up your minds among you by what death she shall die. For she cannot escape being put to death, even if you yourself were on her side, so that even if you said that she should not die yet she shall die" ' (*Mort Artu*, S. 92). The king addressed here, King Yon, one of the knights of the Round Table, succeeds only in getting the sentence postponed till the next day. Gawain comes to the king and renounces his allegiance, 'for I will never serve you again in my life if you commit this act of disloyalty' (*Mort Artu*, S. 93). The fact that the king's actions are contrary to his own juridical laws is emphasised by the subsequent intervention of the Pope who finally brings about a reconciliation between the royal couple, while Lancelot accepts exile and retires to his own lands in France. His lament as he sails from Logres is as moving and noble as any moment in medieval literature:

> Then he said so softly that no one in the ship heard him except Bors: 'Ah! fair land filled with all good things and in which my life and spirit ever dwell, blessed be you from the mouth of him we call upon, Jesus Christ, and blessed be all those who dwell in you, be they my friends or my enemies. Grant them peace! Grant them rest! God grant them greater joy than I have had. God grant them honour and victory against all those who in any way offend them! And indeed they will have these things for no one can be in a country as fair as this one is, who is not happier than any other people and I speak as one who has tested this, for as long as I dwelt there more good things came to me in abundance than would have come had I been in any other land.' (*Mort Artu*, S. 122–3)

It is illuminating to compare the *Mort Artu* with the much better known version which has given the name *Morte Darthur* to Malory's great compilation. Great as Malory's achievement may be, it does not diminish the impact of the 'Freynsh boke' written, it should be remembered, more than two centuries earlier, from which he took his material. The *Mort Artu* is written in spare almost dry prose: the style has none of Malory's luxuriance and suffers therefore by comparison, particularly in English translation, but it has a freshness and sense of historical reality and immediacy that is far removed from Malory's more romantic and imaginative world. In each case the author is looking back to a Golden Age but Malory is doing so at two removes, for the fighting community that inspired the *Mort Artu* had itself changed and evolved. England and France had passed through the appalling disasters of the fourteenth century: the Hundred Years War, the Black Death, the almost complete breakdown of law and order in the wake of fighting, famine and disease. When Malory wrote his *Morte Darthur* he was holding up a mirror to his readers not so much to show them reality but to encourage them with a glorious vision of what had been, an apotheosis of fellowship and nobility: 'And he that was curteyse, trew and faythefull to hys frynde was that time cherysshed' (Malory, XVIII, S.4).

In 1215, the author of the *Mort Artu*, though dealing with a story already nearly a century old, presents an ideal that is much nearer to his readers. More down to earth, almost humdrum. As a result, the characters, especially the principals, are also more accessible and true to the life of the time. When Lancelot comes to court not knowing that Arthur has learned of his liaison with the queen, he is surprised and hurt at the king's unexpected change of manner towards him:

> After supper when the cloths had been taken away, the king called on his knights to go hunting in Camelot forest the following morning. Then Lancelot said to the king: 'Sire, you will have my company on this outing.' 'Fair lord,' the king said to Lancelot, 'indeed you can stay at home on this occasion for I have so many other knights that I shall do very well without your company.' Then Lancelot realised that the king was angry with him but had no idea of the reason and it worried him very much. (*Mort Artu*, S. 88).

In contrast to this personal detail and the description of

Lancelot at court, Malory passes directly from a dialogue between Arthur and Agravain to the simple statement: 'So on the morne kynge Arthure rode an-hunting and sent worde to the quene that he wolde be oute all that nyght' (Malory, xx, S. 1). (In Malory, Lancelot decides to visit the queen, in the French she sends for him.)

The development of the Arthurian prose cycles in the thirteenth century completed, at least temporarily, the eclipse of the Carolingian epics. Some of these, like *Ogier the Dane* or the *Four Sons of Aymon*, survived the great changes of taste at the turn of the century by introducing or expanding the folk elements and the fantasy or even by transforming their heroes into not-quite-courtly lovers. Some were virtually rewritten, like the *Song of Roland* or the *Song of William* (now called *Aliscans*) which were both known to the rest of the Middle Ages and the succeeding centuries only in these later versions. But Charlemagne did not concede the fight to Arthur without one final battle. In some later French romances and their translations in Spanish, Portuguese and Italian, there occurs a scene in which Charlemagne, having conquered Britain with his warriors – such a conquest was a generally accepted part of the poetic biography of the emperor – sees one or more statues of Arthur's knights. The name, number and location of the statues vary. In Italian, there are five: Tristan, Palamedes, Lancelot, Lamorak de Galles and Galahad. Charlemagne finds them and 'seeing their form and their stature declared that King Arthur was worthy of a shameful death having had such knights in his kingdom and power, for he himself would have brought all Christendom and the Saracens too under his rule' (*Tavola Ritonda*, p. 39).

Charlemagne's criticism of Arthur is but a lone voice in the wilderness amidst the chorus of eulogies. The Middle Ages believed in King Arthur's existence because they needed to believe it. His kingdom, and especially the ideals of his knights, represented a golden age to which war-torn weary generations have looked back longingly for nearly a thousand years. Part fact, mainly fiction, wholly believable, this was the ideal of chivalry the Middle Ages needed to invent.

Pagans and Aliens

THE literature of the fighting society, both the 'Matter of France' and the 'Matter of Britain' had of necessity to create enemies, opponents against whom it fought. Although, as we have seen, the starting point of many of these stories is an act of treachery, cowardice or apostasy, or an internal conflict of duty, responsibility or relationship, yet the outsiders, those who do not belong to the community, play an important, indeed a crucial, role in creating the excitement and interest of the *chansons de geste* and the Arthurian romances.

The commonest single group of outsiders are the pagans: a generic term for all non-Christians. Medieval story-tellers made no attempt to distinguish between the Muslims and, say, the Saxons. All are portrayed as idol-worshippers: 'He had the drums sounded in Saragossa. Mahomet was set up on the highest tower and there was not one pagan who did not worship and adore him' (*Roland*, S. LXVIII). However, within each group of pagans there is some attempt at individualisation, similar to that provided for the French barons. Indeed, when the battle of Roncevaux is being prepared for, the pagan king, Marsilie, gives command of the army to his nephew, just as Charlemagne had earlier confided the rearguard to his nephew, Roland. Marsilie's nephew (who is not named) then specifically asks his uncle to 'select for me twelve of your chiefs and with them I will fight against the twelve companions' (*cumpaignons*; *Roland*, S. LXX). These latter are the twelve peers, almost the only named fighters in the French rearguard. This parallelism is maintained and each pagan peer is matched against his Christian counterpart in a long series of very formalised single combats. Since an easy victory brought little credit to the victor, the pagans are naturally presented as valiant fighters and some are clearly shown to be almost equal to the Christians: 'There is a lord from Balaguez with a noble person and a bright proud face. When he is mounted on his horse he bears his arms most proudly. He is far-famed for his nobility and were he a Christian would be a man of great valour' (*Roland*, S. LXXII).

The words used for nobility and valour, *vasselage* and *barnét*, are those normally used for feudal barons. The suggestion that he needs only to be a Christian to be a great warrior is an obvious reflection of the attitude of the time and worth comparing with Voltaire's words, six hundred years later: in the play of *Zaïre* the hero is a noble Turkish sultan who has so many virtues that, 'Were he a Christian what more could he have?' (*S'il était chrétien, que serait-il de plus?*, *Zaïre*, IV.1).

Here and there a vivid little description of the land or people the pagans rule gives an exotic and different flavour to the endless repetitions of single combats. Thus, Chernuble de Munigre – some Saracen names are extremely harsh and cruel-sounding, a technique Tolkien uses to great effect with Orcs in the *Lord of the Rings* – rules over a land 'where the sun never shines nor can corn grow there. No rain falls there nor shower of dew and there is no stone that is not black. Some say that there the devils dwell' (*Roland*, S. LXXVIII). The reference to devils and the use of biblical phraseology emphasise the alien, evil nature of the land and its ruler.

Pagans in the William of Orange cycle are very different from those in the *Song of Roland*, less formalised and more humorous in the way they are presented, even in the early *Song of William*. In the *Crowning of Louis*, William fights in Italy against invading pagan armies on two separate occasions. Each time the conflict is settled by a single combat, but the two battles are skilfully differentiated. The first is arranged by the Pope as representative of the Christians, and our first glimpse of William's opponent, Corsolt, is through the eyes of the 'gentleman in the big hat' (*Crowning*, S. XVIII), as they call him. Corsolt is a giant in size and very ugly – an alien as well as a pagan: 'Ugly and squinting, hideous as the devil. He had eyes as red as coals in a brazier, a broad head with a shock of hair; there was half a foot span between his two eyes and from shoulder to waist he was quite six feet. A more hideous man could never eat bread' (*Crowning*, S. XIX). The fight between Corsolt and William therefore becomes a David and Goliath combat, in the course of which William receives a blow which glances off the nosepiece of his helmet and slices the end off his nose. The fiery count takes this fairly philosophically, declaring: 'I know that though my nose may be shortened, my name will be made longer by it'

(*Crowning*, S. XXVIII). Indeed he is known, henceforth, as William Shortnose (*courtnez* is actually a corruption of *courbnez*, 'hooknose', the form used in the *Song of William*), but his attitude to his injury does not prevent him from rejoicing over the final defeat of Corsolt: ' "God," said William, "I have avenged my nose indeed!" ' (*Crowning*, S. XXVIII).

Roland and his peers only view pagans *en masse* and it is the author of the story who distinguishes them for narrative purposes, whereas in the William cycle much of the character-isation of both Christian and pagan derives from the comments of the protagonist. After the defeat of Corsolt, William takes prisoner the Saracen leader, Galafre, and asks his help to rescue the captured Christian king of Rome, as Galafre had promised. But Galafre refuses to do anything 'until I am held over the font and baptized, for Mahomet can help me no longer' (*Crowning*, S. XXX). William is delighted and the Pope immediately baptises his former enemy with William as one of the thirty godfathers. The question of enforced baptism is central to many of the *chansons de geste* as it was to the whole crusading Christian community. The Church stressed the need to offer baptism as an alternative to death to defeated opponents, but it seems likely that many of the crusaders would have echoed William's words when Otran, king of Nîmes, is reluctant to give up his religion despite urging from the French. 'Then Count William cried out loudly: "A hundred devils take the man who begs him too much." They threw him out of one of the windows and he was dead before he hit the ground' (*Waggon-Train*, S. LVI).

In view of this attitude it is the more interesting that William takes a pagan bride. His wife, Guibourg, who plays such a major role in the *Song of William*, is a converted Saracen princess, Orable. It is her long-lost brother, Rainouart, who leads the rescue force in the later, second half of the poem, armed with his club or *tinel*. At the end of the poem, Rainouart, like Galafre, is baptised with William as one of his godfathers. (It was against canon law to marry your godson's sister, but not, apparently, to be godfather to your wife's brother. It is often overlooked when discussing the forbidden degrees of kinship within which people might not marry, that these included kinship through baptism, so to speak.) The story of the wooing and winning of the princess Orable is told in the

Capture of Orange (*La Prise d'Orange*), one of the central poems of the William cycle. A considerable part of the action of this poem takes place in pagan territory with William confronting them on their own home ground, a feature of these poems which helps to create the unique picture of the pagans that the cycle offers.

A change in the attitude to the pagan is seen very early in the thirteenth century in Jean Bodel's *The Play of St Nicholas* (*Le Jeu de St Nicolas*, see p. 95 below), which has a section describing a battle between the two faiths. The pagan king and his seneschal are depicted as comic characters, though the four emirs the king summons to help him in battle are played more or less straight. At the end of the play, the king is converted by the miracle of St Nicholas and demands that his emirs follow suit. One refuses, and when ordered to obey his feudal overlord tries to return his fief: 'I defy you and give back your fief and my duty to you' (*Nicholas*, 1493). The others then subdue him bodily – albeit with difficulty: 'he is very strong, you'll have to take him by surprise' (1498–9) – and he surrenders, at least outwardly: 'Saint Nicholas, I adore you but against my will and under protest. You will have of me only the bark. In words I will be your man but my trust is in Mahomet' (1512–6). In the light of this change of attitude it is not surprising to find thirty years or so later the character of Palamedes the pagan playing a major role in the *Prose Tristan* romance. He refuses baptism on several occasions because he would then be made one of the knights of the Round Table, which he does not wish to happen until he has had time to match his strength against them – they were debarred from fighting each other – not from any spirit of religious animosity but simply in order to win laurels for himself as a worthy fighter and chivalrous knight.

This more favourable picture of the Saracens found in a number of thirteenth-century texts may have been influenced by the third crusade during which some of the Saracens, especially Saladin himself,[7] were highly praised by their Christian opponents as models of chivalry. Indeed, Saladin becomes almost the hero of a series of tales, beginning with the description of his ancestors in *The Count of Ponthieu's Daughter* (*La Fille du Comte de Ponthieu*) in the thirteenth century where he is credited with French Christian lineage on his mother's side:

'of her was born the mother of the courteous Saladin' (*Ponthieu*, p. 50). By the late fifteenth century the prose text, *Saladin*, though ostensibly part of the Cycle of the Crusades is, in fact, an adventure story in which, among other fantastic incidents, Saladin visits France in disguise and has an affair with the queen. He also conquers England and defeats Richard I ignominiously in single combat. By this time, the enemies of France are not the pagans but the English.

With pagans becoming less popular as satisfactory enemies for the heroes of the changing society, new and interesting opponents had to be found and a wide range of aliens appear in the romances, especially in the later Middle Ages. A small number of them could be classed as monsters, notably the two sons of the demon (*netun*) whom Yvain fights and who are black and hideous and unconventionally armed (*Yvain*, 5506ff.; the term *netun* is a corruption of *Neptunus*, Neptune, and later gave the modern French word *lutin*, a mischievous Puck-like figure); the giant of St Michael's Mount whom Arthur kills; or the same monarch's even more monstrous adversary, the Great Cat of Lausanne (*Vulgate Merlin*, ii, pp. 428–30, 441–4). The best-known medieval 'monster', however, the dragon, who in the modern popular imagination is almost inseparable from knights errant, in fact appears only rarely in medieval literature outside of saints' lives and religious allegory. In French, there is a genuine dragon which plays a minor role in the Tristan story and a maiden who has been turned into a dragon in *The Fair Unknown* (*Le Bel Inconnu*) but the important dragons are found in Germanic and Norse literature, especially in the stories connected with Siegfried.

The role of dwarves like that of giants is ambivalent in the epics and romances: mere size does not in itself imply either good or evil. Vicious dwarves are found in a number of stories, notably Frocin, the evil genius of King Mark in Beroul's *Tristan*, or the ill-mannered dwarf who strikes Guinevere's attendant early in Chrétien's *Erec*. On the other hand, the latter work also includes a noble and valiant knight of small stature, Guivret le petit. Nor is it merely a question of birth. We have already met the noble but hideous pagan giant, Corsolt, who is no uglier than the perfectly benevolent but monstrous herdsman in *Yvain*:

I approached the peasant [*vilain*] and saw he had a head
bigger than that of a nag or other animal; tangled hair and
a scabby brow nearly two spans wide; hairy ears as big as an
elephant's, thick eyebrows and a flat face; eyes of an owl and
a cat's nose, a gaping mouth like a wolf, sharp reddish teeth
like a boar; a reddish beard and twisted moustaches and a
chin that came down on his chest; a long spine twisted and
humped, and he was leaning on his club.   (*Yvain*, 292–306)

When the knight, Calogrenanz, addresses this strange appari-
tion he may be pardoned for asking, 'Tell me if you are a good
thing or not?' and the reply is both succinct and ambivalent:
'And he told me he was a man' (*Yvain*, 328). In the context of
medieval thought, the herdsman has, in fact, said enough to
establish that he is not a creature or a monster. In view of his
zoomorphic appearance, however, it is not surprising that he
adds, when asked what sort of man he is, 'Such as you see and I
am never anything else' (*Yvain*, 329–40). The second assertion
seems to imply that he is not a shape-changer. Werwolves and
other weranimals are less common in medieval France than in
modern Transylvania, and as with other creatures of strange
appearance they may be on the side of good or evil. In *Bisclavret*,
one of the lays of Marie de France, the hero is a werwolf on three
days of each week and this is treated by Marie as merely a
personal quirk, a slight misfortune, until his wife learns the
truth and turns against her husband. In another of her lays,
Yonec, the unhappy heroine, locked up in a tower by her jealous
husband, is visited by a suitor who assumes the form of a hawk
in order to fly in at her window. When she shows some doubt as
to his origins, he offers to take communion with her as proof he
is not a devil but a good Christian.

If Frocin is the best-known bad dwarf, the most famous of the
good ones is Auberon, the lord of faery, who was cursed at his
christening and never grew any bigger after he was five years
old. He plays an important role in the stories of Huon of
Bordeaux (see p. 26 above). However, the fays and their male
counterparts, the mages or sages, are not really aliens. They are
usually of normal stature and appearance – 'beautiful ladies,
richly dressed' (*Play of the Bower*, 387; see p. 98 below) – and like
Morgan le Fay, Arthur's half-sister, or Merlin the enchanter

are more like the Classical deities than the post-Shakespearean concept of fairies. Men and women of exceptional mental stature and with superior control of the natural forces, they are yet essentially part of the community, be it castle, army or court, and not to be confused with the outsiders; when they are wicked, like Morgan, they are portrayed like the traitors not like the enemies; unlike the most alien of all characters, the devils who became increasingly important in the later literature especially the drama and the visions of Hell, these fays are human, part of the created world, or, in the case of Merlin, half-breeds, the offspring of a human woman and a devil (see p. 84 below).

The progressive deterioration of the relations within the Christian forces manifested, for example, in the sack of Constantinople in 1204 also helped to discredit the picture of a united Christendom fighting heroically against the pagans. To this was added the growing sense of national identity and power till by the end of the thirteenth century the vision of a United Christian Europe had disappeared never to return. As a result, the original distinction between historical epic and fictional romance, between the 'Matter of France' and the 'Matter of Britain' became increasingly blurred; a new genre evolved, the chivalrous romance which might feature knights of all traditions. But as chivalry became less chivalrous, the romances became more romantic, even fantastic. Enchanters, giants, devils and vices, Antichrist himself, are depicted as mere stereotyped 'baddies' with little attempt being made to relate them to a realistic social or cultural background. Whether the villains are pagan, alien or Christian, the authors are content to make them merely bigger and nastier Aunt Sallies to be knocked down by equally undifferentiated and standardised heroes.

3. The Quest of the Self

He sees himself in his lover as if in a mirror, not knowing whom he sees.

(Plato)

ALTHOUGH the *chansons de geste* of the 'Matter of France' continued to delight audiences right through the Middle Ages, the new genre, the romance, which developed in the middle of the twelfth century rapidly surpassed it in popularity. The subject matter as we have already seen was drawn from Celtic stories and Classical antiquity but despite the parallels between Arthur's Britain and Charlemagne's France (see p. 36 above) a fundamentally different attitude to the individual informs the two genres of epic and romance. In the former he – the characters are predominantly masculine – is above all a part of the community, national, feudal or family, while in the romances the heroes and heroines – almost equally matched in numbers and importance – are portrayed as isolated individuals seeking to discover their own identity within their community. It is not by chance that in many of the earliest romances a central character remains unnamed until a moment of crisis in the story: Enid in Chrétien's *Erec* is only named at her wedding, while Lancelot is called the 'Knight of the Cart' for the first half of the romance. One result of the stress on personal identity and problems is that the national and religious fervour of the epics, the group emotions, are replaced by more self-centred feelings of love and friendship.

The phenomenon usually called 'courtly love' (*amour courtois*) by modern critics had first appeared in France in the eleventh century when the Provençal troubadours, men and women from many different classes of society, extolled the power of *fin'amor* in their lyric poems. The origins of this ancestor of romantic love are uncertain and much disputed but its nature can be defined with fair accuracy.[1] It is essentially an aristocratic, courtly emotion experienced by both the knight and the lady equally if not reciprocally. In its most extreme

47

form it demands from the lover total subservience to the lady's whim and a grovelling humility: she is so far above him that he can only worship at her shrine and gratefully accept the crumbs of her graciousness. Nevertheless, provided the sentiment is mutual, the lover may attain the bliss of a full physical union with his beloved regardless of whether she is married to another. Just as spiritual grace was manifested in the acts of the saints, inspiring them to superhuman feats of asceticism and suffering for their Lord, so the courtly lover was inspired by his passion for his lady to deeds of valour and acts of courtesy.

The *fin'amor* of the Provençal poets was reflected in Northern France not in lyric poems but in romances where the love between the hero and heroine provided the motive for the action. Many examples of friendship, even of love, between two characters can be quoted from the *chansons de geste*, but they are incidental to the action, whereas in the romances these relationships are pivotal and as such are analysed sometimes in very minute detail, this analysis being one of the distinguishing marks of the new genre. The troubadours of Provence poured forth their feelings in personal lyric poems; the *trouvères* of Northern France created fictional lovers in fictional situations and then analysed and examined their feelings for one another with clinical objectivity.

So successful was the concept of courtly love as a literary device that a code of behaviour based on it was composed in the late twelfth century in Latin, which gave it an authority and status beyond that of the vernacular texts. However, the *Art of True Love (De Amore)* as set forth by Andreas Capellanus seems to have had only a limited influence in its own day. Like its great successor the *Romance of the Rose*, Andreas's treatise became more widely venerated after the literature it codified had been replaced by more popular and less esoteric conceits. The idea put forward by Andreas that ladies held Courts of Love in which they debated the niceties of courtly behaviour is now generally held to be a fictional device with little basis in historical reality. More significant of what the reading public actually demanded is the evidence of the romances themselves which show a far greater range of emotional relationships than the strict courtly ethos would countenance.

This stress on emotion as well as action in the romances

reflects the wider audience for whom they were composed and especially the greatly increased importance of women as readers and patrons. This is also noticeable in the later *chansons de geste*: works like the *Capture of Orange* (*Prise d'Orange*) or the *Siege of Barbastre* from the cycle of William of Orange have a love interest at the heart of the story. A change is also to be observed in the genesis of the tales – the *chansons de geste* were probably composed and sung by anonymous *jongleurs*, minstrels who might be itinerant or part of a great household like the one described in the *Song of William*: 'In all France there is no better singer nor more bold warrior in the battle. He can declaim songs of the deeds of Clovis, the first emperor of fair France who believed in our Lord God, and of his son, Flovent the fighter . . . of Charlemagne and his nephew Roland, Girard of Vienne and the valiant Oliver!' (*William*, S. xcvii). The romances on the other hand were usually composed by named writers and aimed at a public that was at least nominally literate.

The earliest romances to be composed were the *romans d'antiquité*, Bodel's 'Matter of Rome' (see p. 35 above), which date from the middle of the twelfth century and made use of stories from Greek and Roman literature. The four major romances of Troy, Aeneas, Thebes and Alexander were very popular in their day though they had little direct influence on subsequent versions of Classical literature; an exception to this is the tale of Troilus and Cressida, first recounted in the *Roman de Troie* and used subsequently by Chaucer, Boccaccio and Shakespeare whence it passed into the public domain of European literature. The medieval Alexander romances are in a class of their own for they include a range of fantastic journeys which have little to do with either epic or romance (see p. 115).

Springtime of Love: Chrétien de Troyes

FAR more generally influential, however, were the other major group of romances based on the 'Matter of Britain'. The tales of King Arthur and the Knights of the Round Table, especially Gawain and Lancelot, whose epic denouement was considered in the last chapter, started their literary career in the twelfth

century and spread rapidly all over Europe; if Geoffrey of
Monmouth is the father of the legend of King Arthur, the father
of the Arthurian romance is Chrétien de Troyes, one of the
greatest writers in medieval France, who lived in the second
half of the twelfth century in the province of Champagne.

Our information about Chrétien's education and literary
background is only such as can be gathered from his works, and
especially the list of his writings which he gives at the beginning
of *Cligès*: 'The man who told of *Erec and Enid* and translated the
Commandments and the *Art of Love* into French [*romans*] and told
of the *Eating of the Shoulder*; of *King Mark and Yseult the Fair*; of the
Metamorphoses of the Lapwing, the Swallow and the Nightingale, begins here a new tale' (*Cligès*, 1–8). From this catalogue it
is clear that Chrétien knew his Ovid, including the *Metamorphoses* from which he might have taken the tale of Tantalus
offering the gods his son's shoulder at a feast. (Alternatively
the 'Eating of the Shoulder' might refer to the legend of Atreus
and Thyestes.) He was also familiar with the Celtic tales of
King Arthur. Though a romancer, Chrétien never claims
originality for his stories: 'Therefore I delight in telling a story
worth hearing of the king who was so renowned that he is
spoken of far and wide' (*Yvain*, 33–6). Nor is the use of
pre-existent material a peculiarly medieval trait. On the
contrary it remained common practice right down to the
eighteenth century and in certain genres, such as tragedy, it
was considered from Classical times onwards obligatory to use
known stories, since only the knowledge that the events
described had a basis in history or myth could make credible
the extreme situations suitable for tragic drama. Even in the
twentieth century when originality has become such a highly
valued element in literature, the welcome given to new,
independent stories of King Arthur, for example T. H. White's
Once and Future King, shows that the reading public still enjoys
meeting familiar figures in new garments.

Chrétien contributed three major elements to the development of Arthurian romance: the possibility of courtly love's
existing within the confines of marriage; the love story of
Lancelot and Guinevere; and the earliest extant written
account of the phenomenon which came to be known as the
Holy Grail. In each area there are other related texts to be

considered, many of them of very high quality, but no other writer showed such a range of inspiration and few approached his skill in analysing the human heart.

It is above all in the emotions of youth that Chrétien found his principal subject-matter. All his heroes and most of his heroines are young, for despite their married status, Laudine and Guinevere need not be older than their suitors. This emphasis on youth brings with it also the young lover's total preoccupation with his own affairs and needs and desires. The demands of society, religion and even his friends and fellow-knights are largely ignored.

Of all the lovers in Chrétien's romances, no couple is so young and so innocent and so sensitively portrayed as Perceval and Blanchefleur in the *Story of the Grail* (*Conte del Graal*; see p. 68 below). Perceval comes to Blanchefleur's castle when she is under siege from a neighbouring lord who wants both her and her lands. After they have retired for the night, Blanchefleur creeps into Perceval's room: 'Then she left her bed and went out of her room, so scared that all her limbs were shaking and she was covered with sweat.' Perceval is awakened by the tears she lets fall on his face: 'He saw her kneeling by his bed with her arms round his neck. Then he did her the courtesy of taking her in his arms and drawing her to him and asking her: "Fair one, what do you want? Why have you come?" ' She explains at length about the count who is attacking the castle and the fate she fears for her domain and herself and she begs Perceval to fight for her against Clamadeus. Perceval answers with deeds as well as words, inviting her to ' "be comforted, and weep no more . . . come into this bed with me for it is wide enough for us both and you must not leave me again." ' . . . Then he gently and sweetly settled her under the covers . . . and thus they lay all night, side by side and mouth to mouth until day' (*Story of the Grail*, 1960–2068). The innocent sensuality of the scene is a world away from the mature passions of the loves of Lancelot and Guinevere at the end of the prose cycle: all the characters are middle-aged or old in *Arthur's Death*. What Chrétien describes is the spring of love, a time of youthful ardour and freshness very different from the autumnal melancholy of the ageing unhappy queen and her guilt-ridden but still faithful knight (see p. 63 below).[2]

Courtship and Marriage

CHRÉTIEN's romances of *Erec* and *Yvain, the Knight of the Lion* have their counterparts in the Welsh *Mabinogion*, in the tales of *Geraint* and the *Lady of the Fountain*, respectively. The dates of the manuscripts and the very different treatment of the subject-matter make direct borrowing either way extremely improbable, and it is generally accepted today that there was some kind of common source to which each author gave his own idiosyncratic form. That writers from Eastern France and Western Britain should both be familiar with the same stories is less unlikely than it sounds if we remember the existence of the Norman empire and the close political links between England and France all through the Middle Ages and especially in the twelfth and thirteenth centuries.

Chrétien's originality lies not in his subject-matter but in the treatment of it: *Erec* and *Yvain* form a diptych, the two sides of the coin. Both open in Arthur's court and narrate the wooing and wedding of the hero and heroine in the first third of the poem. Then comes a break in the relationship, caused by the hero's immoderation (*desmesure*). In *Erec*, he abandons chivalry in order to devote himself to his bride, while in *Yvain* it is the wife herself who is abandoned while her husband overstays his leave of absence at court and tournament. The rest of the tale, in each case, comprises a series of adventures through which the hero, by implication at least, works his way back into a socially acceptable *modus vivendi* and achieves reconciliation with his wife.

Within these parallel structures, Chrétien presents two very different pairs of lovers. Erec and Yvain are both kings' sons and valiant knights but not only are their characters very distinct: so too are their attitudes to their social rank. The context of *Erec* is realistic, with very few elements of fantasy or marvel. The keynote is struck very early on when King Arthur proposes to revive the custom of the Hunt of the White Stag; Gawain warns him he will have neither pleasure nor profit from it for the custom decrees that whoever slays the White Stag shall kiss the most beautiful maiden in the court: 'And here there are five hundred damsels of high birth, noble, wise daughters of kings, and not one of them but has a knight, bold and valiant and ready to declare rightly or wrongly that the one he prefers is the most noble and most beautiful' (*Erec*, 50–8). Arthur admits the truth of his nephew's criticism but affirms his intention of going ahead with the hunt since he has already declared it, 'and words spoken by the king may not be retracted thereafter' (*Erec*, 61–2). From the beginning of the romance, then, there is a stress on the importance of public opinion. Erec, who is escorting Queen Guinevere instead of going on the hunt, wishes to ride off in pursuit of a knight whose dwarf has insulted and struck the queen's lady-in-waiting. He eventually catches up with his quarry in a distant town. A contest is being held there, with a sparrowhawk being awarded to the most beautiful lady present. The judgement is made by the lady's champion defeating any knights who support a rival claimant. Erec lodges with a vavasour (a minor fief-holder) who has a very beautiful daughter, Enid, for whom he wins the sparrowhawk by defeating the reigning champion, the discourteous knight with the dwarf. Having revealed his identity to the vavasour, Erec then takes Enid, wearing a ragged dress since the family are very poor, to Arthur's court as his bride-to-be. Arthur who had won the White Stag Hunt is able to claim the prize kiss from Enid without offending any one since her beauty is so overwhelmingly superior. The wedding is celebrated with great splendour and magnificent descriptions as befit the rank of the bridegroom and the couple then return to Erec's father's kingdom and settle down to married life together. Gradually Enid realises that Erec is neglecting his duties as a knight in order to be with her and since she loves him she reproaches herself for having diminished him in this way: ' "Therefore indeed I have shamed him utterly, not for anything would I have done so." Then she said to him: "My love [*amis*] alas! for you!" ' (*Erec*, 2501–3). Erec, woken perhaps by her tears falling on his chest, hears these words, wonders why she is weeping and forces her to tell him the truth. It is one of Chrétien's most skilful touches in this story that everything is seen from Enid's point of view and we know Erec's feelings only from his words and actions. His violent reaction to Enid's confession suggests that his pride is hurt; like King Cophetua he has deigned to raise up this ragged beggar-maid to his level and now she dares to criticise him. In his account of Erec's uxoriousness, Chrétien stresses his obsession with Enid's beauty and that he makes her his mistress, his beloved ('*s'amie et sa drue*', 2435), rather than his wife. Only after a series of adventures in which Enid has proved herself as a person – willing to disobey her husband in order to save his life, for example – are the couple reunited and now Erec addresses her as 'Fair sweet sister, noble lady, wise and loyal' ('*Bele douce suer, gentix dame, leax et sage*', 5783–4).

The change in Enid's status starts to show quite early on in this section of the romance. While they are still not reconciled, Erec nevertheless accepts Enid's insistence that she should watch while he sleeps and he even accepts her cloak to cover him. Nor does he now rebuke her for speaking though he had earlier forbidden her to do so. Already Erec is beginning to see Enid as an individual, a person, not just a beautiful toy.

But Erec must still be reconciled to society and this Chrétien achieves by the adventure of the custom of the Joy of the Court (*Joie de la Cour*) where Erec defeats a knight imprisoned by his lady's whim in an orchard paradise surrounded by a wall of air. By overcoming the knight, Erec symbolically defeats his earlier self who was imprisoned in the lovers' paradise of their early married life: 'It was often midday or later before he left her side; this delighted him, whatever distress it caused to others' (*Erec*, 2442–4). The symbolic parallelism of the two episodes is emphasised when we learn that the defeated knight was brought up at the court of King Lac, Erec's father, but never undertook knightly adventures since he 'did not wish to be false and faithless and disloyal' (*Erec*, 6063–4). Having achieved this new mature relationship with his wife and purged his contempt of the demands of his rank and class, Erec is ready for kingship. His father conveniently dies and the romance ends with a long description of Erec's and Enid's coronation.

Although *Yvain*, like *Erec*, opens at the court of King Arthur, there is much less sense in the romance of the social realities. Yvain is a king's son but no mention is made of his kingdom or his duties as a feudal lord. The whole setting is more 'romantic', with the stress on the actions and emotions of the principal characters, and the big set-piece descriptions, wedding and coronation, are replaced by intimate scenes of castle life. The relationship of the lovers is fraught with difficulties since Yvain first sees Laudine and falls in love with her when she is mourning the death of her husband whom Yvain has killed in battle. Whereas in *Erec* the feelings described are almost exclusively those of Enid, here we also have Yvain's, given in the form of interior monologue and authorial commentary as well as in the dialogues with Lunete, Laudine's confidante and friend. There is more concrete description, too, of the lovers' feelings, such as Yvain's desire to hold Laudine's hands to prevent her tearing her hair and face (*Yvain*, 1300–4) or his wish that she should stop weeping and reading her psalter and come and talk to him (*Yvain*, 1424–6). The barrier between the two lovers created by the situation is symbolised by the wall that separates them as Yvain gazes through a small window into the hall where the funeral takes place. In contrast to *Erec*, there is also a considerable amount of humour in the poem, especially in the speeches of Lunete who triumphantly consoles her mistress's distress by pointing out that the knight who killed her husband must be more valiant than the dead man so that she has no justification for claiming she will never see his equal (*Yvain*, 1680–1716). Or when she reassures Yvain as he goes to meet Laudine for the first time and hesitates to approach her or speak: 'Move over there, knight, and don't be afraid that my lady will bite you!' (*Yvain*, 1967–9). This type of gentle mockery adds variety to the tone of the poem and is used in Chrétien's other works too, even in moments of high seriousness, such as Lancelot's first rendezvous with Queen Guinevere when he approaches her window softly: 'and there he remained so quietly that he did not cough or sneeze' (*The Knight of the Cart*, 4576–7). In *Cligès*, too, Chrétien introduces this same tinge of acerbity when he describes Guinevere's difficulty in determining whether the pallor of Alixandre and Soredamours is due to love or seasickness (*Cligès*, 544–54). This implicit criticism of the excesses of lovers is part of the practical, reasonable attitude to life which Chrétien sees as the ideal: reason should govern man's behaviour but love overwhelms him. The same conceit is expressed in the following century in the *Romance of the Rose*.

This attitude also helps to explain Chrétien's treatment of the end of *Yvain*, where the lovers are reconciled by a verbal trick of Lunete's. This has been criticised as unconvincing psychologically but the use of exact formulation of oaths, and verbal niceties of all kinds were much appreciated by the Middle Ages. In the romance of *Tristan*, Iseult swears an oath that she has never been held in the arms of any man except her husband and the beggar who has just carried her across the muddy ford, and is able to emerge triumphant from the ordeal that proved the truth of her words, although she and many other people know that the beggar in question is Tristan. A similar observance of the literal sense of words is used by Lunete when she enables Laudine to receive her husband back after she has sworn never to summon him to her presence; Lunete recommends her mistress should summon the Knight of the Lion and once Yvain, whose sobriquet this is, finds himself in his wife's presence he naturally manages to win his pardon. Laudine, like many of Chrétien's characters is concerned not with moral fears of wrong-doing but with a what-will-the-neighbours-say ethos. If a face-saving formula can be found to enable her to love her husband's slayer then all is well: 'But it must be done in such a way that no one can blame me or say: that's the one who married the man who killed her lord' (*Yvain*, 1809–12). Such sentiments echo those in the *Song of Roland* when the hero refuses to blow the horn to summon help lest people should speak ill of him: ' "May God never allow", Roland retorted, "that any living man should say that I would blow the horn for any pagan" ' (*Roland*, S. LXXXV).

The romance hero's need to be accepted into his society is, however, a very different matter from the concept of community responsibility in the *chansons de geste*. His loss of honour does not reflect on his family or his country as Roland feared would happen in his case. It is a totally personal concept of honour, similar to the *gloire* of the seventeenth century, portrayed in the plays of Corneille: Chimène, the heroine in Corneille's *Le Cid* will not marry Rodrigue, whom she loves, because he killed her father. Each of them is bound by respect for personal *gloire*. Rodrigue sums it up when he tells her that he could only bring himself to challenge Chimène's father (who had dishonoured Rodrigue's own father) by reminding himself that 'a man without honour would not have deserved you' (*Le Cid*, III.iv). The historical Cid had a more practical outlook: having killed

Xiména's father he had to provide her with a new protector. Laudine seems to strike the happy medium between the two approaches; she pardons Yvain, privately, because his killing of her husband had not been intended as a personal affront to her: 'he whom she had rejected she now truly has forgiven for in reason and in justice he had in no way offended against her' (*Yvain*, 1755–7). However, she is careful to conceal from her barons the fact that the new suitor she accepts is the same knight as the slayer of her former husband (*Yvain*, 1855–66).

Although Erec's status as heir to the kingdom of Estregales is stressed in the romance he is not criticised for a failure in any feudal duties but for not going to tournaments, for being a recreant from chivalry. The knight's role in society as clearly spelled out in the romances of *Erec* and *Yvain* is to bear arms, to ride out on adventure and to fight in tournaments. This is a far cry from the *chansons de geste* where nationalism and religious fervour both threaten and inspire the fighting community. A consequence of this shift from the group to the individual is the gradual separation of the Arthurian world from the historical reality. Britain becomes Logres, the crusade is replaced by the search for 'adventure to test my valour and prowess' (*Yvain*, 362–3). Epic has given way to romance.

Faith Unfaithful: Studies in Adultery

ADULTERY was an almost inevitable part of the courtly relationship since one of the basic tenets of the courtly philosophy held that love should be a free gift by each of the partners, based on the beauty and merit of the beloved. Marriages at that date and in that stratum of society in which courtly love was most practised were nearly always a matter of political and dynastic expediency with the parties often being betrothed in infancy, so it was extremely rare in real life for the knight to marry a lady with whom he was 'in love'. Even in literature, Erec and Yvain are among the minority, for in most cases the lady wooed by the courtly lover was already married. Triangles were the norm and two of them have achieved universal notoriety.

The story of King Mark of Cornwall, his wife, Iseult, and his nephew, Tristan the queen's lover, is treated in no fewer than five different poems of the end of the twelfth century and Chrétien also claims to have written about them though his version has not survived. The bare bones of the tale are not particularly courtly but they are extremely individual. The origin of the story is obscure but its location in Cornwall and Brittany is more or less constant and it has certainly got Celtic roots.

The two main French versions, by Beroul and Thomas, are both incomplete; indeed the latter has only survived in fragments but there are sufficient later redactions in French prose and translations in German, Norwegian and English for it to be possible to reconstruct the main lines of the story. The crux of the tale is the overwhelming nature of love symbolised by the potion Tristan and Iseult drink accidentally and which dominates them completely as Iseult explains to a hermit: 'Lord, by God Almighty, he does not love me nor I him except through a potion which I drank and he drank too: that was a sin' (Beroul, *Tristan*, 1386–9). This simple statement recalls the eating of the apple by Adam and Eve: 'She took of the fruit thereof and did eat and gave to her husband who did eat' (Genesis 3:6). The parallel is emphasised by Iseult's final words: 'that was a sin' ('*pechiez*' – the word also meant 'fault' in Old French). In this version, at least, the love of Tristan and Iseult is sinful but inevitable.

The setting of the Tristan story is realistic, in Beroul, with many topographical references to sites in Cornwall, whereas the description of Tintagel in one of the other poems, the *Folie Tristan*, describes it as being built by giants with the outer wall chequered in green and blue (*Folie d'Oxford*, 107–8). In Thomas's version, Mark appears to rule over all of England for Kaherdin finds the court in London. The description of the city is probably based on observation: 'This is the mouth of the Thames, he sails up it with his merchandise and anchors his boat in a creek in the estuary outside the port and continues up river in a skiff as far as London. Under the bridge he sets out his goods' (Thomas, *Tristan*, 5643–9). This is a rare scene of physical reality in Thomas's text which contains a particularly high proportion of emotional analysis and a complex series of parallels and doublings: not only are there two Iseults – Iseult of Cornwall and Iseult of Brittany – but there are also two Tristans since the hero meets another knight of the same name. There are also a pair of statues which Tristan has had made representing Iseult and her confidante Brangane, which provide the opportunity for Thomas to vary his expression of Tristan's sufferings by showing him embracing the statue of his absent beloved and speaking to it as if it were alive. It is 'the delights and pangs of great loves, their torments and pains and distress that Tristan recounts to the image. When he is joyful he embraces it and when he is sad he vents his rage on it' (Thomas, *Tristan*, 941–4).

This complex pattern of love and hate is continually reworked by Thomas as he portrays the changing attitudes of Tristan to his beloved:

> Tristan's feelings constantly change and he debates with himself one way and another how he can alter his desires since he cannot have what he longs for and he says: 'Iseult fair love, how different our lives are and our love is separated by such a distance that it only exists to cause me distress. For your sake I have lost joy and pleasure and you have it day and night; I lead a life of great suffering and you lead yours amidst the pleasures of love; I do nothing but long for you but you cannot help having delight and pleasure and indulge in all you enjoy. The king takes his pleasure with you, his joy and his delight. What was once mine is now all his'.
> (Thomas, *Tristan*, 53–72)

This physical jealousy of the lover for the pleasure he believes his lady is experiencing with her husband, leads Tristan to marry Iseult of Brittany but as soon as he has done so he regrets his inconstancy and does not consummate the marriage. Meanwhile Iseult far from enjoying her husband's embraces finds them loathsome. As Thomas puts it, there are four lives ruined: 'which of the four suffers the worst I cannot say nor give any explanation of it for I have never experienced it. I will put the case to you, let lovers say which of them was most fortunate in love or which suffered the most for lack of it' (Thomas, *Tristan*, 1084–91).

Although Tristan's jealousy and inconstancy seem far removed from the traditional attitudes of the courtly lover, he and Iseult were considered models of true love in the twelfth century and their fame was already sufficiently widespread for Marie de France to preface her *Lay of the Honeysuckle* (*Chevrefoil*) with words that are lapidary in their simplicity and poignancy and therefore virtually untranslatable:

> De Tristan et de la reïne,
> De lur amur que tant fu fine
> Dunt il eurent meinte dolur
> Puis en mururent en un jur.
> (7–10)

> (They tell of Tristan and the queen
> And of their love, the finest seen.
> By many griefs their love was tried
> And of it the same day they died.)

The love of Tristan and Iseult may have been '*fine*' but Iseult's acceptance of the situation of belonging to both husband and lover was not entirely without its critics to judge by the attitude of Fénice, the heroine of the second part of Chrétien's romance of *Cligès*. 'This love was not reasonable but mine shall always be well-founded for my body and my heart shall not be separated in any way. . . . He who has the heart shall have the body and all others shall be set aside' (*Cligès*, 3117–24). Not content with deceiving her unwanted husband – Cligès's uncle who has usurped the throne of Constantinople – with a potion that gives him the illusion of possessing her though she is, in fact, still a virgin, Fénice will not run away with her lover, Cligès, because other people would never believe the marriage had not been consummated: 'My heart is yours and my body yours nor shall anyone by my example learn to act in an uncourtly way. . . . Though I love you and you love me you shall not be called a Tristan and I will never be Iseult for then this love would not be honourable but would be open to blame and reproach' (*Cligès*, 5190–203). Fénice's absolute refusal to be another Iseult leads her to drink a potion which simulates death. Cligès then rescues her from the tomb, which had been warmly and comfortably lined: 'he put a feather bed inside because the stone was hard and, more important, cold' (*Cligès*, 6028–30), and carries her off to a tower in an orchard.

Eventually, of course, they are discovered, flee to Arthur's court and with the king's help recapture Constantinople. Like *Erec* the tale ends with a coronation and this time the wedding as well. There is a humorous coda to the poem, in which Chrétien explains that the knowledge of Fénice's duplicity in deceiving her husband with not one but two potions – her love may have been more courtly but her morals were no better than Iseult's – is the reason that empresses of Constantinople are kept locked up in their rooms guarded by eunuchs: 'For then there is no fear or risk that Love will catch them in his noose' (*Cligès*, 6662–3).

In the absence of Chrétien's own version of the *Tristan* story we cannot tell whether this critical attitude to a triangular relationship was also found there. It is certainly not expressed by any of the extant Tristan authors, who all portray the lovers as victims of fate or the love-potion. Tristan's repeated use of disguise and deception to enable him to meet Iseult is also apparently considered acceptable and it is interesting that in this the texts are so different from the popular image of the lovers expressed in casual references and comparisons, where it is the valour and beauty of Tristan that are stressed or the sufferings and misfortunes of the ill-fated couple (see p. 103 below).

The torments of love are an integral part of the story but in Beroul's version they take the form mainly of physical deprivation. When they are living in the forest after fleeing Mark's vengeance, they have no salt to flavour the venison which is their only food, their clothes are ragged and they must be constantly on the move. The results are expressed in the description of Mark taking the ring from the finger of the sleeping Iseult after he has found them lying with the sword between them: 'Once it was difficult to put it on but now her fingers are so thin it comes off without difficulty' (Beroul, *Tristan*, 2019–21). Beroul's story is firmly rooted in the physical reality of the Cornish countryside and Mark's kingdom, but like Thomas he pays no heed to the social implications of the situation. Tristan is Mark's nephew and vassal but this is not mentioned here though it is implicit in the barons' envy of Tristan. A very different attitude to the relationship between the husband and the lover is to be found, however, in the other great love triangle of the Arthurian romances, the story of Lancelot, Guinevere and Arthur.

Lancelot first appears in the 'Matter of Britain' in Chrétien's romance of the *Knight of the Cart* (*Le Chevalier de la charrette*) which is based, the author tells us, on a story given to him by his noble patroness 'ma dame. de Champaine' (*Cart*, 1), who is identified as Marie de Champagne, the daughter of Henry II and Eleanor of Aquitaine, and the organiser of the courts of love described by Andreas Capellanus. Although Chrétien disclaims any originality in the matter, the source of the romance is not known and despite many more or less probable suggestions over the years Lancelot's origins remain a mystery.

Equally mysterious is the fact that Chrétien left the *Knight of the Cart* incomplete; it has been suggested that he had tired of the subservience of the hero to the exacting and difficult queen but this is only modern speculation though it is true that Guinevere is a complex and rather unattractive character. The excesses of the besotted lover earn him many humiliations described with a certain relish by the not entirely sympathetic author. On one ocasion Lancelot is deep in thoughts of his lady as he approaches a ford guarded by a knight. The horse decides it is thirsty and carries the unsuspecting lover into the stream thus laying him open to attack by the defender of the ford. Only when he finds himself in the water does Lancelot come to his senses and inquire why the other knight has hit him. ' "When I did not know you were in front of me and I had not offended you in any way?" "But indeed you have," replied the other, "and treated me uncourteously for I forbade you to cross the ford three times and shouted it at you as loudly as I could" ' (*Cart*, 775–81).[3]

Chrétien's Lancelot does not seem to have any roots in the Arthurian world at all, he comes out of nowhere and we are not even told his name until more than halfway through the romance. How different is the role of Lancelot in the great prose cycle of Arthurian romances composed early in the thirteenth century and known today as the *Vulgate Version* or sometimes simply the *Prose Lancelot* when only the central core of the romance is meant. At the beginning of the *Prose Lancelot* we have a lengthy account of his family, birth and education, the latter at the hands of the lady of the lake who carries off the baby son of King Ban of Benoic in Gaul and brings him up in her castle which is concealed by a mirage of a lake. At eighteen the young man goes to Arthur's court to receive knighthood and there falls in love with the queen. In this romance, their first rendezvous is a very different thing from the secret meeting in a barred tower described by Chrétien, for the *Prose Lancelot* introduces a more social and less secret element and Lancelot is brought to Guinevere in the garden by his friend Galehaut and the Dame de Malehaut. The youth is so bashful he can only gaze at his lady and Guinevere takes him by the chin and kisses him: 'And the queen saw that the knight dared not do more so she took him by the chin and kissed him in front of Galehaut for such a long time that the Dame de Malehaut knew she was kissing him' (ed. Kennedy, p. 248). This is the scene which inspired the ill-fated love of Francesca and Paolo da Rimini as the former explains to Dante, for they too kissed and 'read no more that day' (*Inferno*, v, 138). This is probably the earliest recorded example from medieval times of the corrupting influence of reading romantic fiction (see p. 222 below).

Forty years later Lancelot and the queen meet for the last time in the abbey where Guinevere has taken refuge from Mordred's treachery. Lancelot has defeated the sons of Mordred who tried to take over the kingdom after the death of Arthur and now comes by chance to the abbey and finds that Guinevere has taken the veil. 'For you well know that we have done, you and I, the thing that we ought not to have done and therefore it is my opinion that we should use the rest of our lives in the service of Our Lord' (*Mort Artu*, p. 265). As on the occasion of their first meeting it is Guinevere who takes the lead in deciding what they should do: she is a more dominant figure in the relationship than Iseult ever was and although the two stories were mutually influential in developing the attitudes and treatment of the characters, there remains a basic difference: Lancelot and Guinevere are part of the great saga of the Arthurian kingdom, and can never avoid the consequences of their actions for other people. Tristan and Iseult were always isolated and set apart and this remains true even in the *Prose Tristan* cycle of the mid-thirteenth century when Tristan becomes a knight of the Round Table and even takes part in the Quest for the Holy Grail. The two heroes, Tristan and

Lancelot, become friends and their affection for each other was developed in some of the later Arthurian texts, especially the sixteenth-century *Tristan* by Pierre Sala who was writing for Francis I. Sala depicts the two knights as close comrades helping each other to visit their respective ladies and quite unperturbed by any considerations of the morality or otherwise of their actions. In this respect he is closer to Chrétien and Thomas than to the prose tales though he does not use the exaggerated language and attitudes of the true courtly love stories.

It is an interesting reflection of literary taste that in England neither Tristan nor Lancelot was originally the major Arthurian hero, that role being reserved for Gawain perhaps because as Arthur's nephew he is a British rather than a French knight. When Malory compiled his *Morte Darthur*, however, in the late fifteenth century, he drew primarily on the French prose romances and his adaptation became and remained the standard English version of Arthurian romance with the well-deserved status of a literary masterpiece. In fifteenth-century France, too, it was abridgements of the prose texts which were chosen for the first printed editions: *Lancelot* in 1488 and *Tristan* in 1489.

A Woman's View-point: Marie de France

OF the two women writers of medieval French literature, Marie is the less generally well known though her works, especially the *Lais*, have been edited and studied more frequently than those of her junior by a couple of centuries, Christine de Pisan.

One reason for the lack of interest in Marie is the absence of any real biographical information on the woman who in the epilogue to her redaction of Aesop's fables merely tells us: 'My name is Marie and I come from France' ('*Marie ai nom, si sui de France*'), and adds that the *Fables* were taken from an English original ('*de l'engleis en romanz treire*', *Fables*, p. 62). Marie uses English words in the *Lais* also, in her explanations of names or titles: the Breton word *laüstic* is 'nihtegale en dret engleis' (*Laüstic*, 6) and the plant the French call *chevrefoil* they call *gotelef* in English (*Chevrefoil*, 115; nowadays it is usually translated as the *Lay of the Honeysuckle*). These lexical asides and the reference to herself as coming from France suggest a Frenchwoman living in England, perhaps at the court of Henry II, but her *Lais* were widely known in the Middle Ages and have survived in many manuscripts as well as in translations into Norse, Middle English and Middle High German.

The *Lais* are Marie's most important and original work. The term *lai*, usually rendered 'lay' in English, was used for a short story in verse which might have been recited or even sung. Marie's twelve *lais* vary in length from a hundred and twenty to more than a thousand lines, the majority being in the five- to six-hundred-line range. They are written in octosyllabic rhyming couplets, the standard narrative verse form used in the romances from the 'Matter of Rome' onwards, a form less obviously designed for oral recitation than the decasyllabic assonanced *laisses*, or sections, of the *chansons de geste* but still more suitable for reading aloud than the sometimes cumbersome, paratactic, narrative style of the thirteenth-century prose romances.

The subject of the *Lais* is love and within the limits of her chosen form Marie gives us a series of vivid and varied portraits of lovers married and single, young or not so young, men and women of various degrees, though she never goes far down the social scale. The lengthy soliloquies and analyses of passion which are important in Chrétien or Thomas have no place in Marie's tales which perhaps helps to give the *lais* a more 'modern' flavour though some of the problems she describes are unlikely to find their way into the pages of *Woman's Own* or a Mills and Boon romance.

Marie is even less a feminist in the modern sense than Christine de Pisan; she has sympathy with an unhappily married woman who takes a lover but severely criticises an unfaithful wife with a good husband. In *Equitan*, the seneschal's wife, fearful that her lover, the king, will marry someone else for dynastic reasons, persuades him to arrange her own husband's death and marry her. They plan to scald the unfortunate man in a bath of boiling water but 'one who pursues another's misfortune may find it recoiling on himself' (*Equitan*, 309–10). Caught *in flagrante delicto* with the seneschal's wife, the king leaps out of bed straight into the bath, feet first, and dies. Grasping what has happened, the husband picks up his erring wife and plunges her into the water in turn, head first.

A less drastic but still appropriate punishment befalls the wife of Bisclavret who, learning that her husband is a werwolf three days a week, bribes her suitor to commit the heinous crime of stealing Bisclavret's clothes, thus condemning him to remain in wolf's form. Years later when the wolf has been taken to court by the king who rescued him from the hounds, the former wife brings gifts to the king: 'When Bisclavret saw her coming no one could restrain him and he ran at her like a mad thing. Now hear how he avenged himself: he bit the nose off her face. What worse thing could he have done to her?' (*Bisclavret*, 231–6). Under threat of torture the lady confesses her guilt, the clothes are found and Bisclavret is restored to his former shape. The lady and her paramour are banished and many of their female descendants were born without noses.

Marie tells us that the word Bisclavret is *bretun* and that the Normans call it *garwaf* and adds that in the past there were many tales of men becoming *garual* and dwelling in the forest. The term *bretun* is used in a number of the lays and probably means Breton though the same adjective was also at that date used for British in a more general Celtic sense. Mention has already been made of her *Lay of the Honeysuckle* about Tristan and there is also an Arthurian lay, *Lanval*, which shows the unnamed queen in a very unsympathetic light, for when Lanval, the hero, rebuffs her advances firmly, saying 'Not for you or your love would I dishonour so my lord' (*Lanval*, 273–4), the queen first accuses him of preferring young men to women (a very serious accusation in the Middle Ages) and then later, like Potiphar's wife, accuses him to her husband of having made improper advances to her. These are the only two lays based on the 'Matter of Britain'.

Marie never uses the same type of character twice and shows very real skill in portraying credible people in a few lines, however fantastic the context may appear to be. In *The Two Lovers* (*Les Deus Amans*) the young princess's suitors have to carry her up to the top of a high hill without resting: a familiar folk/fairy-tale motif. But the treatment of the young lovers is almost mundane. The girl sends her lover off to her aunt in

Salerno to get a strengthening potion and meanwhile goes on a strict diet. (Salerno was the most famous school of medicine in Europe in the twelfth century.) The young man returns triumphant and prepares for his task. Unfortunately he is so full of love and youthful ardour that 'there was in him no sense of proportion [*mesure*]' (179). He picks up his bride who has stripped to her shift, and sets off at a great pace, refusing to pause even long enough to swallow the potion, and reaches the top of the hill only to collapse: 'there he fell and never got up' (204). With pathetic irony Marie tells us that the princess threw away the potion: 'the hill was well sprinkled with it and the whole region and district was much improved by it for many a good herb is found there that had its roots in the potion' (215–9). Then the girl herself died and 'because of the adventure of these young people it was called the Hill of the Two Lovers' (241–2).

Topographical as well as philological references are quite common in the *Lais* and add considerably to their realism. For despite the sometimes fantastic effects, these are essentially very true to life, credible tales written with a vividness and economy of style and a sharpness of observation of behaviour which can stand comparison with any master of the short story. In *Yonec*, for example, which like *Bisclavret* has a shape-changer as hero, Marie describes with great realism the fate of the wretched wife whose husband is elderly and marries only to have a child who can inherit his fortune. The lady is of high rank, 'wise, courteous and very beautiful, who was given to the rich man' (22–3). He locks her in a tower with only an old woman for company and there she pines until her hawkman comes, after which 'the next day she got up in good health and in a week was much restored. She took great care of her person and completely recovered her beauty' (213–6).

In *The Ash-tree* (*Le Fresne*) a man finds an abandoned baby and quickly summons his daughter: ' "Daughter," he said, "get up, get up. Light the fire and the candle. I have brought in this child whom I found out there in the ash-tree. Nurse it for me with your milk, warm it up and bathe it also" ' (197–202).

Not surprisingly, Marie gives us few descriptions of battles and many scenes set indoors in the women's apartments. But it is not just a woman's world. She has compassion and understanding for all her characters of both sexes and nowhere is this better displayed than in the little-known and pathetic tale of *The Maimed One* (*Le Chaitivel*). A beautiful and wise lady, living in Nantes in Brittany, has four suitors all extremely eligible so that she finds it impossible to choose 'which would be the best one to love' (52). She decides to hold a tournament and watches anxiously as all acquit themselves superbly and eventually desperately. At the end of the day, three have been killed and the fourth wounded by a lance 'through the thigh and into the body' (123). The lady laments her lost lovers and plans a lay of the *Four Griefs*, making it quite clear that the surviving knight is permanently crippled and impotent. He tells her that his plight is much worse than that of the others, for he can still see her: 'but I can never have any joy from it, no kissing or embraces nor any pleasure except talking. You make me suffer a hundred evils. I would be better dead' (220–4). They agree to call the lay *The Maimed One*. There Marie ends her tale for 'I heard no more, I know no more, therefore I shall tell you no more' (239–40).

Marie is not a profound writer. Her plots are slight, often merely situations, and her characterisation though acute is not extended to any great depths. But she is a skilled miniaturist with a compassionate, unsentimental approach to the joys and problems of love and a crisp style full of deft touches of character-behaviour, brief, vivid descriptions and occasional flashes of humour; by no means the least bright star in the glittering firmament of twelfth-century romance.

The Quest as Adventure: the Stories of the Grail[4]

PERHAPS no medieval object has had a more varied career in the last eight hundred years than the artefact usually referred to in English nowadays as the Holy Grail. Yet when it first appears, in Chrétien's romance of *Perceval, or The Story of the Grail* (*Conte du Graal*) it features in only one of the adventures by which the young hero gradually acquires self-knowledge; like Lancelot or Erec or Yvain he must come to terms with himself in relation to both society in general and a lady, in this case Blanchefleur, in particular. The adventure at the grail castle forms a turning-point in this process for the young Perceval but it seems unlikely that Chrétien realised how important this one element of his story would become in European, even in world literature and culture. For whatever the ultimate source of the grail, and that is a matter even today for heated debate, it is indisputably Chrétien who may claim the distinction of being the author of the oldest extant text in which the grail is explicitly featured.

In the poem, composed in the 1180s and left unfinished at the poet's death, the hero, Perceval, is brought up by his widowed mother far away from court or chivalry because she does not wish him to become a knight. Nevertheless, as the result of a chance meeting in the forest the half-wild youth does learn of knighthood, abandons his mother and sets out in search of Arthur's court. The first section of the romance describes his adventures and education in social behaviour, first by his mother and then by a knight, Gornemanz. He also meets and falls in love with Blanchefleur whom he defends against a knight who is besieging her in her castle (see p. 51 above). So far the romance is not too different from Chrétien's other tales but at this point Perceval decides he should go home to visit his mother whom he had left in tears at his abrupt departure.

Implicitly, though only later does it become certain, it is this decision that brings about his discovery, the following evening, of the hidden castle where he is offered hospitality by the maimed fisher-king. As they are sitting in the well-lighted great hall they see a procession approaching: first comes a youth carrying a lance from whose head a trickle of blood flows down to the hand holding the shaft. Perceval does not ask 'how this can happen' (*Perceval*, 3205) for fear of being discourteous, for his mentor had warned him against talking too much. The first youth is followed by two others, bearing candelabra with ten candles in each:

> A damsel who came with the two youths held in her two hands a dish [*un graal*]; she was beautiful, well-attired and noble. When she came in there with the dish she was holding there appeared such brightness that at once the candles lost their brightness as the stars do when the sun or moon rises. After there came another damsel who held a silver carving-

dish [*tailleoir*]. The dish [*li graaus*] which went in front was of fine chased gold. There were many kinds of precious stones set in the dish, the richest and most valuable that can be found in sea or land. Without doubt the gems of the dish surpassed all other stones.   (*Perceval*, 3220–39)

The description and context make it quite clear here that the 'grail' is simply a dish (from the Latin *gradalis*): it is an object of marvel rather than of veneration. The parallel scene in the Welsh romance of *Peredur*, the Perceval analogue, has no comparable dish, only a salver carried by two maidens: 'and a man's head on the salver and blood in profusion around the head' (*Mabinogion*, p. 192). Once again, Perceval fails to ask the appropriate question, 'who is served from the dish?' (*Perceval*, 3245). Subsequently he learns that his failure, which has caused great disaster to the land, was the result of his failure in charity when he abandoned his mother in tears. Like Yvain and Erec, Perceval has allowed his personal pride to override his duty of charity to his fellow man.

It is obvious that for Chrétien at least the grail is something important and probably holy: later in the romance a hermit tells Perceval that it contains 'not lamprey nor salmon' (*Perceval*, 6421; this emphasises the idea of a dish not a cup); instead, the grail contains a single host (*oiste*, 6422; a communion wafer) which is carried to the hermit's brother, father of the fisher-king and uncle to Perceval himself. The hermit adds that the grail is a very holy thing (*tant sainte chose*, 6425). Since the romance was left unfinished at Chrétien's death we have no way of knowing how he intended to develop this theme but other writers of the end of the twelfth and beginning of the thirteenth century took up the idea in a variety of different ways.

Almost contemporary with Chrétien's is another poem, *The Romance of the History of the Grail* (*Roman de l'Estoire dou Graal*) by Robert de Boron in which he describes how at the crucifixion Joseph of Arimathea caught the blood of Christ in the vessel 'in which Christ made his sacrament' (Boron, 396). Later in the poem Robert uses the word *graal* (2659). This linking of the grail with the Holy Blood is maintained by many later writers in French, of which there are two groups: those who continue to make Perceval the grail hero and those who replace him by Galahad. The first group includes the authors of the verse *Continuations* of Chrétien's poem and of a series of prose texts based on Chrétien's and Robert's work and including the *Didot-Perceval* and the *Perlesvaus*. The last named both date from the very early thirteenth century.

All the Perceval texts accept the pre-history of the grail provided by Robert de Boron and the vessel becomes linked with the Last Supper and Joseph of Arimathea. By the middle of the thirteenth century this motif was sufficiently widespread for Villard de Honnecourt to include in his sketch-book a crucifixion scene in which Joseph kneels at the foot of the cross holding a chalice beneath the nailed feet of Christ.[5]

This Christianisation of the grail is reflected in the texts in a number of ways: the grail-bearer is no longer a maiden but a youth in the *Didot-Perceval*, for example. In the *Perlesvaus* its nature is ambivalent for when Arthur sees the grail he sees it in five different 'manners' (*manieres*), during the mass: 'King Arthur saw all these changes' (*muances*). The last was into a chalice and the hermit who was singing the mass found a letter on the corporal and the writing said that God wished his body to be consecrated (*sacré*) in such a vessel (*Perlesvaus*, pp. 304–5).

Already in Robert de Boron's *History* Christ had told Joseph that the vessel 'shall be called chalice' (909); however the full association of the grail with the mass is first made in the *Quest of the Holy Grail* (*Queste del Saint Graal*), the penultimate branch of the great *Vulgate Version* of Arthurian romances composed between 1215 and 1225. In this cycle, the grail hero is not Perceval but Galahad, the virgin knight, son of Lancelot whose lineage replaces that of Perceval as the 'grail-family', descended not from Joseph but from a pagan king converted by Joseph. The earliest branch of the cycle, the *History of the Grail* (*Estoire del Graal*), provides a revised and extended pre-history or Old Testament to the material which in the *Quest* is totally Christian and also allegorical. The grail is now the 'dish [*escuele*] in which Christ ate the Paschal lamb with his disciples' (*Quest*, p. 275), and there are two descriptions of the liturgy of the grail which is a High Mass celebrated by a bishop, Joseph himself, and served by angels. In the *Quest* there is a strong influence of the contemporary debate on Transubstantiation and the nature of the Eucharist which had been redefined at the Lateran council of 1215. The quest is a spiritual one in which only the pure or the penitent can succeed and the worldly knights are humiliated and shamed. Much of the didactic material in this text was omitted by the subsequent writers such as Malory, though the nature of the grail as a sacred eucharistic vessel is maintained in almost every case. Nevertheless, despite the careful Christianisation, the enigmatic artefact was never accepted as 'respectable' by the Church. It belonged to romance and never crossed the boundary into orthodox religious literature. Relics of the Holy Blood, miracles of the Sacrament in narrative, dramatic and iconographic form proliferated in the later Middle Ages but the grail remained suspect. Its possibly pagan, Celtic origins, and its indisputable links with the fantasy world of romance were sufficient to taint it with an ineradicable stain of heathenism.

The Language of Love

THE stress on emotional analysis of the self and the beloved in the romances meant that the poets had to extend their vocabulary of feeling and reaction to cope with this new emphasis. As with all aspects of medieval culture, the sources available to them were basically Classical antiquity and the Bible: more specifically, for terms and images suitable for the expression of love, whether Christian, courtly or merely comradely, they turned to Ovid (especially the *Art of Love* and the *Remedy for Love*) and to the *Song of Songs*. All these works were well known to twelfth-century writers and audiences, the Ovid in Latin – and perhaps in French if Chrétien is telling the truth when he claims to have translated it – and the *Song of Songs* in either Latin or the French rhymed redaction composed between 1176–87 for a patroness 'who promised she would pray to God for me and does so I believe' (*Song of Songs*, 3499–3500). It is noteworthy that the translator decribes his work as a romance: 'but this I ask that this romance [*romanz*] should never be put into a child's hands' (3505–6). Elsewhere in the poem he glosses the word 'children' as 'those who have not begun to love' (235). Despite the importance of the *Song of Songs* its actual imagery was rarely called upon: medieval ladies were not given to describing their lovers as a bundle of myrrh, a cluster of cypress or a young hart (Canticle of Canticles, I, 12 and 13; II, 17). More significant was its treatment of the relationship between man and woman in terms of the bridegroom taking delight in his bride, Christ delighting in his Church.

Other sources available to the romancers were the lyrics of the Provençal poets; though direct borrowings are difficult to pinpoint, the general tenor is certainly the same and it was from them that the term *fin'amor* was taken, though the words *druerie* and *dru/e* were the normal ones used in Northern France. In *Equitan*, for example, the king looks favourably on Equitan's wife and declares: 'Alas! for such a beautiful lady if she did not love or have a lover [*dru*]! What would become of her courtliness [*curteisie*] if she did not love in courtly way [*de drüerie*]?' (*Equitan*, 79–82). The terms *curteisie* and *druerie* are almost untranslatable as is the word *fine* used by Marie and others, though in every instance the meaning is clear.

In view of the heavily formalised nature of courtly love and its essentially literary vocabulary it is not surprising that the language put into the mouths of the lovers should be rich in metaphor and symbol. Nor should such a practice be seen as implying artificiality or insincerity in the feelings portrayed. One of the major difficulties for the modern reader of courtly love scenes is that the images have become clichés. Cupid's arrow piercing the lover's heart which was a fresh, new image in French in the twelfth century has deteriorated in the twentieth to an arrow-pierced heart with initials, scribbled on the walls of public lavatories.

The most elaborate development of this Classical image in the French romances is surely that in the *Romance of Aeneas* (*Roman d'Eneas*) which though based, of course, on Virgil shows considerable originality especially in the treatment of the love stories. Aeneas, having received a letter from Lavinia wrapped round an arrow, has fallen in love with her: 'Cupid who was god of love and was his blood-brother held him in his prison' (*Aeneas*, 8922–4; Aeneas, like Cupid his *frere charnel*, is the son of the goddess Venus). Unable to sleep for love, Aeneas rebukes Amor for wounding him with his golden arrow and the brothers have a lengthy discussion:

> 'Be silent, Aeneas, you are wrong.' 'What? I am wounded to death! How shall I be silent? How can a man who is wounded put up with not daring to complain? The arrow which was fired struck me a deadly blow in the body.' 'You lie, it fell a long way from you.' 'It brought with it my death and grievously wounded me.' 'You don't know what you are saying, it never touched you.' 'No truly there is no visible blow or wound but the letter which was round it has given me a great wound in the heart.' 'How could the letter? The skin is quite whole'.   (*Aeneas*, 8961–75)

The situation is here made more complex and also more vivid by the existence of a real arrow – the one used to deliver the letter – and by the particular personification of Love as the brother of the lover. The fact that arrows and the wounds they made were a reality of contemporary life for the readers of these texts is also a factor to be taken into account.

The idea that love provides both the pain of the wound and the ointment that soothes it – another commonplace of the courtly vocabulary – is vividly expressed by Lavinia's mother whose speech mingles the physical and emotional consequences of mutually felt love in a series of antitheses and oxymorons: 'If there is a little pain the sweetness follows it equally. Smiles and joy follow weeping, great delight follows fainting, kissing follows yawning, embraces come from watching, great happiness from sighing, fresh colour from pallor' (*Aeneas*, 7959–66). Similar images, albeit much more briefly expressed are used by Marie de France to describe the fate of her hero, Guigemar: 'young, well-born, handsome and valiant' he 'had so much scorned nature as to have no interest in love at all' (*Guigemar*, 56–7). Inevitably his *hubris* is punished and he meets and falls in love with a beautiful and unfortunate wife who, like Yonec's beloved, is kept locked up in a tower by her jealous husband. 'All night he stayed awake like this, sighing and lamenting; in his heart he remembered and recalled the word and appearance, the bright eyes and beautiful mouth so that the agony touched his heart. Between his teeth he begs her for mercy, and very nearly calls her his love [*s'amie*]' (*Guigemar*, 411–18).

Another common image is of love as a fever, a raging fire. Thus in *Cligès*, Chrétien describes the pangs of nascent love experienced by the hero's parents; Alixandre of Constantinople loves Arthur's niece Soredamours and she him: 'Just as the man who approaches the fire and stands near it cooks himself more than he who stands back from it thus love therefore grows and increases; but each of them is shy of the other and hides and covers it up so that neither flame nor smoke rises from the coals under the ashes. But the heat is not thereby reduced but rather does the heat last longer under the ash than above it' (*Cligès*, 590–600). The gentle humour of the description of the young people who lament their fate and enjoy their suffering at one and the same time (and at great length: Alixandre broods over it for 250 lines and Soredamours for 150) is typical of Chrétien's whole portrayal of these young lovers, who meet during a sea-voyage from Logres to Brittany, so that Queen Guinevere seeing them change colour 'cannot imagine why this is nor why they should behave in this way except it be caused by the sea on which they are travelling. . . . Thus the queen violently accuses the sea and blames it but she is wrong to do so for the sea has done no wrong' (*Cligès*, 536–8, 552–5).

In the second half of this romance Chrétien varies his style and gives us, instead of the interior monologue, a dialogue between Cligès and his beloved, Fénice, in which he describes how during his recent visit to Arthur's court his heart remained with her in Germany, so that 'like the bark of a tree without the wood, my body in Britain had no heart' (*Cligès*, 5120–1). Fénice retorts that she has never been to Britain 'but my heart made a long stay there. I do not know now if that was a good thing or a bad one' (5146–8). This use of a seemingly superficial word-play to reflect the lovers' feelings for each other fits in with another aspect of the courtly romance – the very extensive use of direct speech. Unlike the *chansons de geste*, the romances were written to be read not recited. Nevertheless the markedly dramatic nature of the form and the extensive use of dialogue, monologue and soliloquy, coupled with the fact that many members of the public for whom these tales were composed probably could not read, suggests that reading aloud was a very

likely mode of presentation. However, the introduction of prose
in the early thirteenth-century romances of the great cycles
may suggest a contrary practice. Certainly the very little
precise evidence we have – such as the Paolo and Francesca
reference already quoted – does suggest that by Dante's time
men and women of rank could and did read for themselves (see
p. 63 above).

Whether reading or listening, the audience for these texts,
cultured and aristocratic, included many ladies and the
authors chose their images to suit their readers. Alixandre talks
of the eyes as mirrors of the heart which itself is the candle in the
lantern of the body; he then extends this complex image with a
further patristic metaphor: 'in the same way a window is never
so strong or whole that the rays of the sun cannot pass through
it without damaging it in any way' (*Cligès*, 717–20). The image
of the sun passing through glass without harming it was used by
St Augustine as a figure of the Incarnation: the Virgin Mary
conceived Christ without losing her Virginity. It was a widely
known and quoted image and its use in a secular context is an
interesting example of the intermingling of religious and
mundane language; on another occasion Chrétien also uses
religious terms but in an almost humorous way. When
Lancelot first goes to Queen Guinevere's bed: 'he adored it and
bowed down in worship for he did not believe so devoutly in any
holy relic' (*Cart*, 4652–3).

The taste for these elaborate conceits was not allowed to
dominate the romances to the exclusion of all other linguistic
registers, however, even in the love scenes. Thomas is often
very down to earth, almost cynical in his comments on Tristan
and all other lovers:

> Learn how inconstant and changeable men's hearts can be.
> They cannot give up their bad habits but they can give up the
> good ones. They become so accustomed to evil that it
> becomes their rightful custom for all time . . . they behave in
> such a demeaning way [*vilenie*] that they quite forget courtly
> behaviour [*courtoisie*]. . . . Tristan thought he could give up
> Iseult and put her out of his heart by marrying the other
> Iseult . . . but if he could have the queen he would not love
> the maiden Iseult.   (Thomas, *Tristan*, 286–96, 357–9, 367–8)

However, nothing could be more simple and poignant than the lament he puts into the mouth of Iseult when she arriaves in Brittany to find her lover dead: 'Tristan, beloved, when I see you dead I have in reason no right to live. You have died for love of me, I have in reason no right to live. You have died from loving me and I die, beloved, from tenderness. Since I could not get here in time to cure you and your wound, my love, my love, I shall never be consoled for your death, never know joy nor pleasure nor any cheer' (Thomas, *Tristan*, 3083–93).

Chrétien, too, can vary his language to suit his different lovers, ranging from the very elaborate metaphors of *Cligès* to the simple and sincere farewell between Erec and Enid before the fight with the knight in the Joy of the Court episode; having warned her against grieving before he has been hurt, Erec continues:

> Sweet lady, you do not even know yet whether this will happen nor do I; you are distressed without cause for be assured that if there were no hardihood in me except what love of you has given me I would not fear to meet any man in the world in single combat. I am foolish to boast like this but I do not say it out of pride but because I want to comfort you. Be comforted and let this be.   (*Erec*, 5802–13)

Perhaps the supreme example of the mingling of courtly imagery with natural expression is to be found in the *Lay of the Reflection* (*Lai de l'Ombre*) by Jehan Renart which dates from the thirteenth century and has been compared to a play by Marivaux or Musset, the two French masters of the dialogue of love. There is virtually no plot, merely a situation in which the interest depends on the fluctuating fortunes of the hero as he strives to win the lady whose great beauty and sweet name have wounded him to the heart. Most of the lay is a dialogue between the two as he urges his suit and eventually puts his ring on her hand while she is deep in thought. She will not accept the implied commitment and insists he takes it back: ' "Here." "I do not want to have it." "You must." "Truly I will not." "Would you force it upon me then?" "No truly, lady, I know I have no power to do that, alas so God help me." ' (*Reflections*, 800–5). The lover is now in a quandary: he must not take it

back and he cannot force her to keep it. As the lady points out
with a touch of humour which adds a warmth to the sophisticated word-play: ' "You might as well knock your head against
this stone step as hope to achieve your aim: I advise you to take
it back" ' (*Reflection*, 810–13). However, she has underesti-
mated him. The knight achieves an elegant solution. He agrees
to take it back if he may give it to the one he most loves after her.
' "God," she said, "here's only us. Where have you found her
so quickly?" "In God's name I will show you now the noble,
worthy one who'll have it." "Where is she?" "In God's name,
see she's there! Your fair reflection waiting for it." He took the
ring and held it out. "Here," he said, "my sweetest love, since
my lady does not want it you will take it without argument" '
(*Reflection*, 888–97). The lady is impressed and as Renart tells
us: 'The prudent man who knows how to act courteously at
need, gains all' (914–15). He leaves them embracing by the well
with the suggestion that the rest of the game will shortly be
played out, but he won't talk about it.

The knight in the *Lay of the Reflection* referred to his dilemma
as a *jeu parti* (832–3), a formalised debate in which different
view-points were expressed. Numerous such works have survived in French and the form was also used in other countries
and for other than discussions of love. In some forms of these
debates the protagonist and antagonist are not people but
personified abstractions:

> But Reason who keeps apart from Love tells him he should
> avoid getting in and warns and advises him not to do or
> undertake anything which may bring him shame or re-
> proach. But Reason that dares to speak in this way is in the
> mouth not in the heart; for Love which is deep in his heart
> summons and orders him to mount the cart quickly. Love
> wishes it and jumps in not bothering about the shame since
> love commands and wishes it.   (*Carl*, 356–77)

The use of these elaborately developed allegorisations is
widespread in the twelfth and thirteenth centuries, sometimes
intercalated in other texts, sometimes creating a complete cast
of characters. None is more elaborate or more important than
the allegory of the Rose.

The Allegory of Love: the *Romance of the Rose*

THE *Romance of the Rose* (*Roman de la Rose*) is perhaps the best-known and least-read work of medieval French literature. It was immensely popular in its day: more than three hundred manuscripts have survived and its fame if not its popularity defied even the Renaissance scorn for all things medieval (see p. 165 below).

There are, in fact, two quite different romances under the one name, for the first author, Guillaume de Lorris, writing in the first quarter of the thirteenth century, left his work unfinished and it was completed fifty years later by Jean de Meung who metamorphosed Lorris's vivid sophisticated allegory of the lover's attempt to pluck the rose, the lady's love, into a markedly humorous, philosophical, encyclopaedic study of late thirteenth-century society (see p. 125 below). In the present chapter it is only Lorris's *Rose* that concerns us.

The term 'allegory', used to describe the romance, had a wide range of meanings in the Middle Ages and included texts and images which might more properly be considered as simple personification. We have already noted Chrétien's use of the latter in, for example, the debate between Love and Reason in the *Knight of the Cart*, and in *Cligès* the young lover, Alixandre, describes his beloved in a long elaborate metaphor/personification/allegory as the arrow of love and her hair as the feather on the arrow: 'The feathers are coloured in such a way as if they were all golden, but gilding has no part in this for the feathers as you well know are more gleaming yet. The feathers are the golden tresses I saw the other day on the sea, it is the arrow which makes me love' (*Cligès*, 777–84). After a detailed portrait of the lady's face, the lover concludes that, alas, Love only showed him part of the arrow: 'For then love only showed me the nock and the feathers, for the arrow was in the quiver: that is the tunic and the shift in which the maiden was clad' (*Cligès*, 845–9). This explanation of the allegory by the speaker is also used extensively in the *Quest of the Holy Grail*, where the many elaborate visions and adventures are glossed by the hermits who recur at frequent intervals in the work. But Lorris's work is of a different order.

The *Romance of the Rose* is an unexplained allegory, wherein every character is a personification of some attribute of the lover, the lady or society and every part of the garden in which this elaborate charade is played out has also its significance. The romance begins like many allegories before and since as a dream: 'In the twentieth year of my age, the time when Love takes possession of young men, I went to bed one night as usual and fell sound asleep and in my sleep I saw a vision [*songe*] which was very beautiful and very pleasing to me' (Lorris, *Rose*, 21–7). This dream introduction, used by such diverse authors as Cicero, Bunyan and Lewis Carroll, had a particular function, to make clear the symbolic nature of the story. It is not mere fantasy or *rêve*, it is a true vision, a *songe* (from Latin *somnium*), 'and one can dream such dreams [*songes*] as are not deceits but later prove themselves to be true, and I can quote as proof of this an author named Macrobius' (Lorris, *Rose*, 3–7). (Macrobius was the author of a well-known commentary on Cicero's *Somnium Scipionis* (*Dream of Scipio*) a much-quoted and highly valued text in the Middle Ages.)

In narrating his dream, the poet uses the first person throughout, becoming himself the Lover of the story and from time to time talking of the lady he loves and to whom he is recounting the dream. This duality provides the necessary personal element in the allegory, which would otherwise be merely a fantasy. But although this is therefore the earliest example in French of a first-person narrative romance, the Lover remains a lifeless and uninteresting character, lacking even the visual reality of the other abstractions in the garden, for he naturally enough does not describe himself in terms of his physical appearance.

As so often happens in stories and in drama, it is the unpleasant characters who are the most vivid. Covetousness has hands that are 'bent and crooked [*recorbelees et crochues*]' (188); the French words, especially the first which has five syllables, are extremely effective visually but have no moral implications. Avarice is 'thin and wretched and green as a leek' (199–200). It is typical of the intensely visual nature of the whole work that these particular details should be found in a series of descriptions of images painted on the wall of the garden in which the Lover has seen the rose, for they have as much life as the three-dimensional beings he meets inside, like Idleness (*Oiseuse*), the doorkeeper with her arched eyebrows (527) and the dimple in her chin (536); Pastime (*Deduit*), the youth, who is dancing 'shod most cunningly in cut-away laced shoes' (824–5); or Generosity (*Largesce*) who has given away the clasp (*fermail*) of her dress, 'but it did not ill become her that the bodice was open and displayed her bare throat, the whiteness of the skin showing through the shift' (1168–72).[6]

The *Romance of the Rose* is primarily a picture-book, containing a whole iconography of courtly behaviour and language; an elegant formal ritual of the wooing of the lady by the lover. But this medieval mating-dance has none of the flesh-and-blood reality of the lovers in the tales of Chrétien or Marie de France. It is a text-book, not a story; a work of art to be appreciated like a tapestry or stained-glass window for its colours, shapes and workmanship rather than for the emotion or the story it may be illustrating. Guillaume de Lorris has codified and encapsulated the principles of behaviour of the courtly lover at a time when the courtly love story has mutated into the prose cycles, retaining the knowledge of human psychology and emotions but expressing them now in less formal and stereotyped language. As a treatise, a text-book on love, it survived unscathed the changes of taste of the later Middle Ages which caused the Arthurian and Carolingian tales to be constantly revised and reworked, but unlike them it could not outlive the ultimate end of the aristocratically dominated world except as a wonder to be venerated, a relic of the past, beautiful but dead.

Miracles and Marvels

HOWEVER true to life the descriptions of battles and warfare, however subtle and convincing the analysis of the psychology of love, neither the *chansons de geste* nor the romances set out to be naturalistic stories; like Adam and Eve in the Anglo-Norman *Adam* play whose pre-Fall nakedness was covered by rich vestments, the reality of the situations and characters was adorned and thus their appeal was enhanced: 'The gown became her so well that she was more beautiful than before ' (*Erec*, 1633–4). Many kinds of embellishment were used, numerous ornaments of style and description and among them the range of exotic, mysterious people, places and things which may collectively be referred to as the 'marvellous' (*merveilleux*).

In epic texts such as the *chansons de geste*, the marvellous is generally, and in early examples exclusively, Christian and biblical in its inspiration: Roland's deathbed is glorified by the presence of the archangels Michael and Gabriel and 'the angel Cherubim' (*Roland*, S. CLXXVI), and a similar kind of escort is provided for the soul of Lancelot at the end of the *Mort Artu*, but in this case the fact is narrated by the archbishop to Blioberis as a dream-vision he has had of a great company of angels 'who were bearing up to heaven the soul of our brother Lancelot. So let us go and see if he has passed away' (*Mort Artu*, S. 202). It was generally believed in the Middle Ages that every dead person's soul was taken in charge by either an angel or a devil to escort it to the appropriate location: this accounts for the presence of an angel on the shoulder of the penitent thief and a devil by the other thief in many representations of the crucifixion. It is not the presence of angels, therefore, that is marvellous in the epics but their quality and quantity.

When Charlemagne is pursuing the pagan king Marsilie, the sun is halted to give him a longer day, a device used in the Bible for Joshua (Joshua 10: 12–14), and a similar kind of miracle occurs in *Cligès* when King Arthur is besieging Windsor Castle which is held by a traitor, the Count of Angres, to whom Arthur had entrusted the realm during his visit to Brittany. The parallel with Arthur's war against Mordred in Geoffrey and Wace is obvious and the tone of the scene is epic, so it is not unexpected to find a miracle occurring: the count and his men creep out to attack Arthur's forces at night when 'neither star nor moon had shown their beams in the sky. But before they came to the tents the moon began to rise; I think she began to rise earlier than was her custom so as to hinder them, and God who wanted to do them harm illuminated the dark night' (*Cligès*, 1672–9).

This kind of marvel was widely used in epics and saints' lives, but even when the heroes are inspired and strengthened morally and physically by divine grace and power, they retain their free will and therefore remain human, fallible and interesting; God tells Adam this quite explicitly:

> In your person I have put good and evil
> Who has this gift is not a fettered slave.
> Now all things you can weigh up equally.
>
> (*Adam*, 65–7)

The least human character in the *Quest of the Holy Grail* is Galahad, who is a type of Christ, without weakness, foible or sin and consequently without much pyschological interest either. But the author is well aware of this result of depicting perfection and the major part of the story concerns the other knights and their greater or lesser success in measuring up to this perfection: the saints, Perceval and Bors, who like Mary and Martha are types of the contemplative and active life; the penitent sinners, especially Lancelot; and the recreants such as Gawain, or Lancelot's half-brother Hector.

The non-Christian marvellous, found mainly in the romances and the later versions of the epic stories, works in substantially the same way: it is either functional or ornamental. Many of the magic elements are really only technology, enabling the story to function: magic boats that bring hero and heroine together as in *Guigemar*; the ring of invisibility that saves Yvain's life by hiding him from the search parties (*Yvain*, 1023–37). Arthur C. Clarke has claimed that any really advanced technology is indistinguishable from magic, and the reverse is also true. Whether the reader is blinded by science or dazzled by the sleight of hand, the effect is to advance the story in an entertaining way and add 'verisimilitude to an otherwise unconvincing narrative'. The same may be said of the 'medical' marvels, like the ointment that heals Yvain of his madness. Here Chrétien concentrates our attention not on the action of the ointment but on the character of the damsel administering it: 'she was so eager for him to be cured that she set to work to anoint him all over and used up all of it, quite heedless of her lady's warning'. She had been told to use it sparingly but instead rubbed it all over him 'right down to the toe' (*Yvain*, 2989–3005). Marie de France has a similar attitude to potions as we see with the strength-giving drink the young man fetches from Salerno in *The Two Lovers* but never uses, or the herb which Eliduc uses to bring back to life his young bride after he has seen a weasel use it to resuscitate its mate (*Eliduc*, 1043–53).[7] Even the exceptionally strong living-death potion that Thessala gives Fénice in *Cligès* does not make her invulnerable and when she awakens she is seriously hurt as a result of the torments inflicted on her by the imperial doctors to test whether she is really dead. Snow White and Juliet are spared such realism.

Sometimes the pagan doctors are shown in a more favourable light as in an interesting passage in one of the *chansons de geste* of the cycle of the crusades. Peter the Hermit introduces a captured Saracen doctor – 'I assure you there is no wiser man in heathendom or Christendom' – and he is taken to the tent where Raimbaut Creton lies seriously wounded and heals him with a mixture of medicine and miracle:

> He probed the wound in his side and ribs and found that none of the bowel was touched; he cleared away the coagulated blood which was causing him much distress and then washed the wound lavishly in white wine; then he went to his chest and unfastened it and took out a great quantity of that holy ointment with which our Lord had his body anointed when he was laid to rest in the Sepulchre. He put as much as he wanted of it on the wounds and then bound him up well in a rich silk cloth. I do not think you would have had time to walk half a league before Raimbaut was quite cured and fully restored to health. (*Corbaran's Christianity*, p. 42)

The enchanters and fays may have superior powers but are limited in their use. They can neither protect themselves entirely from harm nor impose their will on others beyond a very clearly defined point; Morgan le Fay can imprison Lancelot, she cannot make him love her; while Merlin, though he could help Uther deceive Igraine, is himself entrapped by the wiles of another woman. The shape-changers cannot usually metamorphose others, though an exception to this rule is found in the romance of *William of Palermo* (*Guillaume de Palerne*) who is befriended by a wolf which is really a Spanish prince transformed by the traditional folk-tale character, the wicked step-mother; and even she can only alter the exterior, not the mind or heart of the prince. As Lunete tells Yvain when explaining the magic ring to him, it hides the person like the bark of a tree hides the wood (*Yvain*, 1036–7). Magic affects only the exterior not the heart or mind.

Side by side with the useful marvels are those which seem only to serve as ornament to the story. The sword-bridge which Lancelot must cross to enter the land where Guinevere is imprisoned, or the wall of air which surrounds the orchard in *Erec* differ only in type not in function from the double portcullis which traps Yvain as he pursues the dying knight of the spring and which has been shown to have been the latest thing in castle-defences in the late twelfth century. Like the descriptions of the rich clothes or the detailed portraits of the hero and heroine, these descriptive marvels are used sparingly by Chrétien and with increasing frequency by the romance writers of the thirteenth century and later. But the romances are not fairy-tales nor are they myths. Many of the elements which today seem unreal were everyday normality to the audiences in court and castle. Others are of the very stuff of story: the knights who boldly go through the forest of adventure on endless quests for hawk or hound or Holy Grail are ordinary human beings, albeit in extraordinary situations, and so are the people they meet, dwarfs and maidens, kings and courtiers set in a world of 'magic casements, opening on the foam of perilous seas, in faery lands forlorn'.

For this reason, the miraculous may also enter the marvellous world of romance, especially in such works as the *Quest of the Holy Grail* where the hermit introduces Galahad as 'the one by whom the marvels of this land and other lands will be brought to an end' (*Quest*, S. 7). The Middle Ages were keenly attuned to the concept of divine intervention in human affairs – their theology was strongly incarnational – and both writers and readers could distinguish between the truly divine and the false glamour of devil-inspired conjuring tricks. In the Chester play of *Antichrist*, the prophets are not deceived by the apparent miracles of the imposter. They see fruit suddenly growing on trees or dead men raised to life and know 'these are not miracles but marvellous things'.

4. The World Upside-down

> 'and if you're not good directly,' she added, 'I'll put you
> through into Looking-glass House. How would you like
> that? . . . the books are something like our books, only
> the words go the wrong way.'
>
> (Lewis Carroll, *Through the Looking-Glass*)

ALTHOUGH epic and romance dominated vernacular literature
in the twelfth century, other genres did begin to develop and by
the early thirteenth century were sufficiently well established to
pose a real challenge to the pre-eminence of the serious
aristocratic literature of castle and court. The fighting values of
the *chansons de geste* with their emphasis on loyalty to God and
one's overlord; the preoccupations of the courtly lover and his
lady; the self-serving adventures of knights errant in the
fantastic world of the romances – all these tales had only a
limited appeal for the new bourgeois society that was evolving
at the turn of the century and becoming sufficiently wealthy
and socially aware to be interested in patronising the poets and
artists who had previously looked only to the barons and the
aristocratic world for their inspiration and their commissions.

If we are to judge the taste of this new society by the works
they wrote and read and had copied, the major innovations
were the emphasis on humour, often with a tinge of satire, and a
general questioning of social and moral values, coupled with a
delight in incident and plot rather than characterisation. It is a
literature of deeds and actions more than feelings, but without
the high seriousness which informed the greatest works of the
epic period. Some of the courtly romances were refurbished and
extended in the immense prose cycles, others were continued in
verse, new ones were composed, but the heyday of the
psychological romance was over: Chrétien's *Knight of the Cart*
gave way to the *Prose Lancelot* with its vast network of interlaced
stories covering a time-span of almost a century and with a
huge cast of characters.

At the other extreme of length, although lays continued to be

read and written, a new genre arose: the *fabliau*, a short story
with a non-aristocratic setting and characters, normally
humorous, frequently bawdy, often obscene. But of all the
innovations perhaps the most original was the vast and
influential beast-epic, the cycle of stories centred on the
character of Renart the Fox, which combined the court setting
of the epic with the bawdy humour of the *fabliau* and a lusty
uninhibited enjoyment of physical reality which is the keynote
of thirteenth-century literature.

Hero and Anti-hero: the Knight and the *Vilain*

ONLY a mature and confident society can laugh at itself and
there is considerable evidence that the thirteenth century had
this kind of maturity. Although the *Vulgate Cycle* took itself
seriously, unashamedly appealing to the emotions of love,
honour and loyalty which had been the hallmark of the earlier
romances, it included also a wide range of marvels and
incidents that appealed to a more varied reading public, one
that would not appreciate too many soliloquies on the niceties
of courtly love. This trend is even more marked in the later
prose cycles which leaned ever more heavily on adventure and
shifts of fortune, with the setting becoming progressively more
fantastic and exotic. Nor was this the only concession to a
changing taste. The author of the *Prose Tristan*, writing in the
middle of the century, introduced a new character, Sir Dinadan
the critic and sceptic, renowned for his sharp tongue and acid
comments but also very much part of the Round Table and
well liked by Arthur who enjoys his irreverent mockery of the
traditional norms of knightly behaviour, such as the custom of
challenging every knight you meet regardless of whether there
is anything to fight about. The originality of Dinadan lies in his
being part of the system he mocks: he is a valiant fighter and
worthy knight. Chrétien's humorous portrayal of the follies of
the excessively amorous Lancelot was only lightly sketched by
an indulgent outsider looking in on the game. Dinadan is
inside, part of the community, laughing at them, with them.

A very different kind of anti-hero in the later romances is the villainous Sir Breus Sans Pitié who tramples fallen enemies, carries off damsels and generally breaks all the rules of chivalry unchecked, as if the great company of the Round Table had lost its power to right wrongs and bring justice for all. The ethics of force have become considerably more complex and the situations as a result are morally though not physically more realistic.

The real anti-hero of the period, however, is not the knight at all but the *vilain*, a term used often and loosely in the *fabliaux* for a wide range of non-aristocratic social types, some of whom exist barely above subsistence level while others are clearly in comfortable circumstances. A good example of the hero and heroine who have replaced the baron and his châtelaine, the knight and his lady, are the *vilain* and his wife in the *Tale of the Partridges* (*Dit des Perdrix*). A man finds two partridges in the hedge and gives them to his wife to cook while he goes to fetch the village priest to share the banquet. The centre of the tale is a minute description of the wife gradually eating the partridges while she waits for her husband's return: 'And when she could not see him coming, her tongue began to flicker over the remaining partridge: if she doesn't have a little more she'll go raving mad. She drew the neck out very carefully and ate it most delicately, licking her fingers all round' (*Partridges*, 39–46). By the time the husband eventually returns, she has consumed both birds and tells her husband the cat ate them. He attacks her furiously and she hastily retracts this, shouting 'It's a joke, it's a joke' (63), and sends him out to sharpen his knife ready to carve them. Meanwhile the priest arrives and greets the wife with significant familiarity: 'he came to the lady without delay and embraced her gently and at once she said to him: "Sir, flee, run away. . . . My husband has gone outside to sharpen his great knife and says he intends to cut off your testicles if he can catch you" ' (80–9). The priest believes her (guilty conscience?) and runs off while the lady at once tells her husband the priest has stolen the partridges. The story concludes with a splendidly visual cartoon-film ending as the husband pursues the fleeing priest, knife in hand and shouting: 'You'll lose them if I catch up with you' (118). The moral of the tale is one of the commonest in the genre: 'Woman is made for trickery. She makes lies become truth and truth become lies' (151–3).

These stories frequently portray trickery and deceit, often of the husband by the wife with a priest or monk as the third member of the triangle. Students are also popular choices for the second man – a second woman is a comparatively rare character – especially in the stories that are set in towns where an itinerant student might well be offered accommodation by a kindly disposed bourgeois household. It is noticeable that cases of 'wife-swopping' are very rare. The *vilain* and the bourgeois seem to have enough to do to satisfy their own wives.

The humour in the *fabliau* is often very black, with violent and cruel practical jokes being played, and the characterisation is almost uniformly uncomplimentary; notwithstanding the cruelty and obscenity, the anti-feminism and the use of uncourtly characters, there is little reason to suppose that these tales were not enjoyed by the same audience as the romances; for despite an unrefined narrative style, *vilain* rather than *courtois*, they treat the same subjects. Adultery and violence are the mainsprings of courtly love and chivalry, and the portrayal of women as venal, lecherous and treacherous is an inevitable reaction against the excessive adulation and worship of the lady under the code of *fin'amor*.

Not all *fabliaux*, of course, treat of sexual themes, though there are few that do not involve some kind of verbal trickery or cunning, for the conventional characters of these tales, who are rarely distinguished by a name, are almost uniformly articulate and quick-witted. One of the most unusual and entertaining of the one hundred and fifty or so surviving stories in this genre is the tale of the *Peasant who argued his way into Heaven* (*Vilain qui conquist Paradis par plait*). A peasant dies but neither angel nor devil comes to collect his soul which therefore follows an angel escorting another soul up to the gates of Heaven. St Peter challenges his right to enter, unescorted, and adds that, anyway, 'we don't want any low types [*vilains*] here' (28). At once the peasant retorts: 'There can't be a lower type [*plus vilains*] than you are' (p. 30), and goes on to remind the saint that he denied Christ while the soul has always been good and loyal. St Peter summons St Thomas to help him, with predictable results. St Thomas is reminded of his unworthiness to be in Heaven for he doubted the resurrection of the Lord. Bewildered by these arguments the apostles now call on St Paul who orders the peasant out, in vain. 'St Paul the bald' (82) finds himself reminded of his part in the martyrdom of Stephen. As a last resort the saints appeal to God himself, who questions the soul's right to stay in Heaven when he has forced his way in without leave and been very rude to 'my apostles' (117). At this point the soul lists in detail all the good works he has performed and insists he has fulfilled the Church's requirements of final confession and communion, concluding: 'They tell us in sermons that if anyone dies in this way God will pardon his sins. You ought to know if I am telling the truth' (139–41). Thus challenged, God accepts the soul's argument and allows him to stay, praising him for his skill in pleading his case. The moral of the tale is a common one also, 'cunning is more effective than force' (160) and it is clear from the choice of language – *plait* and *plaidier* are legal terms – that it is the lawyers who are being satirised here for their skill in making right seem wrong and wrong seem right. This ironic praise of the lawyer matches the wry admission of many of the tales that women, too, are quick-witted and verbally clever. All the professions, the law, medicine and the Church are fully represented in the *fabliaux*, together with the merchant and the student, indeed all the members of the new fighting community; the wars between Christians and aliens, vassals and feudal families have been replaced by a less bloody but equally bitter struggle; cunning has superseded muscle; *Dallas* and *Coronation Street* compete with *The Saint* and *Dr Who* for the mass audiences.

Man and Beast: *Renart the Fox*

IF the true lovers of the courtly romances had their mirror-images in the hen-pecked husbands and wanton wives of the *fabliaux*, the fighting community found itself reflected in the struggles of King Noble the Lion and his barons with the renegade, treacherous Renart the Fox, whose exploits (like those of Roland or Arthur) were first chronicled in Latin, in the twelfth century poem *Ysengrimus*, then developed in French whence they spread all over Western Europe, winning for their cunning, vicious, hypocritical hero a high place in the popularity charts for several centuries and replacing the Old French word for fox, *goupil* from Latin *vulpiculus*), with the Modern French form, *renard*, in the process.

As with the 'Matter of Britain' and the 'Matter of France', the different stories, or branches as they are called, of the *Romance of Renart* were composed by many different authors over a period of more than a century. There were also other, separate redactions using the same characters composed in later centuries, but these were usually heavily moralised and didactic (see p. 107 below). The earliest writer in French is Pierre de St-Cloud, in the twelfth century. In the preface to his tale *How Renart got Isengrim into the Well* (Branch II in the cyclic manuscripts), the author tells us plainly what he is trying to do: 'Now, I must tell you something which will make you laugh, for I am well aware that the truth is you don't want sermons or to hear the lives of saints. That's not what you want, but rather something to entertain you' (*Renart*, 3256–63).

St-Cloud's story is based on an old folk-tale and tells how Renart, thirsty after his midnight raid on the monks' poultry-yard, goes to the well, and seeing his reflection in the water believes it is his mate, Hermeline, whom he truly loves ('*d'amor fine*', 3416). Wishing to reach her he treads in one of the buckets which immediately drops down the well and the fox is trapped. Fortunately for him, Isengrim the wolf, his fellow baron and principal butt arrives, looks in the well and seeing Renart and his own reflection believes they are his mate and his enemy together. With the mixture of human and animal behaviour which is a feature of beast literature from the *Fables of Aesop* to *Watership Down*, Isengrim upbraids his wife for her treachery in both words and wolf-howls. The cunning fox sees his chance and proceeds to talk himself out of the well as the *vilain* talked himself into Paradise. Only in this case Renart claims he is already *in* Heaven: 'My body lies on the bier in Hermeline's earth and my soul is in Heaven sitting at the feet of Jesus' (3517–20). Only the word 'earth' (*taisnière*) in this statement reminds us that it is animals talking, not men. Renart goes on to expatiate on the pleasures of Heaven where there are woods and meadows filled with good things: 'And oxen, cows and sheep, hawks, goshawks and falcons' (3529–30). Isengrim, who is very hungry, eagerly begs to be allowed to join him and eventually Renart explains that the two buckets on the well are the scales of justice, and if the good weighs heavily enough the wolf will descend to join him. ' "But no man can ever under any circumstances sink down here unless he has made his confession. Have you renounced your sins?" "Yes," he said, "to an old hare and to the goat, Dame Hersent, most truly and devoutly" ' (3563–9). After the wolf has howled his repentance, Renart tells him he is pardoned and may step into the bucket. Immediately the wolf, being heavier than the fox, sinks down into the well, like Hoffnung's bricklayer, passing the other bucket as it bears the delighted fox to the top. For as he explains: 'When one goes, another comes, that's the usual custom. I am going up there to Heaven and you are going down to Hell' (3607–10). Renart rushes off leaving Isengrim in the well where he is found by the monks who haul him up, beat him severely and leave him for dead. He limps home eventually, meeting his son who plans vengeance on Renart in epic style, swearing 'by God who suffered martyrdom, that if he can get his hands on him he'll make him pay for his actions' (3713–16).

Many of the branches of the beast-epic turn on similar tricks, and every time Renart escapes the consequences of his misdeeds or involves Isengrim in some painful plight for the fun of it. In this respect, the fox has much in common with the *fabliau* heroes, combining cruelty and black humour with the cunning which in the *fabliaux* is more often the prerogative of the women. But Renart is in no sense a 'popular' hero, a poor man using cunning to defend himself against a corrupt and powerful aristocracy. Renart, like Isengrim, is a feudal baron, one of the principal vassals of King Noble who has as little success in controlling Renart as ever Charlemagne had with Roland, Renaud or Raoul. The audience for these stories appreciated power, whether physical or mental, for it was a world in which only the strong survived. Renart, like Roland, is strong, but like Oliver he is also wise. His actions and those of the other anthropomorphic beasts are an inextricable interweaving of natural/animal and social/human behaviour. On one occasion, King Noble sends Renart a letter, written and sealed by Baucent the boar, warning the fox he will be hanged for his crimes unless he can defend himself in the king's court by 'right and reason' (*droit et raison*, 1019). Renart breaks the seal and reads the letter, two totally human actions. He then confesses his sins to the badger and is pardoned – but the human characters are suddenly replaced by animals, for on their way to court, Renart sees the nuns' hen-yard and suggests a raid as any fox might do.

The range and variety of Renart's adventures cannot be adequately and briefly described. The context is also very detailed and consistent: the court of King Noble and the household of Renart and his mate are those of feudal lords, but the scene of the action is also the farms and villages, abbeys and nunneries with fish-ponds and wells, a whole panorama of rural life compared to the mainly urban locations of the *fabliaux*. The story of *The Fox and the Crow*, taken by Pierre de St-Cloud from the *Fables* of Marie de France, and which in La Fontaine's celebrated seventeenth-century version is eighteen lines long, runs to one hundred and fifty verses in the romance where it begins with the Crow, Dant Tiecelin, stealing the cheese: 'He saw a thousand cheeses which had been put out in the sunshine, and the woman who was supposed to be looking after them had gone into the house so Tiecelin saw his chance to win, and swooping down, seized one. The old woman sallied forth into the street to rescue it and saw Tiecelin; she hurled stones and pebbles at him, screaming: "Vassal, you shall not carry it away" ' (*Renart*, 5573–84). While Tiecelin is eating the cheese, 'the yellowest and softest part of it' (5603), he drops a crumb which falls in front of Renart who is lying in the shade of a tree. The traditional dialogue follows but the story does not end with Renart getting the cheese 'for in addition, if he can, he wants to have Tiecelin too' (5649–50). He ignores the cheese and claims the smell of it is killing him and begs the crow to come and take it away as he himself has hurt his foot and cannot run. 'Tiecelin believes he is speaking the truth because he begs him with tears' (5669–70). The foolish crow is lucky to escape at the cost of some feathers, and from a safe distance rants at the fox who 'answered not a word but gently soothed away the pain by eating all the cheese himself' (5693–6).

The intention of the authors of *Renart* is laughter, and at the expense of the foolish and the weak, but there is in the original

Romance of Renart only implicit satire and no authorial criticism or moralising. It is a comedy of manners with the animals used as types, focusing the readers' attention on particular characteristics in an almost allegorical manner. Though Renart fights and betrays, murders and assaults, blasphemes and corrupts, it is 'but jest, poison in jest, no offence in the world', for the humour insulates us from the horrors of the reality of the actions in the same way as in a *Tom and Jerry* cartoon. But the animal literature of the Middle Ages is not written for children and it is a far cry from the cunning, violent, lecherous wolf-baiting Renart to the heroic outlaw-fox in lincoln green who stars in Walt Disney's animal-cartoon version of the *Story of Robin Hood*.

The Wheel of Fortune: Drama and the Town of Arras

THOUGH the *fabliaux* and the beast-epic may have been written by and for the members of the new urban society, they shared these literary genres with the aristocratic communities of court and castle who enjoyed also *chansons de geste* and romances. But the new literary phenomenon of the thirteenth century, the vernacular play, was indisputably the preserve of the towns and of one town in particular: Arras.

A centre for banking and the cloth trade – it gave its name to a kind of wall-hanging – Arras in the thirteenth century was one of the most important towns in France. It was ruled by a small number of patrician merchant families, so wealthy that they lent money both to municipalities, like Bruges, and to local potentates, like the Counts of Flanders, and were also considerable patrons of the arts and literature, so that the status of the town at this period was not unlike that of Florence under the Medici two centuries later.

By the end of the twelfth century Arras had already a flourishing *confrérie* or *Guild of the minstrels and burghers of Arras*, with the usual aims of mutual aid, death grants, regular reunions and a certain number of spiritual benefits. In addition to this general association, there was by the middle of the thirteenth century a literary guild or *puy* whose membership was limited to the leading patricians and poets. Such societies developed all over Europe at this period, side by side with the trade guilds and the religious confraternities and became the focus of urban artistic and literary patronage, especially in the fields of lyric poetry and drama (see p. 186 below).

Six plays have survived from the thirteenth century, four of them from Arras, all of high quality and two at least acknowledged masterpieces. Though no two of the six are in the same style, they possess one common element: they portray rapid changes of fortune in the life of the principal characters. Blind Fortune with her wheel was a popular figure in medieval art and literature: the men living in the so-called age of faith were not unaware of the uncertainties of the human condition. Trust in God and the saints not only did not preclude awareness of the risks of war, disease and famine, it did not protect the individual from the machinations of the ungodly, who in this kind of literature are not necessarily the genuine pagans; as in the *chansons de geste*, the threat from within the Christian society was the commonest catalyst for good stories.

There are three religious plays among the six, two of them from Arras – a miracle of St Nicholas and a biblical parable – and one from Paris, based on a miracle of the Virgin Mary. The earliest, the *Play of St Nicholas* (*Jeu de Saint Nicolas*) was written by Jean Bodel of Arras in 1200–1; at the time he was planning to take the cross, but fortune intervened to prevent his actually setting out on crusade: he contracted leprosy. In a number of lyric poems, the *Congés*, he appealed to the local *echevins* or town-councillors for assistance, which seems to have been granted for he ended his days in one of the local leper-houses maintained by charitable and civic donations. He died in 1209.

The story of the *Play of St Nicholas* derives from what is now a little-known aspect of the saint, his role as a guardian of treasure. The theme was popular in the Middle Ages, occurring in a number of narrative legendaries while two plays on this subject are among the small number of Latin saints' plays to have survived from the twelfth century. This play is set in a pagan land whose ruler summons his emirs to fight the invading Christians, and after the victory takes prisoner a *preud'hom* who has a statue of St Nicholas which he assures the king is infallible

as a guardian of treasure. Determined to test the claim, the king
orders the statue to be laid in the treasury, the *preud'hom* to be
put in the dungeon and his messenger, Auberon, to declare to
all the people of the town that the royal treasure is unguarded.
These opening scenes establish the unusual nature of the play
with its mixture of seriousness and humour. The king demands
from his idol Tervagan – the play is to some extent a conflict
between two statues – a sign: 'If I am going to win, then laugh,
if I must lose, then weep. What do you think, seneschal?
Tervagan has wept and laughed: this is very significant!'
(*Nicholas*, 180–5). Tears and laughter alternate in the ensuing
scenes which range from the epic seriousness of the Christians'
heroic words before the battle in which they are all killed to the
comic threats of the gaoler to whom the hapless *preud'hom* is
entrusted: 'While you are in my care my pincers will never be
idle while you have a tooth in your head!' (547–9).

The most original feature of the play, however, is the bold
step which Bodel takes when the messenger, Auberon, leaves
the pagan king's palace and stops to slake his thirst in a French
tavern in Arras where wine from Auxerre is sold, and which
numbers among its clientele a group of petty thieves whose
subsequent behaviour makes it quite clear that they are at least
nominally Christian. So skilfully is this transition managed and
so outrageous is the premise that it is immediately acceptable
as a dramatic convention to introduce the naturalistic comedy
of the tavern scenes into the already heady mixture of saint's
life, *chanson de geste* and farce. After a long scene of dicing,
drinking and quarrelling (which can still be effective today when
staged though it is somewhat tedious to read, and we probably
miss many a local allusion and joke), the thieves go off to the
palace, steal the treasure and return to the tavern. The king
discovers he has been robbed and threatens the *preud'hom* who
beseeches St Nicholas to save him. The saint now appears in
person to the thieves, addressing them in very uncanonical
language and threatening them with divine retribution and the
gallows if they do not replace the treasure. It is interesting to
notice that here, as in the epics and romances, the supernatural
characters do not influence the personality of the humans, only
their actions. The thieves return the treasure as ordered then go
their unregenerate petty-thieving ways. Since they are already

Christians (albeit bad ones) they are not converted like the king and his emirs (see p. 43 above). Tervagan's smiles and tears are proved to have been a true prophecy even though he is a false god.

The mixture of serious and comic elements is also found in the second of the four Arras plays, the dramatisation of the biblical parable of the prodigal son, *Courtois d'Arras*, composed about 1230. The fluctuating fortunes of Courtois, who spends his patrimony of sixty *sous* in riotous living with two whores in a tavern and then finds himself reduced to feeding pigs, are reflected in the variety of language registers used, from the familiar tones of the scenes with his father to the crude tavern dialogue and the formal beauty of the speech of repentance. It is also shown in practical terms: in the opening scene Courtois scorns the 'bread and peas' his father offers him (*Courtois*, 50), but later he tries to eat the peas in their pods that the pigs are trampling and finds them sour and rotten (550). This emphasis on a detail of the different type of life he is leading prepares the way effectively and naturally for the killing of the fatted calf by Courtois's father to celebrate his son's return home. The wheel has come full circle.

The third of the religious plays is not from Arras. The earliest surviving dramatisation of the very popular legends of Our Lady, the *Miracle of Theophilus* (*Miracle de Théophile*) was written about 1260 by the Parisian poet Rutebeuf, one of the major lyric poets of the thirteenth century. Like Courtois, Theophilus experiences rapid changes of fortune from poverty at the beginning of the play, to which he has been reduced by the local bishop, to a summit of wealth and power in the Church when he has sold his soul to the devil, to repentance and fear when he appeals to Our Lady. She demands Theophilus's charter from the devil, and when he refuses she warns him: 'I shall trample on your belly [*je te foulerai la pance*]' (*Theophilus*, 585) and does so, treading the devil underfoot in good biblical style (see Genesis 3:15). Theophilus does public penance before the congregation to whom the bishop reads the charter as a warning to others. *The Miracle of Theophilus* is a lively and effective piece of theatre particularly rich in poetic imagery and variety of verse forms, but it lacks the humour and the visual, dramatic impact of the Arras plays. The latter is also absent from the oldest farce, *The*

Blind Man and the Boy (*Le Garçon et l'Aveugle*), which dates from the thirteenth century. It was left to Arras again to produce, in the two plays of Adam de la Halle, the earliest and most original secular plays of medieval France.

The slighter of Adam's two works, *The Play of Robin and Marion* (*Le Jeu de Robin et Marion*) has been called the first musical comedy, for the story of Robin the shepherd and his shepherdess love, Marion, is interspersed with songs and dances whose music is included in the manuscript. A passing knight tries to persuade the shepherdess to change her love and favour him instead but she remains faithful to Robin despite the knight's condescension: 'Really I'm making an ass of myself by coming down to an ass's level' (*Robin and Marion*, 378–9). After the knight's departure, the shepherds feast, dance, sing and play the game of Kings and Queens.[1] The play ends with a dance led by Robin. One of the manuscripts of the play, which was composed about 1283 in Italy whither Adam had accompanied the Count of Artois, contains a short dialogue called *The Play of the Pilgrim* (*Le Jeu du Pèlerin*) in which a pilgrim tells some citizens of Arras that he has come from foreign lands, and in Italy he heard much discussion of Adam: 'He was called Master Adam the hunchback [*le bochus*] when he was here, and there he was known as Adam of Arras' (25–6). Now, says the pilgrim, Adam is dead, mourned by the count who showed the pilgrim his tomb. This little dialogue with its introduction of real people, though too brief to be considered a play is typical of the Arras drama tradition with its unique mixture of reality and illusion, a tradition which reached its apotheosis in Adam de la Halle's *The Play of the Bower* (*Le Jeu de la Feuillée*), a unique hybrid work containing elements of farce, satire, comedy, fairy-tale and revue set in the most naturalistic setting possible: the streets of Arras peopled by the author himself, his father and his friends – a sort of nightmare blend of *A Midsummer Night's Dream* and *Under Milk Wood*.

The play turns on a simple question: should Adam leave Arras and the wife he has grown tired of and return to his studies in Paris? – 'I have been with a wife and now am going back to study [*clergiet*]' (*Bower*, 2). The speakers in this elaborate debate include several of Adam's friends: a doctor and a monk collecting money with his relics, who seem to represent the two ways to health and sanity; a fool and a madman whom they are unable to cure; Adam's own father who is diagnosed as suffering from avarice; and the local whore, Dame Douche. The play is strongly satirical but in a very individual, personal way. Half the major families in Arras are mentioned in unflattering terms. Having wrung all the humour he can out of the subject, Adam then introduces an element of the marvellous, from the romances, for this is the night when the fays visit the town. A table is laid for them and after the monk has been made to put his relics out of the way as they would prevent 'Dame Morgue and her company' (564) from coming, Adam and his friends hide to watch the 'great marvel' (572). The author having become actor now changes his role again and becomes spectator.

The fays are accompanied by Fortune with her wheel and there is more talk of local people and their changing fortunes; some are on the way up, others about to fall. Seeeing the table prepared for them, the fays prepare to give gifts to those who have thus honoured them. Unfortunately, there is no knife at one of the places and in a scene which foreshadows the christening scene in *Sleeping Beauty*, one of the fays gives bad gifts while the other two give good ones. For Adam, the angry fay, Arsile, condemns him to stay in Arras with his wife and forget all about his ambition to go to Paris. Morgue regrets this but has no power to change the curse. At length the fays depart with Dame Douche on some mysterious women's business: 'We have been waiting for you all night at the Cross in the Meadow, watching for you in the streets, you've kept us waiting too long' (854–7). The hidden spectators emerge and the play concludes with a cheerful drinking-scene in the tavern during which the monk falls asleep and the others creep away, leaving him to settle the bill.

Bodel and Adam de la Halle both treat reality with a casual insouciance which is unequalled in medieval drama. They apparently limit their stages to realistic locations, a palace, tavern, battlefield or street, but they introduce also an element of supernatural: the angel and the saint in *Nicholas* and the fays in *Feuillée*, and thus extend their range upwards to the sublime, while the tavern, which was a well-known medieval image of Hell, provides the ridiculous, the depths, the other end of the scale. Like the epics and romances and their humorous counterparts, the *fabliaux* and the beast-epic, early medieval drama is conceived on a cosmic scale. A mirror of the world and of man's fluctuating fortunes in it, the new urban literature has found in the theatre its most successful mode of expression.

A Looking-glass World: *Aucassin and Nicolette*

'OF all pretty tales the prettiest': such was a nineteenth-century verdict on the *chantefable* of *Aucassin and Nicolette*, composed in the first half of the thirteenth century in a highly original form which alternated sung verse sections – 'Now it is sung [*Or se cante*]' – with prose narratives – 'Now they speak, narrate and tell the story [*Or dient et content et fablent*]'. The music for the sung passages is in the manuscript and it is obvious that *Aucassin and Nicolette* is an oral, almost a dramatic work.

In the verse prologue, the author tells us that 'the song is sweet, the tale is good and courtly and well told' (*Aucassin and Nicolette*, S. 1, 8–9). It is also witty, gently satirical and extremely funny. It would be unfair to Aucassin to call him an anti-hero for he is young and handsome, valiant and very much in love – the very model of a young and courtly knight. But he has one serious flaw: 'he was so overcome by love the all-conquering, that he did not want to be a knight, nor take up arms, nor go to the tournament nor do anything at all that he ought to do' (S. 11, 16–18). Truly, compared to Aucassin the uxorious Erec was the epitome of chivalrous behaviour.

The story of the *chantefable* is based on the opposition between the effect love ought to have on Aucassin and the effect it actually has. His father's castle is being besieged but Aucassin will take no part in the fighting till his father bribes him with the promise of a few minutes' meeting with his beloved Nicolette and a kiss or two. At once all is changed and, well-armed and mounted, the young man gallops out into the fray. But, like Lancelot, he cannot keep his mind on anything but his lady and deep in thoughts of Nicolette he allows himself to be captured, only coming to his senses when he hears his captors discussing ways of executing him. 'If I have my head cut off I shall never be able to talk to Nicolette my sweetheart whom I love so much', he reasons (S. x, 20–1) and he manages to keep his mind on the job long enough to capture his enemy and drag him back to the delighted father. But the count does not want his son to marry Nicolette who is a slave girl, bought from the Saracens, baptised and educated by the viscount. To prevent the marriage, Nicolette is locked in a tower from which she escapes by tying the sheets together. For Nicolette is the perfect heroine: beautiful, intelligent, courageous and very much in love with her somewhat lackadaisical lover. The two run away together and are shipwrecked in the kingdom of Torelore, a really topsy-turvy land where the king is in bed celebrating the birth of a son and the queen is out leading the army. Perversely, Aucassin himself now becomes energetic and active, stripping the bedclothes off the king and beating him, then interfering in the battle and killing many people before they can stop him. 'It's not the custom for us to kill each other', he is told (S. xxxii, 15) for in Torelore the battles are decided by more peaceful means: they throw cheeses and rotten apples and big mushrooms into the river and see who can make the biggest splash (S. xxxi).

Throughout the lovers' stay in Topsy-turvydom, Aucassin remains the dominant partner and Nicolette is content to be meek and submissive, but soon the author moves them on again. This time they are kidnapped by slavers and Aucassin is again shipwrecked, near his own home town of Beaucaire where he finds his parents have died and he is the lord. He settles down passively to lament the loss of his beloved Nicolette. She, meanwhile, is carried to Cartage, the Saracen capital (probably Cartagena in Spain) and recognised as the king's long-lost daughter. Energetically determined to be reunited with her lover, however, she takes lessons in playing the viol; then, disguised as a minstrel, runs away again and eventually comes to Beaucaire. Once convinced that Aucassin still loves her in his inactive way, she promises him to restore his beloved to him in a week and spends that time with her former foster-mother, getting the stain off her face and making sure she is as beautiful as possible. 'Then she dresses herself in rich silk of which the lady had plenty and sits down in the bedchamber on a silken coverlet sending the lady to fetch Aucassin her lover' (S. xl,

39–42). Thus at long last the lovers are permanently united.

The tone of *Aucassin and Nicolette* is light-hearted and amusing, with a strong dramatic element: it was staged in Paris in the eighteenth century, and has been a successful radio play and a delightful cartoon-film in the twentieth. But it is not just a pretty tale nor a parody of Chrétien's romances, though it is both these. The strength of the story lies in the constant reversals of the norm. It is a looking-glass world as irrationally logical as that of Lewis Carroll. One of the most interesting passages is that where the viscount warns Aucassin that if he makes Nicolette his mistress, his soul will go to Hell for ever and he will never enter Paradise.

> What should I do in Paradise? I don't want to go there unless I have Nicolette my most sweet beloved whom I love so much. For the only people who go to Paradise are these I tell you about: old priests go there; and the old cripples and the maimed, who day and night crouch before the altars and in the old crypts; and those dressed in old worn cloaks and old garments, naked, barefoot and barelegged, who die of hunger and thirst and cold and wretchedness. They go to Paradise: I have nothing to do with them! But I want to go to Hell for that's where the fine clerics go and the fine knights who die in tournaments and great wars and the good men-at-arms and noble men. I want to go with them. And the beautiful courtly ladies go there, for they had two lovers or three as well as their husbands. And that's where the gold and silver goes, the ermine and squirrel-fur, and the harpers and minstrels and the kings of this world. I want to go with them, provided I have Nicolette my most sweet love with me.   (S. VI, 26–43)

This virtuoso piece of rhetoric has been interpreted in many different ways, but in the artless mouth of the young lover it cannot be a serious satire. Its humour has the naïve edge and simple directness of a child: far from swearing 'all for love and the world well lost', Aucassin is even prepared to give up the attractions of Hell and go to Heaven, provided he can have his Nicolette. Yet another example of the paradoxical logic of this original and entertaining work.

Disguise and Delusion

IF the mainspring of the action in an epic is a conflict, and in a romance usually a quest, in the new humorous literature it is most frequently a trick. Deception is, of course, far from unknown in the earlier literature, and is a common ingredient of the marvellous (see p. 84 above), from the potions with which Orable (*Enfances Guillaume*, 1971–2013) and Fénice (*Cligès*, 3296–304) delude their unwanted husbands, to the ring of invisibility which enables Yvain to escape his pursuers. Disguises may be used against the hero as well as for him, especially by the devil and his followers, who take the form of hermits, or damsels in distress (see, for example, *Quest*, pp. 110, 177 etc.). But then the devil had been a deceiver from the beginning, masking his temptations in fair words and his evil nature under the guise of an angel of light or a serpent, which in many medieval plays and paintings appears with a human, normally female, face.

Deceptions of a purely human kind are also integral to the concept of courtly love with its emphasis on adulterous liaisons and the need to conceal the relationship from society or the lady's husband. Disguise is, however, rarely used in these stories, except in the Tristan romances where it is often combined with verbal trickery as in the scene already mentioned of Iseult's trial by ordeal (see p. 36 above). Outstanding among the disguise stories are the two versions of *Tristan's Madness* (*La Folie Tristan*) in which the hero, having been banished from Mark's court, disguises himself as a madman in order to visit the queen, taking great pains to make the disguise effective. He changes clothes with a fisherman and, in addition, 'Tristan had a pair of scissors which he was accustomed to carry about with him; he valued them very highly for Iseult had given him the scissors. With these scissors he cut his hair very short all round so that he looked like a madman or an imbecile and afterwards he cut himself a cross-shaped tonsure. Tristan was very adept at changing his voice and he also dyed his skin with a herb he had brought with him from his own land. He anointed his face with the juice and it changed his colour and made it very dark.' As a final touch Tristan cuts himself a staff from the hedgerow and sets off for Tintagel (Oxford *Madness*, 195–223).

William of Orange also uses disguise to visit his future love, darkening his skin 'with alum and dark stain so that they looked just like Saracens or heathens' (*Capture of Orange*, 14–15). Both these masters of disguise thoroughly enjoy the role-playing into which they enter with zest, especially Tristan pretending to be mad and telling Mark his mother was a whale who lived like a siren in the sea. There is a very poetic element in the description he gives of the castle in the air to which he will take the queen if Mark will exchange her for the madman's sister: 'Up there in the air I have a hall which I visit, it is large and beautiful and made of glass, pierced through with sunbeams. It hangs in the clouds high in the air but the wind does not rock nor shake it. Within the hall is a room made of crystal and fine panelling and when the sun rises in the morning it is filled with light' (Oxford *Madness*, 299–308). The mixture of nonsense and poetry quite deceives Mark who allows the madman to wander freely round the court, thus enabling Tristan to visit the queen.

Sometimes verbal deceit is used without disguise, as in the very famous scene from the Tristan story in which the king, having been told that Tristan and Iseult are planning to meet in the garden, hides himself in a tree. The lovers see his reflection in a pool, however (or in some versions actually see him in the tree), and deliberately use the opportunity to deceive him about their relationship, with Tristan begging the queen to intercede for him with his uncle who has got this ridiculous notion his nephew is in love with his wife (Beroul, *Tristan*, 176–211). This scene was often represented in art, for example in misericords in Chester and Lincoln Cathedrals.

This theme of 'the biter bit' is also common in the *fabliaux*, for example the *Burgher's Wife of Orleans*. In this tale, when the wife realises that the cloaked figure she meets in the garden is her husband and not her lover, she turns the tables on him. While her husband is spending a cold night locked in a cellar she is disporting herself with her lover. Later she tells her servants to throw the man out and give him a good beating. On her husband's eventual return she 'innocently' tells him how she has avenged them both on the man who was pestering her for a rendezvous. In later centuries the theme was often used in stories and plays, most memorably perhaps in Beaumarchais's play of the *Marriage of Figaro*.

A common form of disguise in medieval literature is that of a minstrel, probably because they had considerable freedom of movement and the entrée into all kinds of society, as witness the exploit of Blondel whose search for and finding of his master, Richard the Lionheart, is related in the thirteenth-century collection of anecdotes by the *Minstrel of Rheims* (*Ménestrel de Reims*, 77–79). When Tristan goes to Ireland to be healed of his wound he calls himself Tantris, a harper; and Renart, whose appearance has been transformed by falling accidentally into a vat of yellow dye (from which he escapes as usual by a trick) introduces himself to Isengrim as a minstrel from Britain and proceeds to speak broken French, mispronouncing common words in such a way as to make obscenities of even simple statements like 'I was [*je fous*]' (*Renart*, 2418; a similar device is used by Shakespeare in *Henry V*, III.iv). In two texts girls disguise themselves as minstrels. Nicolette does so in order to escape from Cartage and find her lost love, Aucassin, and the heroine in the *Romance of Silence* (*Roman de Silence*) leaves home and travels with a couple of minstrels. In each case an integral part of the disguise is the staining of the face, for ladies in the Middle Ages always had white skins (compare Celia in *As You like It*: 'and with a kind of umber smirch my face, the like do you', I.iii).

A change of sex is perhaps the ultimate disguise and several stories describe a travesty, both romances and *fabliaux*. In Robert de Blois's *Romance of Floris and Liriope* (*Roman de Floris et Liriopé*), the youth, Floris, is living as a girl among girls, like Hercules at the court of Omphale. His winning of Liriope's love under these circumstances is treated with remarkable delicacy. Their son is the ill-fated Narcissus whose death in the Middle Ages was never, however, viewed as the result of this somewhat unfortunate heredity. In the *Romance of Silence*, the heroine, Silence, is brought up from infancy as a boy because her parents will lose their lands if there is no male heir. This unusual subject is developed in the form of a conflict between

Nature and Nurture, heredity versus environment. Edgar Rice Burroughs's original story of *Tarzan of the Apes* (1914) was created with a similar purpose and both stories show the ultimate triumph of Nature over Nurture. Silence realises that when she is eventually recognised as a woman she will have no feminine skills to occupy her, so she decides to learn those of a minstrel which will either serve her 'in the women's apartments' or if she remains a man but is not very good as a knight, 'for I never saw a woman carry any sort of arms in this way' (*Silence*, 2843–4), she will be able to be a minstrel (2864). *Silence* is a late romance, composed towards the very end of the thirteenth century and using many clichés of the genre, but the basic theme is unique.[2]

The epitome of humorous disguise is probably the *fabliau* of *Trubert*, composed in the second half of the thirteenth century, in which the hero plays a series of jokes on the local overlord, Duke Garnier of Burgundy, a mythical character. At the beginning of the poem, Trubert is almost a simpleton who is sent by his mother to sell the cow and is cheated as in *Jack and the Beanstalk*. However, unlike Jack, Trubert is corrupted by his change of fortune and soon the kindly youth who was trying to help his mother and sister becomes a cruel, unprincipled, practical joker – a Perceval in reverse. He seduces the duke's wife and plays a crude joke on the duke, then disguises himself as a carpenter and while in the castle again tricks them both, this time beating the duke severely. Then he comes to court disguised as a doctor – a common theme in farce and *fabliau* – and the duke gets beaten again. Gradually the exploits become more outrageous and cruel. He disguises himself as a knight, pretends to win a battle, causes the death of the real knight and to escape the consequences of his actions finally changes clothes with his own sister and, as Couillebaude (Bawdyballs), joins the maidens who attend the duke's daughter, with predictable results. Unlike the scene in *Floris and Liriope*, the seduction of the princess by the supposed girl is described in far from delicate terms. When the duchess comments on her daughter's unwonted pallor, Couillebaude claims 'she' has seen a dove (*colon*) (2587) visit Rosette each night and believes it is a winged angel: 'Be assured without any doubt she is filled with the holy ghost! she's full of little angelkins [*angeloz*]!' (*Trubert*, 2599–

601). Trubert's final triumph is to be married to King Golias instead of Rosette and on the wedding night the supposed bride tricks 'her' husband with the aid not of a potion but a stout leather draw-string purse. Later that night the bride retires to the other room, where 'she' seduces the waiting maid then sends the girl into the king's bed promising her a husband and a crown. On this unexpectedly cheerful note the *fabliau* ends abruptly.

For the tricksters it is not enough to await the turn of Fortune's wheel. Taking advantage of her blindness they take their fate in their own hands and clamber up by themselves. Nor were such actions condemned by the medieval audience who could laugh at the story of the *Three Blind Men of Compiègne*, who are tricked by a pretended charitable offering, or the farce of the *Blind Man and his Boy*, in which the unfortunate cripple is cheated out of his savings by the unscrupulous youth. Trubert and Renart are as sympathetic to the readers as Tristan or William Shortnose, characters to laugh with rather than at, for their disguises are physical not moral. They make no claim to sanctity or even to common decency.

However, for later writers Renart became himself a disguise and a delusion: Guillaume le Clerc in his *Bestiary* (*Bestiaire*) reminds his audience of what they 'have heard in stories [*oï fabler*]' (1307) about Renart who lived by 'robbery, stealing and trickery' (1313–14). He then talks of the fox as described in the *Bestiary*, with his cunning trick of feigning death in order to entice the birds nearer and catch them. This is the real fox, whereas Renart 'signifies the evil fox . . . the devil who wars against us' (1343–6).

This diabolical Renart is the hero of the satirical works, the *Crowning of Renart* (*Couronnement de Renart*) and the *New Renart* (*Renart le Nouvel*), both of the later thirteenth century, while in the fourteenth-century poem *Renart Disguised* (*Renart le Contrefait*) the author reverses the process and disguises himself as Renart, 'to relate in covered words what he dares not speak openly' (*Contrefait*, 121–2). A rather different view of Renart is implied in the fourteenth-century Anglo-Norman book of courtesy which advises a young man who cannot keep himself from swearing to 'swear without peril to yourself by the cat or the fox, by Saint Renart or Saint Tibalt' (*Edward*, 225–7). Hero or villain, saint or devil, Renart became the symbol of cunning, the archetype of deceit. Rutebeuf summed it up in his short satirical poem, *Renart the Hypocrite* (*Renart le Bestourné*): in an upside-down world, 'Renart Rules OK!' (*Renart regne*, 544).

5. Macrocosm and Microcosm

> Suppose there were a great big hollow sphere made of looking-glass and you were sitting inside. Where would it stop reflecting your face and begin reflecting your back? The more you think about the problem, the more puzzling it becomes.
>
> (Jean Webster)

MEDIEVAL writers had a clear understanding of the fundamental difference between man and beast: not only did the former have a soul he also had reason, and to live without using it was to live like an animal. The ancient philosophers 'did not think like animals who only want their food, like those nowadays whose only concern is to live like pigs and rest themselves in comfort' (*Image of the World*, p. 68). 'We should call such men beasts' (*Book of Fauvel*, 277). Three hundred years later Hamlet is saying the same thing: 'What is a man if his chief good and market of his time be but to sleep and feed? A beast, no more' (*Hamlet*, IV.iv).

To satisfy the needs of those who sought for their minds food with more substance than mere entertainment, the vernacular writers of the twelfth and thirteenth centuries produced translations and anthologies of philosophical and scientific texts, 'honey culled from many flowers', as Brunetto Latini called it in the preface to his *Book of Treasure* (*Livre du Trésor*), the treasure of the title being the sum of human wisdom and knowledge condensed 'briefly' (*Treasure*, p. 2). That a public for such works existed is clearly shown in the preface to the *Image of the World* (*Image du monde*), one of the most popular of the medieval encyclopaedias, compiled in the middle of the thirteenth century because, says Gossuin,

> I found some men in my time of good sense and intelligence who could have learned many useful things if they had had any knowledge of Latin [*clergie*]. I saw many who asked me about the making of the world, what supported the earth,

how the firmament turned and many other subtle things which they were eager to learn about. And I often marvelled how any layfolk had the sense to ask about such things since they had no books nor commentaries. (*Image*, Prologue 17–30; Harley MS 4333)

A few such works were already being written in the twelfth century – the *Bestiary* of Philippe de Thaon or Wace's verse redaction of Geoffrey of Monmouth's *History of the Kings of Britain* – but it was in the thirteenth century, the age of the universities and scholasticism, of Aristotle and Albertus Magnus, of the *Speculum Historiale* (*Mirror of History*) of Vincent of Beauvais and the *Summa Theologica* of Thomas Aquinas, that a flood of encyclopaedias and compendia, mirrors and bibles presented the enquiring layman with a comprehensive picture of the world and its inhabitants, described, discussed, analysed and satirised in a whole library of information, instruction and edification.

Many of these works retained their popularity throughout the Middle Ages, were translated into other languages, even occasionally into Latin, and in the late fifteenth century received the ultimate accolade of print. Alas, with the exception of some of the historical writings they are today virtually unknown, many unedited and most unread. This is partly the fault of the original compilers, whose enthusiasm for knowledge or desire to castigate the sins of their contemporaries often led them into interminable digressions and tedious elaborations, culminating in the middle of the fourteenth century with the cautionary tale of the *Epicier* (pharmacist) from Troyes who kept himself from idleness in retirement by writing the *Renart Disguised* (*Renart le Contrefait*), using the famous fox as a mouthpiece through which he himself could expatiate on the evils of his age. Not content with his first version of a mere 32,000 lines, he started work again ten years later and spent another fifteen years revising and extending his work so that the second redaction comprises more than 40,000 lines of verse and a prose section of over sixty folios. Renart, accused before Noble the Lion of many misdeeds, proceeds to talk himself out of it. The foxy Scheherazade includes the story of Alexander (10,000 lines), the history of the world from Augustus to 1328

(50 pages in the printed edition), dissertations on the seven liberal arts, the nature of the universe and the deadly sins. Other sections of this massive 'Inquire Within Upon Everything', include a number of Renart's own adventures, many *exempla* and numerous references to contemporary events, local customs and abuses culminating in a satirical, but not therefore necessarily inaccurate, picture of the different orders of society from barons to bishops, courtiers to clerics, with a collection of portraits of the different trades – carpenter, tiler, carter, etc. – and their restrictive practices, frequent 'tea-breaks' and general reluctance to get on with the job, that could have been composed in the mid-twentieth rather than the mid-fourteenth century (see p. 142 below).

Ripples from the upsurge of thought and theology which stimulated the growth of learning in the cathedral schools of the twelfth century and led, in the thirteenth, to the foundation of the universities where Aristotelian dialectic replaced neoplatonic culture, produced a spirit of enquiry which joined to the medieval taste for reason and measure created a demand among the laymen for books, written sources at which they could slake their growing thirst for knowledge. Learning broke free from the stranglehold of Latin as books on the world, the universe and society became widely available in French. Nor was it only the rich and famous who owned them: from catalogues, wills and *ex libris* comments we can build up a picture of the wide range of owners and readers of these popular and widely diffused works, text-books for the medieval open university.

The Image of the World

ABOVE all things is God, 'the mirror of that which endures [*pardurableté*]' (*Placides*, S. 34). All other things are created, forged by Nature, the handmaiden of the Creator, and set to work by her priest, Genius (Meung, *Romance of the Rose*, 16740–754). Although Jean de Meung wrote in symbolic terms of the created world, his basic picture is the same as that expressed in less elegant language in many texts of the thirteenth century, works like the *Image of the World* and the *Book of Treasure* already mentioned, or the philosophical dialogue of *Placides and Timeo*, or the ancient work of Eastern origin known as the *Book of Sidrac* which purports to be the work of a Jew, Sidrac, answering the questions put to him on all kinds of subjects by King Bocthus (although the Jewish element is improbable, the work is certainly very ancient, its earliest known form dating from seventh-century Syria). Some of these vernacular works claim to be translated from the *De Naturis Rerum* (*Of the Nature of Things*) by Solinus as the author of the *Mappemonde* explains: 'Pierre has worked hard and set himself the task of translating from the Latin into Romance a description of the world as it turns so steadily, as Solinus has described it. One of the books from which, as well as from others he has clearly set out the substance to hear and know the form of the world where we dwell and the elements from which we are made' (*Mappemonde*, III, pp. 123–4; Pierre dedicated his work to his patron, Robert of Dreux, who died in 1218 and for whose brother he had already translated a bestiary). What is the form of the world for the thirteenth century?

The world is round: like an apple (*Sidrac*, III, pp. 233–4), or a ball (*Image*, p. 90), surrounded by concentric circles of the firmament and the ether like an egg (*Sidrac*, III, p. 234). The starry firmament is the white, the air is the yellow and in the centre the germ of the egg from which the chicken emerges is the earth (*Mappemonde*, III, p. 125). The egg simile is used also by the author of the *Image* in a slightly different way: for him the four elements are the concentric circles of the egg, with the earth as the heaviest in the centre, surrounded by water, air and fire (*Image*, p. 92). The earth is in the centre because it is the heaviest element and all things fall towards it by virtue of this attraction: 'For that which is heaviest falls lowest and attracts all things that have weight towards it' (*Image*, p. 93). God created the world and the universe in this round form because it is the most perfect one and moves very easily – an important point since all the parts of the cosmos are in constant rapid motion (*Image*, p. 99). If there were no obstacles in the way, men could circumnavigate the globe like flies walking round an apple; two men walking in opposite directions, one going east and one west would meet in the antipodes (*Image*, p. 93).

But such a journey would not, in fact, be possible: there are too many obstacles, mountains, deserts 'where nothing can be seen', and the chasm into which falls the 'solid sea' (*mare concretum*, from Plato's *Timaeus*; *Sidrac*, III, p. 236). Are there men in the antipodes? Yes, they are men like us who see day and night, sun, moon and stars as we do; they live by work and digging as we do; 'all is by the roundness of the earth' (*Sidrac*, III, p. 243). If a hole were bored in the axis of the earth, right through to the other side, we could see the stars of the antipodean skies, but any object dropped down such a hole would come to rest in the centre because of the attraction of the heavy element (*Image*, p. 94).

These stars and planets are a great distance from the earth: a heavy weight dropped from the stars would take a hundred years to reach the world's atmosphere (*Image*, p. 101); they are in different layers, and some which seem very small to us are in fact the largest but further away (*Sidrac*, III, p. 244). The beauty of the stars is part of their nature: they express the glory of God who created them. In a beautiful Classical image, Jean de Meung describes how Night,

> when she sits down to her table makes them her candles so that she may appear less hideous to her husband Acheron . . . for she thinks when she sees her reflection in her pantry or cellar or storeroom that she would be too ugly and livid, her face too sombre if she did not have the bright joy of the glowing heavenly bodies shining through the dark air as they turn in their spheres as God the Father established them.
> (Meung, *Rose*, 16896–8, 16909–18)

The planets are different from the stars. They are nearer to the earth and they govern the actions of men. Gautier gives some details of the size and distance of the planets, based on the work of the Greek cosmographer Ptolemy from whom most medieval astronomy was derived. The circumference of the earth is 20,428 miles, its diameter is 6500, (actually it is 7927 miles at the equator). The moon is distant from the earth some 34 diameters or 221,000 miles (actually 239,000). The sun is 585 diameters from the earth and the smallest star is more than 10,000 diameters away. Not surprisingly the greater the distances the greater the errors of calculation. Gossuin goes on

to remark that it will surprise people to know that the sun is 166
3/20 times the size of earth. He too was surprised, but it has
been calculated geometrically 'and I would never have written
it down if I had not seen it to be true' (*Image*, p. 193). Gossuin is
clearly making a serious attempt to present scientific facts to his
intelligent if unlearned readers (cf. also *Treasure*, p. 136).

In addition to the cosmography of Ptolemy, Gossuin and his
fellow vulgarisers describe the geography of the world, the
three continents of Asia, Africa and Europe and the many
countries and people who live there. There are also long lists
and descriptions of the flora and fauna of the universe, some of
them peculiar to an individual author, most of them taken from
the traditional bestiaries, herbals and lapidaries. All levels of
creation are arranged in a hierarchy: the highest among the
beasts is the lion, among the birds the eagle (Philippe de Thaon,
Bestiary, p. 225). Not content with descriptions of the different
species, the authors often give also the symbolic meaning and
associations of the different creatures who all have their place
within the hidden purposes of God. In the *Book of Sidrac* the
information is interspersed with a bewildering variety of
questions: Which animals are the most intelligent? Monkeys
and dogs. How do you recognise a good horse? Four things
long, four short and four broad (*Sidrac*, III, p. 264; this is
believed to be the oldest extant example of the celebrated
standard for horses still in use today).[1] Some of the questions
are those of a naïve but not stupid child: Where do thoughts
come from? Why did God make man feel hunger daily and not
weekly? (*Sidrac*, III, p. 225). Timeo asks Placides more subtle
questions, such as: Do Siamese twins have one soul or two?
(*Placides*, S. 329).

The sources for all this scientific and philosophical information are Latin writings, most of them translations from earlier
Greek texts, Plato's *Timaeus*, Aristotle's *Physics* and Ptolemy's
Almagest being the commonest. To these were added Pliny's
Natural History and the encyclopaedia of Isidore of Seville, itself a
compendium of earlier writings. The geography and history of
some of the countries described is, however, also culled from
other sources, from eye-witness accounts like the travels of
Marco Polo the Venetian, or the mysterious but widely
credited account of the marvels of the East in the *Letter of Prester
John*.

Travellers' Tales

A VERY large number of people travelled in the Middle Ages for a variety of reasons. Lords with their vassals and men-at-arms went on crusades; men and women of all classes made pilgrimages to the three great shrines of Christendom: Jerusalem, Rome and St James of Compostella, as well as a host of lesser holy places; merchants travelled on business to the great fairs and foreign ports; messengers travelled on behalf of their lords; architects and builders went in search of work or because they were recommended by one patron to another – the sketch-book of Villard de Honnecourt records his travels to Hungary and other parts of Eastern Europe in the mid-thirteenth century; monks and friars travelled from one religious house to another; minstrels and performers also travelled widely, sometimes as itinerant entertainers, making a living by playing and tumbling in the marketplaces or the stopping points on the pilgrim routes, sometimes in the suite of a great lord, as Adam de la Halle went to Southern Italy with Robert of Artois. That some of these travellers made unscrupulous use of their adventures is clear from Gossuin's reference to the *vilains* who have been to Rome or Constantinople and use the opportunity of talking about what they have seen to gain advancement or money (*Image*, BN MS 25343, f. 23).

Two of the best-known travel books of the earlier Middle Ages are cast in story form. The *Voyage of St Brendan*,[2] constructed on the basis of the traditional Irish *immrama* or voyage literature, was immensely influential but its main relevance to the present chapter is that it describes travel to the west from Europe while the bulk of medieval travellers went east, as far as India and the great barrier beyond. Such a one was Alexander the Great, whose conquests were the subject of the important and influential *Romance of Alexander* (*Roman d'Alexandre*) first composed about 1150. Not content with the historical reality of the feats of the great Macedonian, the medieval author added two other unique journeys: one to the bottom of the sea and one up into the atmosphere.[3]

In accordance with the usual French habit of making the real as fantastic as possible and the imaginary as real as possible, these two voyages are described in very sober, restrained terms. Having conquered most of the known world Alexander looks round for fresh worlds to explore: 'I have come and gone a great deal on the earth; now I want to know the truth about those who dwell in the sea' (*Alexander*, 396–7). Despite the protests of his followers the king has a bathysphere made: 'the workmen made him a very fine vessel entirely from clear glass. No one ever saw one finer. They set lamps all round the barrel [*tounel*] which blazed inside it so that it was a joy to behold. No little tiny fish in the sea but the king would be able to see it clearly' (422–7). Alexander enters his sphere with two youths and they are taken out to sea in a boat to avoid the rocks, then lowered on a long chain fastened to a ring in the top of the globe. The vessel is well sealed with lead. When the king is deep in the water he sees all the fish, the great ones preying on the lesser so that he concludes 'that all this world is cursed and damned' (448). The blazing lights keep all the fish at a distance and the vessel lies safely on the gravel of the sea-bed while the king looks his fill, then the fair-haired monarch gives a signal to his followers and they are hauled up to the surface again and the king opens up the barrel with his own hands. The possibilities of such a scene in the hands of a Jules Verne are obvious. The twelfth-century author ignores them. He gives neither real nor fanciful details about the fish, merely reiterating constantly the theme of the large ones eating the small ones and moralising on this fact of nature. 'Covetousness has caught and defeated all of us, and indeed the world is confounded by avarice' (508–9).

Encouraged by his success the king later decides to take another journey of scientific exploration:

I want to go up into the sky and see the firmament; I want to see the tops of the mountains from above, the sky and the planets and all the stars and all the fifteen signs through which the sun passes and how the four winds blow around the world. I want to survey the world and see how the earth goes; the clouds contain water and I want to know how.   (4969–75)

Compared to such space-travellers as the Roman Lucan,

Cyrano de Bergerac or Captain Kirk, Alexander is merely planning to go up in a weather satellite. His means of travel is ingenious: he captures some huge dragon-like creatures called griffons and attaches them to a leather chariot in which he is ensconced with a long lance and a large supply of fresh meat. By holding the lance with meat on it above the heads of the griffons he makes them fly up into the sky carrying him with them. The extravagant nature of the description is sobered by a nice attention to detail: the king's hand that holds the lance is covered in a heavy leather glove so that it does not show (and get eaten by the griffons) and the king also does not risk the harness pulling away from the *engin* – he wraps the ends of the leather straps round himself, up his legs like a charioteer. When they have passed the raincloud and the sphere of the winds they come to the region of untempered heat. The king is almost stifled, his little room 'crisps in the burning' (5053). Afraid it will break, the king turns the lance downwards and is safely borne back to earth by the famished birds who 'set it down on the ground in the midst of the meadow with the king inside it: he'd had a good day' (5060–1).

When he has recovered, the king informs his men he has seen and measured the length and breadth of the world, and of what he had seen he had conquered all except Babylon. 'We'll move against it in the morning' (5098). Alexander is well aware of the kudos he has acquired by going where no man has gone before (4985–6) but there is no attempt to colour up the marvels, no fantasy – just sober facts; the deed is its own first cause, the journey its own justification.

A very different motive inspired the greatest of all medieval travellers, Marco Polo the Venetian, whose book of his journey to the realm of Cathay was written not in Latin or Italian but in French, being ghosted for him by a certain Rusticien from Pisa while the two were prisoners of war in Genoa in 1298. French was probably chosen as the language to use because, as Brunetto Latini explains, 'the speech is the most pleasing and most widely used by all people' (*Treasure*, p. 3). Rusticien had already composed a version of the Arthurian romances, also in French; it is still unedited and is known simply as the *Compilation de Rusticien de Pise*.

Marco Polo always insisted that his descriptions of people,

places and events were scrupulously accurate, and later evidence has supported many of his claims, so that it is particularly interesting when he describes a man or a place also known from less authentic sources. Most striking of these is the reference to Prester John.

The celebrated priest–king is first mentioned in Latin chronicles in the early twelfth century as a powerful Christian ruler from distant Asia who, although a Nestorian heretic, was interested in helping to free the Holy Sepulchre from the Infidel. St Louis on the seventh crusade looked in vain for him, but Marco Polo discovered the province of Tarduc where all the towns and castles belonged to the Great Khan (i.e. Kubla Khan), 'for all the descendants of Prester John serve the Great Khan. The principal city is called Tarduc and the king of this province is of the lineage of Prester John' (*Marco Polo*, I, pp. 209–10). The Venetian never found out any more about the illustrious ruler who was by then long dead, but all Europe knew him from the text of the *Letter of Prester John* sent to the emperor Manuel Comnenus in Constantinople in 1160–80, and rapidly translated from Latin into many vernaculars including French prose and Anglo-Norman verse. The sovereign expresses his desire to learn about orthodox Christian worship and invites the emperor to send learned theologians to enlighten him. But the important part of the letter for the average reader was the long account the king gives of his own country with its strange animals, its giants and its black cyclops 'which have only one eye in their forehead like a mirror' (*Letter*, III, p. 50). It is a paradise where everyone is rich and there are no thieves, traitors or hypocrites. Lying is unheard of. The letter goes on to describe the palace built by St Thomas the Apostle (a detail taken from the apocryphal Acts) which contains a very unusual mirror: 'the mirror is broad and round, supported on a single pillar underneath', and this in turn is supported on a complex, multiple arrangement of pillars dividing into four again and again. The structure sounds a little like the multiple arches of a gothic spire. By means of this mirror Prester John can watch out for any attack by enemies so that he has no need to employ spies (*Letter*, III, p. 68).

With the exception of Marco Polo, who had been there, the medieval travellers' accounts of Asia are all very similar.

Writers like the anonymous French author of the book widely known in English as *The Travels of Sir John Mandeville* claimed to have visited the places they describe but this does not prevent them talking freely of dog-headed people and other fabulous races. Moreover, the Middle Ages believed Marco Polo without losing faith in the ancients whose authority was not yet questioned by laymen, at least not on matters like geography. The gradual undermining of the authority of the written Latin, usually Classical, texts which is a feature of the later Middle Ages and led to the tensions between the establishment and the individual which found their expression in the writings of Hus and Wyclif and ultimately the whole Protestant and reforming movement, is still hidden from the readers of the late thirteenth century. Avid for information and lacking the discrimination to distinguish true and false, they greedily absorbed even mutually contradictory stories: after all, there was no limit to the creative powers of God or to the hearers' appetite for stories on every subject under the moon, whose sphere represented the boundary of created beings in pre-Copernican cosmology.

Man the Microcosm

'THE author of the *Six Principles* claims, and reason does not contradict it, that the world is called the macrocosm and man is the microcosm, which is to signify and be understood as the greater and the lesser world, for each closely resembles the other' (*Book of Fauvel*, 993–9). The author mentioned here is Gilbert de la Porrée, a schoolman who died in 1154 and was the author of commentaries on Aristotle and Boethius's *Consolation of Philosophy* which, in the translation by Jean de Meung, was an important source for much of the vernacular philosophy of the thirteenth century, especially the concepts of Fortune. Man, like the world, is composed of the four elements whose qualities combine to give the four humours. This may be tabulated as follows:

Fire	= hot and dry	= Choleric
Air	= hot and moist	= Sanguine
Water	= cold and moist	= Phlegmatic
Earth	= cold and dry	= Melancholic

This conventional medieval picture is given some unusual variations in the encyclopaedias. The *Secret of Secrets* (*Secreta Secretorum*) which purports to be based on a letter of Aristotle to Alexander the Great giving advice on the art of kingship, includes a section in which the philosopher is supposed to say that man is a microcosm because he has in him all the attributes of the animals: 'bold as a lion, simple as a lamb, lazy as a bear, lustful as a pig' (*Secret*, III, p. 112). The dialogue between the sage Timeo and his pupil Placides on the other hand contains a quite different comparison: 'Know first of all that just as the world is round so a well-proportioned man is round. For a well-proportioned man should have the same span between his outstretched arms as there is in his height in order to make a true circle. And the ancient philosophers claim that the head of man signifies the sky and fire, the chest is the air, the stomach is the water and the base of man, the feet, is the earth' (*Placides*, S. 214–15). This comparison is then extended and developed: for example, the eyes represent the two luminaries of the sky, the sun and moon, for the eyes are the luminaries of the body.

The close link between man and the universe is at the basis of most medieval medicine. Medical treatises were being translated into French by the end of the thirteenth century, including the *The Regimen of the Body* by Aldebrandin of Siena, or the *Surgery* (*Chirurgie*) by Henri de Mondeville, who was royal surgeon to Philip the Fair, and much medical lore is included in the encyclopaedias. King Bocthus in the *Book of Sidrac* shows a particular interest in obstetrics: How does the child come out from its mother? Can a woman have more than two children at once? 'Woman can carry seven children in one bellyful' (*Sidrac*, III, p. 225). Timeo instructs Placides on the physiology of reproduction in some detail, and claims that the information about women is first derived from a very wise woman called Trotula; later Hermaphroditus disguised himself as a woman and learnt much that way. A third authority is another woman, Cirenis (*Placides*, S. 297). There is also a good deal of attention paid to health and hygiene and diet in these works, notably in the *Secret* where Aristotle advises on baths and washing for his royal pupil: take a little exercise first thing in the morning, and in summer the extremities may be washed in cold water as an appetiser. Next the king should rub his teeth and gums, chewing a suitable plant: this is good for preventing bad breath and is also a stimulant for the appetite; rhubarb taken as a purge in the morning does wonders for the wind, and so on (*Secret*, III, p. 93).

The lore here and in other texts is a mixture of sound advice, old wives' tales and pseudo-Greek medical practice. Aristotle's *Physiognomy* and Plato's *Timaeus* are cited together with Galen and Hippocrates, but the references to herbs and medicinal plants also lead into long discussions on plant life in general and a detailed discussion of wine (*Secret*, III, p. 103). Occasionally the authors actually query some of the more extreme claims of their sources. The French translator of the *Secret* is very scathing about a section on stones in the Latin: 'But in truth what he says in this place of stones and plants and trees is false and more like fictions [*fables*] than truth or philosophy. And all the clerks who understand Latin know this. . . . And from this we realise that Aristotle did not compose the whole of this book in the manner in which it has come down to us for in no other of his books do we find blatant falsehood' (*Secret*, III, p. 108–9). At all costs the authority of Aristotle must be upheld even when it is evident that a book purporting to be written by him contains obvious error.

Above all, man's life should be governed by order and measure. It is important to eat at fixed times and take food according to the season of the year. Sidrac even advises on the right choice of women: brunettes are better in cold weather and blondes when it is hot. And always prefer young ones (*Sidrac*, III, p. 248). Clocks, first invented by Ptolemy (*Image*, p. 178), are valuable because they encourage regularity in prayer which is pleasing to God, and it would be good to regulate the whole of one's life the same way. But alas! men are so busy chasing after money that they shorten their lives by the lack of order and method: 'There are many men dead today who would have been still alive if they had ordered their business as they should have done at fixed hours each day' (*Image*, p. 179). 'Although no one can prolong the life of the body . . . many shorten their lives . . . through bad management . . . sleeping too much or staying up too late, resting or working too much . . . in enjoying oneself too much or wallowing in grief, eating or drinking to excess. . . . They could easily protect themselves from death if they would refrain from the excesses and follies which shorten their lives' (Meung, *Rose*, 16957–17006). Nature's complaint which is long and detailed makes it obvious that the rat-race was well established already in the thirteenth century.

Man is not only a body, he is also a rational soul made in the image of God, an individual part of the species which must continue. As Jean de Meung explains, Nature continually forges pieces to replace those death has destroyed and this Aristotelian theory of the continuation of the species is approved by Reason as part of God's plan. Aristotle's *Treatise of Generation and Corruption* was on the syllabus of the University of Paris in the mid-thirteenth century, and it is quite probable that Jean de Meung would have studied it. As a body, man is subject to the influence of the planets, but as a rational soul he has free-will to resist the effects of their power. This dichotomy is constantly reiterated by medieval writers but nowhere so cogently argued as by Jean de Meung's loquacious Nature who, in the course of her 3000-line confession to her priest, Genius, includes a clear and scholarly discourse on the nature of free-will and its reality *vis-à-vis* the omnipotence of God. 'For free-will is so strong, if a man truly knows himself, that he can always control himself if he is aware in his heart that sin is seeking to become his master, whatever the celestial bodies may do' (Meung, *Rose*, 17543–48).

The most original and effective of all the studies of man as an individual is that in Philip of Novara's *Four Ages of Man* (*Quatre Ages de l'Homme*) written when the author was over seventy after a long life in public service, much of it spent in the Middle East (*Outremer*) where he had been on many ambassadorial missions after taking part in the sixth crusade and the war between the king of Cyprus and the emperor Frederick II. He died about 1264. He wrote poetry in his youth and in middle age compiled, in French, a volume on the laws, customs and usage of the *Assises* of *Outremer*, Jerusalem and Cyprus. Finally, full of years, he composed his last book, a study of man which was not merely a compendium of other writers' views, as so many such works tended to be, but a personal and original work based on his experience and enriched by quotations from a wide and idiosyncratic range of books. Nor is this originality his only claim to fame; he has another rare quality compared to his contemporaries: he writes briefly to a fixed pattern and with relatively few digressions.

The four ages of man are childhood, youth, middle age and old age which Philip measures arbitrarily at a score of years each, equating them also with the seasons of spring, summer, autumn and winter. In the *Book of Fauvel*, the ages are divided at fifteen, thirty and sixty with the seasons being linked also to the four humours, 'the first of which is phlegmatic, then sanguine then choleric and the fourth is melancholy' (*Fauvel*, 3023–5).

Children are not like the young of birds or beasts for they are born with the power of speech and with reason, and from the age of ten at least they 'have free-will to do good or evil' (*Four Ages*, S. 6). It is fortunate for children, Philip explains, that God gives them a special grace to inspire love in those who care for them 'and this is very necessary for them, for otherwise they are so dirty and troublesome when they are tiny, and so wicked and contrary when they are a bit older, that none of them would ever be looked after' (*Four Ages*, S. 3). This love is found particularly in father and mother and in grandparents, and goes on increasing all the time while the child's natural love for those who nurse or play with it decreases and disappears as it grows older. An even less affectionate attitude to children is expressed by the *jongleur* author of the *Whirling World* (*Riote du Monde*) early in the thirteenth century: 'I never liked tiny children, nor small ones nor big. The tiny ones are troublesome to feed and they keep people awake at night; small ones get out into the street and have to be kept away from the horses and the carts, and the big ones quarrel with their parents, wanting their rich inheritance, and in the end have to have their tavern bills paid' (*Whirling World*, p. 282).

Nor is there any purpose in trying to save and leave something to your children, 'for if they are sensible they will manage without, and if they are bad they'll soon squander all you leave them' (*Whirling World*, p. 282). Philip is equally aware of the potential for evil in children and insistent on the need to educate them carefully while they are young enough to be impressionable, for the father is responsible for his child's actions while it is young, though thereafter every man is responsible for himself. The importance of the father's role in the upbringing of the child is vividly dramatised by the Italian writer Feo Belcari, who introduces into his play of the *Last Judgement* two couples, a saved son and father and a damned son and father: the former thanks his father for his care in bringing him up while the damned son curses his parents for their part in his fate (Belcari, *Last Judgement*, ed. Ancona, III, p. 504).

The first things to teach a child, says Philip, are the Creed, the Our Father and the Hail Mary; later, 'when the child has more understanding the two principal commandments', namely to love God with all your heart and your neighbour as yourself (see Luke 10:27). The next step in education is to teach the child a trade or profession (*mestier*) and this should begin as soon as possible, especially for the two highest and most honourable professions, *chevalerye et clergie* (knighthood and the Church). Philip adds what is obviously a personal comment that 'he who does not learn young will never ride well' (*Four Ages*, S. 14). As a member himself of the knightly class it is not surprising that Philip favours it; the education he recommends is very similar to that found in the romances, such as the early part of the *Prose Lancelot* or the *Prose Tristan*: courtesy and good manners, generosity above all, for as Philip practically, if perhaps a trifle cynically, points out, it 'covers a multitude of sins in a great man, for if he should not be valiant in his person, if he dares to give and pay out generously he'll have plenty of other valiant men so that he won't lose his land' (*Four Ages*, S. 19).

A girl should also be carefully brought up to be obedient and submissive, to her parents in youth and later to her husband or if she enters religion, her superior. She should especially avoid 'using her body improperly either in appearance or in fact, for however small the fault may be the reproach will be very widespread. And the shame is much greater for a woman than a man' (*Four Ages*, S. 22). Philip is certainly no advocate of Women's Lib but he is far from being as anti-feminist as many of his contemporaries. Formal education is unnecessary 'unless specifically to become a nun' for much evil has resulted from women reading and writing: they can send and receive letters from lovers, and the devil is so cunning he will lead them into temptation very easily (*Four Ages*, S. 25). However, all women should be taught to spin and sew, for the poor will need the skill and the rich should be able to oversee the work of their attendants. For this reason also all women should be taught housewifery and none should scorn it, for the Mother of God deigned and wished to work and to spin. Daughters need fewer accomplishments than sons anyway because a woman, provided she is chaste and modest, will retain a good reputation, 'whereas a man who wishes to be well thought of has to have many good qualities: he must be courteous, generous, bold and wise' (*Four Ages*, S. 31).

Youth is a dangerous age for then the 'heyday in the blood' is strong. Life and death are both perilous to the young because of the sin of lechery and the other great sins of youth. Love, for Philip and others, is folly, contrary to reason. As soon as Jean de Meung took over Guillaume de Lorris's *Romance of the Rose* (see p. 79), he brought back the character of Reason who had been rapidly rejected by Lorris's Lover; Jean gives her a long scene (about 3000 lines) in which she tries to convince the Lover of the folly of obeying a lord like the God of Love who treats him so badly and will bring him to destruction. In a passage which recalls in its construction the description in the *Romance of Aeneas* (see p. 74 above), Reason describes love: 'Love, that is hateful peace, love that is loving hate, loyalty disloyal and loyal disloyalty . . . healthy languor and sickly health, raging hunger in abundance, covetous sufficiency; the thirst which is always drunken, drunkenness made drunk by thirst . . . it is sweet hell and wretched paradise' (Meung, *Rose*, 4263–98). The Lover is unimpressed by this rhetorical *tour de force* and asks Reason to define love rather than describe it, 'for I never heard it defined' (Meung, *Rose*, 4345). Reason is willing to oblige: 'Love, so it seems to me is a sickness of the thoughts between two persons freely linked together of different sexes, the result of a fire born of disordered vision, that makes them embrace and kiss to find physical relief' (Meung, *Rose*, 4347–54). These relationships, adds Reason, should always be for the purposes of procreation since this is Nature's will.

Jean de Meung is warily anti-feminist. Nature interrupts her confession to Genius to warn every man most urgently never to entrust a secret to a woman since they are constitutionally incapable of keeping it. The Friend (*Ami*) to whom the Lover appeals after rejecting Reason is equally uncomplimentary about women, although he also encourages the Lover to be faithful in his quest. An unusually witty approach to this theme is that of the *Gospel of Women* (*Evangile aux Femmes*), where each quatrain is based on a sudden inversion of meaning in the fourth line: 'it is not right or reasonable to speak ill of women: they are wise and discreet and full of courtesy, whatever anyone says he is a fool who does not trust them as much as the shepherd trusts the wolf which has seized his sheep' (*Evangile*, S. VIII).

Philip of Novara is aware of the frailty of both men and women in their youth and writes scathingly of the fools who encourage the seduction of wives and daughters under the guise of 'love'. Since all men and women are weak in this matter it is the duty of the sensible older man to correct and rule his younger kin as a good monarch brings order and justice to his country. Being a practical man, Philip recommends that the young should be married off as soon as possible to avoid the sin of fornication. Nor is the married state a bad one for Philip, unlike the author of the French translation of the thirteenth-century satire the *Lamentations of Matheus* (*Lamentations de Matheolus*), who concludes a diatribe against woman of all kinds with a scene between the writer and God, in which the deity admits that marriage is a more severe penance than being a monk and assures the frantic husband that married men have a high place in Heaven as martyrs (*Lamentations*, II, pp. 276–80). For Philip, however, there is both good and bad in marriage, the best being children, and on the whole 'the good exceeds the bad' (*Four Ages*, S. 78). He has also an unusually rosy view of women who, despite their lack of stability and sense, have been given grace by the Holy Spirit and many of them have remained chaste virgins while others have made true marriages; and a great many of them are saved and will be, who are and will be in eternal peace (*Four Ages*, S. 52).

Another writer of fairly moderate views on women is Robert de Blois, author of a whole range of different works, among them a romance, *Floris and Liriope* (see p. 105 above), and a number of didactic works including the brief and lively *Reproach to Women* (*Chastoiement des Dames*) where he mingles conventional advice on good table-manners ('don't forget to wipe the grease off your mouth before drinking'), how to turn away unwanted suitors and whether or not to sing in public, with some less conventional warnings, especially when he cautions against peering into people's houses as you pass them: 'It is not sensible or courteous to gaze into someone else's house nor to linger there. Often a man is doing something privately in his house which he would not want anyone to see if they came past his door. And if you want to go in, you should wait at the entrance and make your presence known by speaking or coughing' (*Chastoiement*, 480–90).

Many writers give advice on social behaviour for both men and women but mainly the latter. Jean de Meung's Old Woman (*La Vieille*) combines the least agreeable characteristics of all the attendants, companions, chaperones and nurses in literature from the old women in the towers in Marie de France's *Guigemar* or *Aucassin and Nicolette* to Juliet's Nurse or the venal and vicious duennas of eighteenth-century fiction and opera. Echoing a view of women attributed to Plato, she explains that women are sexually insatiable and the only way to treat a woman is to dominate her sexually and frequently. The harridans and viragos, the wilful, wanton wives of the *fabliaux* and farces, are part of the same medieval tradition.

Middle age, the autumn of life, is also in many ways the best season, says Philip. The lover and the soldier give way to the justice 'full of wise saws and modern instances'. At this age, declares the medieval Montaigne, 'First of all one should know oneself and control oneself, giving up the follies of youth, and reasonably and voluntarily make amends for one's faults to God and the world' (*Four Ages*, S. 96). It is a time to prepare for old age by prudent and careful saving and organising, and everyone who can should acquire wealth before old age, for honourably acquired wealth can be used both for one's family, for God and for the world. A middle-aged man should have good sense (*sens*; Philip constantly reiterates this theme) for it is always needed and always useful 'and those who have no book-learning nor the grace of subtle knowledge can still look after the mundane matters which they find in front of them each day' (*Four Ages*, S. 120). Philip also criticises those who make no attempt to reform and repent and rely on a deathbed repentance. Even if they are able to save themselves from Hell by such means, 'they will still be in purgatory for a very long time' (*Four Ages*, S. 126). In everything a man should aim at moderation: lords should use it in the treatment of their dependants, and the poor lest they attract punishment from those greater than they. 'By enduring and serving one can win great possessions' (*Four Ages*, S. 138). Philip has nothing but condemnation for the men who try to claim that present behaviour does not matter since there is no afterlife anyway. Such people are foolish and wrong and run great risk of damnation (*Four Ages*, S. 148).

Philip then gives suggestions for a planned and ordered day, beginning with prayer and thanksgiving. Next, select from the different possibilities what task should be undertaken today, for yourself, your family or your country. Having chosen the most suitable, say it over to yourself three times firmly so as not to forget it. Then should follow three actions, two for the soul and one for the body: the first, to go to church, hear mass and say appropriate prayers; the second, to give alms of some kind, much or little according to your means even if it is only a penny; then the third action, for the body, is to go home and perform some small attention to your person, even if only to file your nails. Thereafter, set about the day's tasks (*Four Ages*, S. 154–7).

This mixture of generalisation and particular detail is continued throughout the third and fourth ages, for it is in these that Philip is really writing personally and from the heart. The account of the evils of old age with its ailments and weakness has the ring of truth. Those are honoured in old age who take heed to amendment of life and the salvation of their souls, men as well as women. A good old woman looks after her household and her children, arranges marriages for them and keeps herself from sin; but there are bad old women who still pursue men, though now they have to buy the men who formerly gave them gifts. Such women use make-up and dye their hair, a habit which was obviously widespread to judge from the beauty hints in such works as the *Adornment of Women* (*Ornement des Dames*), translated into Anglo-Norman prose from the Latin text which claimed to be by the woman doctor Trotula of Salerno (see p. 120 above). The Anglo-Norman version includes recipes for dyeing the hair black, blonde or red, removing wrinkles or clearing the skin of spots.

Philip's study of the *Four Ages* concludes with his summing-up (*Somme*) on old age. Remember, he tells all old people, you are on the edge of your graves and should keep your eyes open lest you fall in unprepared. Because he is a layman and a lawyer and a man of moderation, Philip does not attempt to harrow his hearers with gory details of the pains of Hell and the laments of the damned. He is neither priest nor preacher, just a plain, practical, elderly man with a good understanding of the society in which he lives. He was also a learned lawyer, and although the *Four Ages* treats mainly of man as an individual, there is throughout evidence that he thought also of man as part of a social whole. Like his contemporaries, he quotes many anecdotes and *exempla* from history and literature, citing the *Prose Lancelot* or the story of Alexander, a *fabliau* or a fable, as the matter in hand demands. As a lawyer and an educated man he could, of course, read Latin but by the middle of the thirteenth century even the unlearned layman could read history, as well as literature and natural science, in the vernacular.

The Mirror of History

MANY of the vernacular historical works of the twelfth and thirteenth centuries come under the general heading of historical novels, even when the subject is a contemporary one. As well as the Carolingian epics which, as has been shown, were closely linked with Latin saints' lives and chronicles – without thereby becoming more historically accurate, let me hasten to say, many chronicles are far from objective documents – there existed by the middle of the twelfth century a cycle of *chansons de geste* on the life and family of Godfrey of Bouillon, a major figure in the first crusade and the first ruler in the newly conquered Holy City until his death in 1100, when he was succeeded by his brother, Baldwin I, king of the Latin kingdom of Jerusalem. The group of poems known as the Cycle of the Crusades includes a serious historical account of the siege of Antioch (*La Chanson d'Antioche*) and a partly historical one of the capture of Jerusalem (*Conquête de Jérusalem*) as well as the fabulous tales of the Swan children and the Swan Knight (*Chevalier au cygne*). This mixture of fact and fiction, much of which was written in

Syria, where the victorious French crusaders were living, is rarely treated as serious source material for the first crusade, which is a pity since the battles described are almost contemporary with the poems and much of the material derives from eye-witness, personal reporting.

Biographical romances based on contemporary families and individuals are not uncommon in Anglo-Norman – *Guy of Warwick* and *Bevis of Hampton* are two names that spring to mind – but such works are very rare in continental French, perhaps because the numerically limited French-speaking aristocratic society of Norman England was a more suitable public for such works of literature. Godfrey of Bouillon seems to have been chosen as a subject because, like Arthur and Charlemagne, he was a larger-than-life historical figure, a legend in his own lifetime; he became widely known as one of the three Christians in the list of the Nine Worthies, who are first mentioned in French literature in the *Vows of the Peacock* (*Vœux du Paon*), an Alexander romance composed by Jacques de Longuyon in the early fourteenth century.

Alexander himself, one of the pagan Worthies, was well known to medieval readers from the *Romance of Alexander* and his fellow Greek, Hector, from the *Romance of Troy*; their third member, the Latin pagan Julius Caesar, received more 'historical' treatment from the thirteenth-century writers. The *Deeds of the Romans* (*Li Fet des Romains*) though freely translated was intended as a serious history of the Roman emperors from Julius Caesar to Domitian, but only the first section, on Caesar himself, was completed. The work was immensely popular in the Middle Ages. Its sources were Caesar's *De Bello Gallico* and the histories of Suetonius, Sallust and Lucan. They are translated, adapted and where necessary enlarged or embellished by the author whose purpose in writing was twofold: as he explains in his prologue, he wished to be one of those whose efforts to record the deeds of others makes him worthy of praise, and also to give instruction, for 'from their deeds one can find much teaching on doing good and eschewing evil' (*Fet des Romains*, p. 2). One at least of the Jewish Worthies, Judas Maccabeus, was also given the historical treatment in a thirteenth-century poem, *The Knightly Deeds of Judas Maccabeus* (*La Chevalerie de Judas Macabé*), whose author stressed that the

Jewish leader had been one of the first of the *chevaliers* and was a worthy example for others to follow.

Historical figures who had first appeared in the *chansons de geste* and the romances were sometimes given new authenticity by being written up in prose vernacular texts which claimed the authority of the Latin chronicle. The French version of the *Pseudo-Turpin Chronicle*, for example, was composed by a certain Johannes for Count Renaud de Boulogne in 1206, 'and because rhyme seeks to adorn itself with words extraneous to the story, the count wants the book to be unrhymed like the Latin of the history which Turpin, archbishop of Rheims, treated, writing of what he saw and heard' (Johannes, Prologue). Although he obviously believed in the authenticity of the Latin chronicle which was his source, Johannes treated it with great verbal freedom, despite his comments about the inaccuracy of rhyme. There are also sections where his emendations result from a need to 'tidy up' the carelessness of the original author. What is perhaps more significant for the relationship of chronicle and romance is that although Johannes has achieved a very respectable style at a time when French prose was almost unknown, his spare, dry narrative is but penny-plain compared with the twopence-coloured of the *chansons de geste*. Johannes's text is questionably more accurate than the *Song of Roland*; it is indubitably much less memorable.

Other prose writers of the thirteenth century were more fortunate, having no polished poem to compete against. Moreover, Robert de Clari and Villehardouin in their accounts of the crusades are writing as eye-witnesses, and the same is, of course, true of the great biography of St Louis by Joinville, in which, however, the author unashamedly uses literary narrative techniques in his portrayal of the saintly king. Thus, when describing the siege of Damietta, Joinville recounts an incident during a night attack by catapults and Greek fire. One of his companions, Sir Gautiers d'Escuiré, urges the crusaders to pray for safety:

Lords, we are in the greatest peril we have ever known, for if they burn our siege-towers and we stay at hand we shall be burnt and destroyed, and if we abandon these defences we

Have been left to guard we shall be shamed, and no one can help us in this plight except God himself. Therefore I counsel and advise you that every time they dispatch fire against us we should get down on our knees and elbows and pray to God to guard us in this peril.   (Joinville, S. 204)

The form and length of this speech are very similar to the speeches used in the *chansons de geste*, but what is more, Joinville is giving verbatim words which the nature of the occasion makes it impossible for him to have recorded and unlikely to have remembered in this detail. This technique is, of course, commonly used by biographers and in no way impugns the authenticity of the account. Similarly, Joinville describes the king's actions during the same incident as though he himself had been in the king's tent: 'Every time our holy king heard that they were sending Greek fire against us he sat up in his bed, stretched out his hands to God and said, weeping, "Fair lord God, protect my people for me." And I truly believe his prayers were of great benefit to us' (Joinville, S. 207). Obviously the king's actions could have been described to Joinville by one of the chamberlains but this is also true of the actions and words of characters in, for example, the *Conquest of Jerusalem*. Certainly the account of travelling through desert regions has the ring of total authenticity: 'The princes and the barons dismounted. The forepart of their hose over the foot was cut, worn and broken up to the ankles for they had walked and travelled over so much sand which is very sharp, that they were very weary' (*Conquest*, S. xxvi).

Few individuals, as we have seen, were considered sufficiently important to be written about in detail, but from the thirteenth century onwards personal accounts of the national events of the day began to be recorded, and although written officially for a patron were probably also composed with an eye on a wider readership. Froissart, whose account of the Hundred Years War is vivid and accurate in its detail, also composed poems and a romance, *Meliador* (see p. 211 below), and in the fifteenth century when nearly all literature was markedly individual in its angle of vision, the *Memoirs* of Philip de Commynes reveal a very real gift of observation and a shrewd eye for the incidents which made political history, and they are also intensely personal, with Commynes seeming intent on justifying his own changing allegiance.

The shift in stress from the bare Latin chronicle of events of the early Middle Ages to the more idiosyncratic and detailed French historical writings, parallels the gradual evolution of fiction from the idealisation of the saint's life and the epic to the would-be naturalism of the bourgeois literature and the satirical attacks on manners and society. A very considerable body of anecdote and incident from contemporary life exists half-buried in the traditional and sometimes excessively verbose criticisms of these writers which will be considered in the next section.

Man in Society

PAST, present or future, the state of society is always a subject of interest and from the twelfth century onwards numerous writers in verse or prose held forth didactically or critically but rarely succinctly on the contemporary scene.

'The world was good in the olden days when justice flourished and faith and love' (*Life of St Alexis*, 1–2). Looking back wistfully to the good old days, a favourite human occupation, is also a literary commonplace which in French dates back to one of the oldest surviving vernacular texts, the fragmentary tenth-century *Life of St Alexis*. Three hundred years later the same theme is still being orchestrated. One variation is that sounded by the Seigneur de Berzé in about 1230: 'There was once, formerly a time when the world was fair and full of many idle pleasures' (Berzé, *Bible*, II, p. 99). The term *Bible* used here and in a slightly earlier work by Guiot de Provins, merely indicates a work of a general nature, a mirror of the world, without any scriptural connotation. From the many surviving texts we can build up a comprehensive picture of medieval attitudes to their own society and its shortcomings. Not all these writers are rabid reformers or revolutionaries: some are harshly critical of their fellows, many are cynically satirical, a few are cheerfully tolerant. None is optimistic.

(a)   *The Allegory of Life*

Then they left their first way of life and henceforth became
false and treacherous and unceasingly wicked. Then they
began to own property and divided even the lands themselves, setting up landmarks at the boundaries. And when
they set up these boundaries they often fought among
themselves and took from each other all they could, the
strongest having the largest share. And while they were out
seeking more possessions, the idle who remained behind
went into their caves and stole what they had collected. Then
it became necessary to choose someone to guard the dwelling
places and capture the malefactors and ensure justice to the
plaintiffs: and no one dared deny this. Then they got together
to have an election. They chose a big fellow from among their
number, the largest and toughest, and him they made their
lord and prince.   (Meung, *Rose*, 9557–82).

This description of the 'Origin of Inequality among Men' comes
not from the pen of Jean-Jacques Rousseau in the eighteenth
century but Jean de Meung in the thirteenth, who took over
Guillaume de Lorris's *Romance of the Rose* fifty years after the
first writer and transmuted the theme of *fin'amor* of the original
allegory into a study of love in society and among all mankind.
'Thus they lived peacefully together, for these simple good-
living people loved each other naturally' (Meung, *Rose*, 9493–5).
That is how it was before sin entered the world and led to all
the evils of possessions, society, law and kings. It was the
beginning of the division of society into the three estates: the
Church, the nobility and the people, for the knights forgot that
'Good sense is worth more than noble folly' and that gentlemen
should remember all men were equal in their mothers' wombs:
'Did they come out from there on horseback?' (*Book of Fauvel*,
1088, 1103).

The third estate in the Middle Ages filled the role of the third
world today. The majority of its members were disadvantaged,
underprivileged and inarticulate. The critics of privilege and
corruption among the aristocracy and the clergy come almost
invariably from the estates they are criticising: men like Adam
de la Halle or the author of the *Renart Disguised*; clerks, students,
members of the learned professions, *clergie*; or that most

1. William prepares to capture Nîmes with barrel-loads of armed knights. (p. 22)

2. Lancelot forces his way into Guinevere's bed-chamber—with her permission. (p. 63)

3. The secular clergy were often on very friendly terms with their parishioners. (p. 88)

4. The world is round, like an apple, with all matter falling towards the centre. (p. 113)

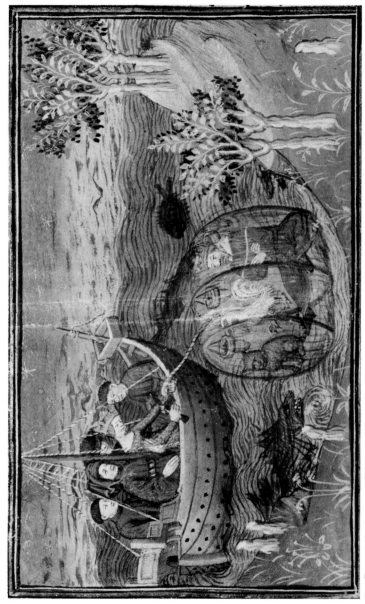

5. Even at the bottom of the sea, Alexander discovers the strong preying on the weak. (p. 116)

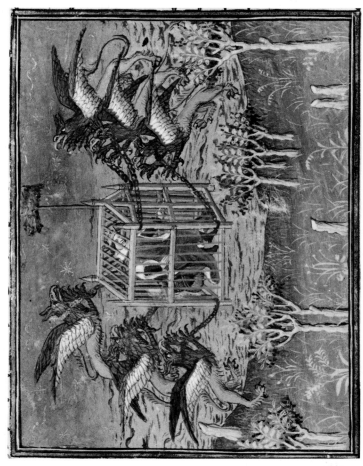

6. Alexander is raised to new heights by a team of gryphons. (p. 117)

7. This mirror offers the ladies a warning image of what they will one day become. (p. 163)

8. The Pilgrim nearly falls into the clutches of Avarice. (p. 203)

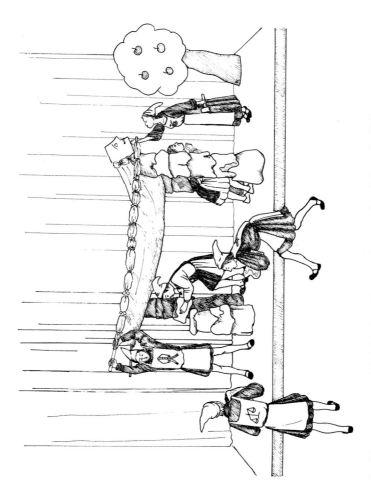

9. The *sots* construct their ideal world on very insecure foundations. (p. 199)

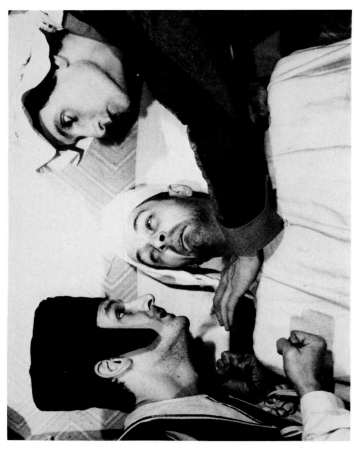

10. With his wife's help, Pathelin makes delirious fun of his creditor, the gullible draper. (p. 203)

outspoken of medieval tavern poets, François Villon, who was a Master of Arts of the University of Paris (see p. 239 below).

Not surprisingly, the writers from the first estate did not rate nobility of birth very highly. 'Nobility comes from a good heart, for gentle birth is not true gentility if goodness of heart is lacking', claimed Jean de Meung, adding that such nobility of heart is more easily learned by educated men, 'and I will read you the reason, for the learned [*clercs*] see in their books, with the proofs of the knowledge reasonably demonstrated, all the bad things one should avoid and the good things one can do' (Meung, *Rose*, 18607–14). Robert de Blois made the same point but in different terms: the contrast between a gentlemen and a *vilain* is not who his father was but how he behaves: 'A valiant, courteous peasant's son is worth fifteen wicked sons of kings' (*The Instruction of Princes*, 793–4). The teaching these texts contain is not limited to such general moralising, however, though there is plenty of that, but most writers season their ethics with etiquette, making manners the spice to morality.

(b)   *The Three Estates*

'Death, the mirror in which the soul sees itself when it is rent from the body' (Helinand, *On Death*, S. xi). Although all men were equal in death, there was considerable variation between the three estates in life, and the advice given to them varies also from one author to another. Much of the instruction and invective is of a fairly obvious kind: kings should rule wisely and only listen to good councillors, not to the false flatterers; churchmen should practise what they preach and avoid hypocrisy; the *vilains* should work hard and avoid quarrelling and drunkenness. Many texts, however, include also some details or original ideas which add colour to the reflection they present.

In the *Secret of Secrets*, for example, Aristotle includes advice to his royal pupil on the proper choice of servants and officials: royal secretaries should be chosen from men of great eloquence and good memories for 'spoken words are the body but writing is the clothing that covers the words' (*Secret*, iii, p. 114). Sidrac also rates writing very highly as the most difficult of the arts: 'whoever writes is working with his whole body, his eyes, his brains and his loins, and dare not think or look or laugh or speak or listen or harken to anything but his writing, and those who do not know how to write do not believe writing is an art' (*Sidrac*, III, p. 232). A king, of course, has no need for such a skill himself: like a modern business man he has secretaries to write for him.

Alexander is not the only former ruler held up as an example to later kings. Guiot de Provins, like his contemporary Chrétien de Troyes, condemns the modern king for being inferior to King Arthur. Instead of taking counsel from his wise barons he listens to the advice of mere fighting men: 'cross-bowmen and miners, catapult-machinists and engineers are henceforth the ones in favour' (Guiot, *Bible*, 183–5; it is interesting to note that already in 1180–90, Arthur was an accepted ideal even outside the world of romance). In contrast to Guiot's viewpoint, the author of the *Book of Fauvel* compliments St Louis and his grandson, Philip the Fair, for tackling the problem of the corruption of the Templars. But then the Church, and especially the religious orders, are the most popular target of all for moralist and satirist alike.

(c)   *Arts and Sciences*

The *clergie* of the first estate comprised all those in orders whether regular – monks, nuns and friars who lived under a rule – or secular – those living and working in the world. Many of the former, especially members of the recently formed orders of Franciscan and Dominican friars, were teachers and scholars at the new universities, such as the Sorbonne in Paris. By the middle of the thirteenth century these modern teachers are being unfavourably compared with the great philosophers of the past, just as the kings and rulers had suffered by comparisons with Arthur or Alexander. The *Image of the World* is particularly outspoken on this theme, describing how many poor men would willingly study the seven arts, the basis of all learning, but are prevented by lack of funds, while the rich *clercs* with libraries full of fine books look only at the bindings, admiring their treasured volumes for their appearance but not studying the contents: 'and so the arts are dying' (*Image*, p. 74). Criticism is also levelled at those who only study just enough grammar (the term covered all aspects of written language) to enable them to proceed to more rewarding studies leading to the lucrative professions of the Church, medicine and the law. Such was not the behaviour of those who first invented the arts and later saved the knowledge of them from the Great Flood by copying them on strong clay tiles or huge slabs of marble. After the waters had subsided they were found again by the sons of Noah, who 'were able to read' (*Placides*, S. 386; see p. 153 below).

The importance attached to the seven arts outside the formal schools and universities is also attested by the existence of two different versions of the poem *Marriage of the Seven Arts* (*Mariage des Sept Arts*), both dating from the thirteenth century and describing in the form of an allegorical dream-vision how each of the six beautiful daughters of Dame Grammar chose a husband from one of the Christian virtues: Grammar herself announces she will wed Faith, and the other Arts choose Alms, Prayer, Love, Abstinence, Confession and Penitence – or Obedience – with a brief explanation in each case of the reasons for their choice. The two poems both depend on the Latin writings of the influential Alain of Lille but show considerable originality. The earlier poem, by Jean le Teinturier from Arras, has a more intellectual bias in the descriptions the Arts give of their choice of husband. Thus Geometry chooses Abstinence, 'for as it is shown in the books, she wants to live by measure and has no taste for excess and I know so much about measuring that by my skill [*sens*] I would measure the whole world if I could see it in front of me clearly' (*Mariage*, I, 175–81). In the second, anonymous, poem, Geometry stresses the need for measure in more mundane terms: 'for who lives by measure does not lose but amass', but if someone lacking in measure were teamed with measure, 'the alliance would be bad, for everything he acquired he would put straight in his belly' (*Mariage*, II, 104, 111–12). Nor do the two poems give identical lists of pairings, for Jean includes Astronomy who is married to Love, while the anonymous text omits Astronomy and includes Theology as the spouse of Love.

This kind of freedom even in handling traditional material is typical of much medieval allegory and symbolism (as we shall see in the next chapter), and the different authors of the encyclopaedias did not hesitate to give varied sources for their knowledge. Timeo even advises Placides to consult another philosopher, 'for we do not all agree but as I told you on another occasion, each one says what he believes about things and thus we are like champions openly hitting out at each other and no one says anything that he does not believe to have some reason in it' (*Placides*, S. 420). This statement ultimately derives from St Augustine who accepted that men might legitimately see different interpretations of the same truth: 'But from these truths each of us chooses one or another to explain the phrase "In the beginning God made heaven and earth" ' (*Confessions*, XII, S. 20). Therefore, says Timeo, he has put together a *somme* or summary of the truths of the philosophers, for as Aristotle has said all men eagerly desire to know naturally the secrets of nature (*Placides*, S. 1).

Although theology, and to a lesser degree philosophy, were the proper subjects of study for the Church, and knowledge, reason and logic the tools for such investigation, the clergy were also supposed to set an example of moral rectitude; but the reflection of the Church in the mirror of the satirists is far from being one of an enlightened and charitable Body of Christ.

(d)   The *Mirror of Charity*

The twelfth century which saw the composition of Anselm's *Mirror of Charity* (*Speculum Caritatis*) was also the age of the earliest great attacks on the established Church, especially, even at that date, the Roman curia. 'Ah! Rome, Rome, you kill us every day and Christianity is in a bad state. . . . All is lost and destroyed when the cardinals have come, who come, I know, burning and alight with greed, . . . without reason, faith or religion, for they sell God and his mother and betray us and their father [the Pope] whose eyes they have put out as they have blinded others. . . . Body of Rome you are filled with the vilest sins' (Guiot, *Bible*, 661–711). Guiot described his work as a mirror: 'This bible will be a mirror to all people . . . and all the orders there are can see themselves reflected in the fine sayings and fine words that I have written; let those with understanding see themselves, and the wise reform themselves with care' (Guiot, *Bible*, 7–22).

Occasionally the attacks are very personal in tone and detail, and even humorous, as when Guiot, speaking from his own experience as an ex-Cistercian and Cluniac monk, severely criticises the austerities of this life that is worse than death, whereas the canons of St Augustine 'have plenty of good food and good wine and are finely dressed. These I could well endure for I would rather live than die' (Guiot, *Bible*, 1690–94). The most significant point about Guiot's comments is that he is sincere in his praise of the canons. He is not being sarcastic at their expense. The situation is very different in two allegorical works, one from the beginning of the thirteenth century and one a hundred years later, which both present a uniformly critical view of all aspects of the religious life of the period.

The Reclus de Moliens in his poem *Charity* (*Carité*), composed about 1220, begins by bewailing the absence of charity in the world today. He has sought it among the laity and the intellectuals, the monks and the recluses. He has even been to Rome for he had heard that the Pope used to follow the advice of charity. But no more. Everything in Rome is dry. Hinges and palms alike have to be greased, and that frequently (*Charity*, S. 13–17). Nor is Charity in England, where since the murder of Thomas of Canterbury the ruler of the country is sterling (*estrelins*) (*Charity*, S. 25). Finally having sought charity throughout Europe and the Holy Land, the Reclus turns to France.

The next section of the work consists of a series of studies of the different estates and orders, with mention of their duties and responsibilities. The main targets of criticism and advice are the clergy. The parish priest is described in detail, though with none of the wit and pertinent observation of a Chaucer; instead the Reclus makes use of numerous and often laboured puns on the names of the different orders. The priest should govern himself and his household by reason, and his 'leisure and speech should be moderate and give no cause for scandal' (*Charity*, S. 69). The *prestre* should *preche*, the *abbé* should *aboie* (bark), the *eveche* (bishop) should *éveille* (watch). The good watch-dogs should protect the flocks against the wolves, but instead 'the bad dogs have themselves become wolves' (*Charity*, S. 118). Nor is it only the behaviour of the secular clergy that is criticised: the Reclus spares more than a passing glance for the fashions of the monks in their religious houses where, instead of the wide shoes, wide sleeves and wide tonsure of the Rule, they wear pointed shoes, short robes with tight sleeves and live on rich food (*Charity*, S. 134–5). The Reclus is by no means the only writer to criticise the fashionable clothing worn by the religious. A very bitter attack is launched a century later by Gilles li Muisis, who complains that nuns who should spin and weave their veils at home get permission to go out to the shops: 'they will buy fine cloth to deck themselves out; then they go on to the *fichus* and have them displayed. If they are going to spend their money on these trinkets they also know where to go for amusement' (*Gilles*, p. 217).

A century after the Reclus had set out on his vain Quest for Holy Charity, the author of the *Book of Fauvel* created a different but equally critical allegory of the world of the day, especially the clergy. Fauvel is a beast whose name is the initial letters of the vices: *f*lattery, *a*varice, *v*illainy, *v*anity, *e*nvy and *l*ascheté (cowardice). It is the age of Fauvel for the beast rules everywhere and all kinds and conditions of men are engaged in currying Fauvel (*étriquer Fauvel*; the English version of this popular text has given us the phrase 'to curry favour'). 'A beast is Fauvel, and those who worship him are beasts' (*Fauvel*, 281–2). Even the Pope 'rubs Fauvel's head saying, "This is a fine beast", and to please him the cardinals reply, "You're quite right, holy father." Then they all stretch out their hands and begin to curry him' (*Fauvel*, 113–18).

It is natural that satire and criticism should always be directed against the powerful and the great, those whose actions can influence the society in which they live. But there is also a considerable body of general commentary and criticism to be culled from these writings on the less influential but increasingly numerous groups of the professions, merchants, trade guilds and even occasionally the poor who, despite their lowly position, do not entirely escape the vitriolic pens of the *moralistes*.

In the *Book of Enanchet* (*Livre d'Enanchet*) a father gives his son advice on the possible careers open to him. The angle of vision is from lower down the social scale than Philip of Novaro. Although the author shares Philip's ideal of knighthood as a 'precious order' whose job is to ensure peace for all, he does not suggest his son should become a knight but talks instead of the minor court functionaries, including messengers and attendants. The Church, however, is open to all and is considered first as being pre-eminent. 'He who wants to become a *clerc* should excel at reading and singing so that he may deserve his benefice' (*Enanchet*, p. 7). He should wear the proper clothing of his profession, 'to show he is a wise man he should wear his hair cut all round, as becomes members of the holy church, with the tonsure of his order according to local custom; long robes down to his shoes' (p. 7). The references to clothes recur constantly, not only for religious and priests as we might expect, but also in other secular professions. The doctor, for example, should 'be well-dressed as his means permit and in long robes, for rich clothes carry with them great respect and comfort, and long robes are a sign of wisdom and humility' (p. 14). A doctor must also be very careful not to laugh too much, which is a sign of folly, and should be careful always what he says, for his words will be watched more than those of ordinary men, 'and if he speaks foolishly that will be remembered more than a hundred words of wisdom' (p. 13).

The father is determined to give his son a wide choice of careers, for he includes the skills and behaviour necessary for a farmer and those of the merchant or 'workers in other arts'. The child who would become a farmer must learn to look after animals so they do not damage the crops or possessions of others. 'He should spend more time in the fields than in the town and learn to plough and sow, to make carts and ploughs and other things necessary for his work' (pp. 10–11). The merchant, on the other hand, should first of all learn about profit, then different money systems, 'so that you may not be tricked if you are in another country' (p. 11). When you want to trade you must enquire about other countries to find out which is the best market, and when you are there you should use your intelligence in what you acquire, for it is shame and disgrace to lose your possessions by foolish actions; in particular beware of whores and dicing (cf. *Courtois d'Arras*, p. 97 above). In an unexpectedly modern phrase, the father then mentions other skills: 'anyone who wants to learn another skill [*art*] should

begin with the one he likes best. But if he does not learn it
immediately he should not give it up but persevere once he has
begun, for practice makes perfect, both in hand skills and in
more abstract learning' (p. 12).

Enanchet does not specify what these other *arts* may be, but it
seems likely he was meaning the skilled trades which were
highly organised in the later Middle Ages under the aegis of the
different guilds. The author of *Renart Disguised*, in the fourteenth century, includes them in his survey of the social world
and finds an unusual and ingenious way of introducing the
criticism of these particular groups. A Tigress is searching for
food and can only eat 'good workmen'. She comes to the town
and talks to the various craftsmen whose spokesman makes it
quite clear that none of them is suitable food for such a dainty
eater: to begin with, he explains, he never arrives at work on
time because he is always busy checking that no one else is
being paid more for the job than he is, for if so he will go
elsewhere even if he has a year's contract, for under no
circumstances will 'I hire myself out for less than another'
(*Renart Disguised*, 40530). He also passes part of the time sitting
and chatting with his mates, so that when he does get to work
and the overseer asks what he has been doing, he claims he has
sent someone else to do the job, but only by paying him six
deniers over the rate 'which you will pay me back for you have a
good conscience' (40548–9).

Other practices quoted include sitting up on the roof (it is a
tiler speaking) playing with the tiles, whistling, or lying down
in the gully between two roofs for a sleep. 'I could very easily
have put eight or ten in position, I promise you, before I
actually lay a single tile' (40586–91). And all of them are alike,
he says, for 'if we wanted to work properly we could prove in
one day that without difficulty we could complete in six days a
job that takes three weeks' (40625–8). A carpenter joins in the
discussion agreeing with the tiler, and adding that anyone who
tried to work too hard would be in trouble with the others. He
also has to have a mate, paid at the full rate though he is
unskilled, and the mate is sent to get things while the carpenter
sharpens his axe or his saw or meditates on the job for a while,
'and then it is dinner time and we go and drink in the tavern
and stay there a long time' (40719–22). The Tigress finally

abandons any hope of finding food, having rejected in turn the dishonest workmen, lying lawyers, deceitful merchants and a whole corrupt society.

If brevity is the soul of wit, prolixity is the curse of critics. Although they consistently advocate measure and order, the medieval *moralistes* (writers who describe the *mœurs* or manners of society) are with very few honourable exceptions, such as Philip of Novara or Robert de Blois, conspicuously lacking in both order and measure. Their nuggets of originality are concealed in a vast quantity of dross through which the reader must patiently sift if he is to find the precious specks of gold. One of the worst offenders in this respect is Gilles li Muisis who outrambles Polonius, though it may be said in his defence that he dictated his work in 1350 when nearly eighty and blind. (He had a successful operation for cataract in 1351 and died the following year.) Other writers, almost as prolific, lacked even these excuses of age and infirmity.

There are many vignettes of contemporary life and manners scattered through these works, and much information both for the medieval reader and the modern one, but nowhere is there a writer with the gift of portraiture of a Chaucer or the rapier-sharp satire of a Dante. The portraits are most often mere caricatures and the weapon used is a bludgeon not a scalpel; they hammer home their lesson or their complaint with all the heavy-handedness of Jean de Meung's Lover as, armed with the staff and bag that Nature gave him, he forces his way into the shrine of the rose: 'Vigorous and athletic I knelt without delay between the two fair pillars, for I had a great desire to worship this fair and noble shrine with a devout and pitiful heart . . . I had to assault it strongly, often striking it, often thrown back . . . I had worked so hard that I was covered with the sweat of effort' (Meung, *Rose*, 21559–64, 21587–8, 21598–9). We are a far cry from the eager, timid young man who first saw and adored the rose in the perilous mirror of love.

Words and Pictures

By the end of the thirteenth century, the rising number of

people who could read at least French had led to an enormous increase in the range of books copied for the laity and also, paradoxically, encouraged the visual arts as well. Pictures were no longer merely a substitute for words – books for the illiterate as they are often called – nor was art restricted to the adornment of life and ritual. Treatises and encyclopaedias included diagrams and drawings to aid the comprehension of the text; the exploits of William of Orange, Lancelot or Renart were lovingly illustrated; Bible stories, miracles and saints' lives were impartially recorded in words or windows, sermons and sculpture.[4]

This compulsive desire for both information and decoration combined to produce the explosion of colour, form and line which is still visible in surviving manuscripts and stained-glass windows, though the vivid wall-paintings and polychromed carving which once covered the interior and exterior of cathedrals, churches and even some secular buildings have faded or disappeared.

Art in the Middle Ages was largely narrative or didactic while literature was often strongly visual. The decoration of a great church might involve a number of well-known stories or themes: the labours of the months or the psychomachia (the battle of the vices and virtues) rubbing shoulders with the creation and fall of man or legends of the saints. Even the apparently merely decorative creatures wreathing a capital or writhing up a pillar can often be shown to belong to a known sequence of metaphors or allegory, to a bestiary or fable.

The mixing of Christian and secular subjects is also typical. Figures from romance: Alexander borne aloft by griffins or Yvain having his spurs cut off by the falling portcullis; figures from the fable or beast-epic: Renart preaching to the geese or the funeral of the cock, Chantecler; scenes of domestic life: the brawling husband and wife or the toper with his tankard; all these and many others are found carved on the misericords in medieval chancels side by side with Noah or Abraham. Equally common are the biblical subjects decorating a secular object: a comb, or mirror or box. Some subjects are ambivalent in their significance. The windows of Chartres Cathedral include a sequence of scenes from the *Song of Roland*, while a Wheel of Fortune is carved in the exterior stonework of a rose window in the church of St Stephen in Beauvais. Neither of these themes can arbitrarily be labelled religious or secular, the distinction between the two areas being extremely nice in medieval culture.

The strongly visual nature of much medieval literature has its own consequences also. Many manuscripts contain sequences of illustrations like strip cartoons, and such pictorial narratives may also be secular or religious ranging from the Book of Genesis to the stories of Renart the Fox. The proportion of image to writing in a text can vary enormously, some manuscripts being virtually comic books, while others would incur Alice's condemnation for having 'no conversation and no pictures'.

In most instances the verbal story predates the pictorial narrative but an exception is the *Book of Fauvel* whose author, Gervais de Bus, starts by saying that 'they often see him [Fauvel] depicted in art in such a way that they cannot tell if he figures mockery, sense or folly' (*Fauvel*, 5–7). A manuscript in the Bibliothèque Nationale has conserved a series of forty line-drawings of Fauvel with a commentary by a certain Raoul le Petit (who may have come from Arras) and other series are also known (*Fauvel*, pp. civ–cv).

Very often only one or two striking elements of a story are represented time and again, the choice depending on either a possible symbolic meaning for the scene, or the likelihood of identifying the characters concerned. 'When we see a monk sitting on a rock looking tranquilly up to heaven with a human skull beside him and without other baggage, we know that that is St Jerome. Because we know that he always went flying light in the matter of baggage. When we see a party looking tranquilly up to heaven, unconscious that his body is shot through and through with arrows, we know that that is St Sebastian' (Mark Twain, *Innocents Abroad*, ch. XXIII). Perhaps under the influence of such religious trade-marks and attributes, some secular subjects acquired a similar set of semiotic labels: when we see a man and woman drinking from a cup, with a ship in the offing, we know they are Tristan and Iseult. Other figures are less easy to label, which may account for the absence of, for example, Lancelot from medieval illustrative schemes.

In biblical stories the relationship between words and pictures is not always without its own kind of problem. Obviously the original plots are all older than the church building being adorned, but often an individual detail or association may have a much later source. This can lead to very delicate situations in the relationship between the plastic arts and that most visual of literary genres, the drama. Many attempts have been made to link a particular visual sequence with a specific play. For example, the combination of prophets and creation scenes on the façade of the romanesque church of Notre-Dame-la-Grande in Poitiers was linked by the art historian Emile Mâle with the Anglo-Norman play of *Adam*, which also combines the Fall of Man with prophecies of Redemption.[5] In this instance it is fairly easy to refute Mâle's claim, for the prophets in Poitiers have scrolls on which their prophecies are scribed and they differ in name and text from those in the play. On the other hand, an engraving in a Book of Hours of some shepherds listening to the angels announcing the birth of Christ includes labels giving their names which are identical with those in a play from Huy near Liège (see p. 176 below). Since these names are not traditional a link between the two works may surely be postulated. The illustrations actually occurring in a play text are also a potential hazard, for it is tempting to see them as illustrative of the performance of the text when they may have no such significance. The manuscript of the Arras Passion contains miniatures of several scenes – the shepherds guarding their sheep or the soldiers with infants impaled on their bloody swords – but they are set against backgrounds of natural landscapes, not stage sets, so that it is very difficult to determine whether these are stage pictures or merely the artists's creative reaction to the text.

Illustrations in manuscripts of the romances or the *chansons de geste* are often painted hundreds of years after the original story was written down so that the details of clothing or armour may be either contemporary with the original and copied, or contemporary with the particular manuscript, or merely the artist's impressions of the kind of clothes worn by the characters. Medieval art and literature had no interest in strict temporal historicity, but it did often have symbolic ways of showing certain historical events and these might remain standard for centuries. On the stage, of course, costumes were never intended to be 'historical' in a limited sense: such a concept did not come in until the eighteenth century. The use of manuscript illustration for any kind of historical dating is a dangerous pastime.

The other element common to medieval art and literature beside the narrative is the didactic. The paintings that covered the interior, and often the exterior, too, of castles and churches might include schemes representing the Creed and the Lord's Prayer, a saint's life or a Doom painting (depicting the Last Judgement). But although didactic, medieval art was by no means childish, we are not *Watching with Mother* or learning with *Sesame Street*. The counterpointing of worship with word, image or music has more in common with *son et lumière* today than with *Playschool*. Television offers the modern viewer much of the information and culture that his medieval counterpart found in the historiated capitals, glowing windows or richly coloured wall paintings. But the schemes of meaning are often very sophisticated and there is also the difficulty of studying carefully the significance of a stained-glass window high up – in French Gothic churches exceedingly high up – in the walls of a cathedral without the aid of a telephoto lens.

Medieval artists delighted in pattern. Two or more themes or stories may be juxtaposed in the squares or roundels of a single rose-window; an illuminated capital letter may have a series of little pictures set among its curves and lines. Often immense skill is shown in adapting the theme or story to the deliberately chosen odd-shaped area which is being decorated: the triangular space between the tops of pointed arches or the hooked curve of a bishop's crozier. Most medieval art is enclosed in a framework which, like the structural corset of rhyme and rhythm controlling a poet's exuberance and intensifying the impact of the words – Victor Hugo claimed that verse is to prose as tempered steel to mere iron – emphasised the form by restricting it so that a deliberate extrusion from the framework, Goliath's head or an angel's wing, stressed the constant tension between the formal created universe and the infinite eternity of God.

Patterns are not merely structural, they may also be found in the meanings and associations of the themes, such as those found in the thousands of extant sets of pictures in manuscripts, on church walls or in tympana which present a bewildering complexity of line and thought. Stories are equally complex. The multi-stranded framework of incidents in a romance, the ordered complexities of an allegory, the elaborate prosody of a lyric poet all testify to this same love of order and measure, a vast tracery of ideas and associations blended into that unity in diversity of which the epitome is the greatest monument of medieval creative genius – the Gothic Cathedral.

6. The City and the Pilgrim

> Mirrors are the doors through which death comes and
> goes. Look at yourself in a glass every day and you will
> see death working like bees in a glass hive.
>
> (Jean Cocteau)

THE universe and the world, the society of past and present in
which he lived and worked and had his being – these were only
part of the reality of existence for medieval man who knew
himself to be, in Augustine's words, a citizen of two cities, the
city of the world and the city of God. 'Here is no abiding city':
man is constantly on the move, a quester, a seeker, a pilgrim on
his way to the new Jerusalem.

Christianity was a fact of life for the dwellers in Christian
Europe. A man might be a good Christian or a bad one, he
might be a Jew or a heathen, he was only rarely an atheist. The
careless and the wicked might break the commandments but
were normally quite aware of the reality of the hereafter. They
were not like the heathen who say let us eat and drink and be
merry for tomorrow we die. It was usually rather a question of
eat, drink and be merry for tomorrow we repent and only the
next day shall we die, we hope.

In view of the immense importance of religion, it is not
surprising that a vast amount of specifically religious literature
was composed in addition to the general Christian element in
fictional works such as the *Song of Roland* or the *Prose Lancelot*, or
the moral teaching of the critics and satirists. Critics might
complain and *moralistes* mock but only the Church could save.
This it did in three ways: by examples of virtue, by admonition
and by encouragement to personal devotion and spirituality.

The Literature of Edification: Exemplary Lives of Christ and the Saints

(a) *The Vernacular Bible*

ALTHOUGH the earliest French versions of the Bible date only

149

from the twelfth century, the idea of translating the Scriptures into vernacular was already put forward by Charlemagne, and a capitulary of Louis II (dated 856) ordains that the Lord's Prayer and the Creed should be learned by everyone 'both in Latin and in the vulgar tongue so that what is professed by the mouth should be believed and understood by the heart'.[1]

The Psalms, the Books of Kings and other parts of both the Old and New Testaments were translated into prose in the twelfth century; in 1140 Herman of Valenciennes produced an abridged verse redaction of the whole Bible, and by the mid-thirteenth century the University of Paris had commissioned a complete prose translation of both Old and New Testaments. The quality of this prose text is very high and it remained the standard vernacular version until the sixteenth century. However, only a few manuscripts of it have survived, for at the end of the century it was conflated with the extremely popular vernacular translation of Peter Comestor's *Historia Scholastica*, one of the most influential of medieval biblical commentaries, and the two texts together, in the form known as the *Bible Historiale*, or illustrated Bible, became the commonest French Bible of the later Middle Ages. That keen bibliophile, the Duc de Berry, had nine French Bibles in his library, and more than seventy copies of the *Bible Historiale* are extant, most of them richly illuminated and many having belonged to the royal house or the great nobles. Others were copied for English kings and nobles who were, of course, all French speaking, and it seems possible that the existence of a vernacular version of the Scriptures, available to those who could afford it, may be one reason why there was no pressure from the rich patrons of English society for a comparable translation of the Bible into English before Wyclif.

The *Bible Historiale* had one great disadvantage: it was very expensive because of its size and many illustrations, and the bulk of medieval society made do with partial texts or with the vernacular verse adaptations of the life of Christ usually known in French as *Passions*. The earliest of these, the *Minstrels' Passion* (*Passion des Jongleurs*) was composed in the thirteenth century and includes many of the apocryphal and legendary accretions to the gospels which had become popular over the centuries. Some of these accretions are extremely ancient, deriving from the apocryphal gospels, texts written in the early centuries of Christianity but not considered part of the strict canon of scripture. One such text is the *Protevangelium* or *Gospel of St James*, which contains details of the birth and childhood of Christ and was well known in Latin in the Middle Ages before being translated into French as the *Evangile de l'Enfance* in the thirteenth century. More important and influential, however, was the *Gospel of Nicodemus* which contained the narrative of the Harrowing of Hell: Christ's visit to the place of the dead to bring Adam and Eve and the patriarchs out of Hell after the Crucifixion and before the Resurrection. The brief reference in the Apostles' Creed, 'he descended into Hell', was enough to give the story particular authority and it is found even in texts like Greban's passion-play which claim not to use apocryphal material (cf. Greban's *Passion*, 1720). The *Evangile de Nicodème* was translated into French several times in the twelfth and thirteenth centuries and the scene of the Harrowing was portrayed in numerous sculptures and wall-paintings throughout the Middle Ages.

Much of the apocryphal material is of the 'gap-filler' kind, common in historical novels and plays where areas of the hero's life are developed in detail which were left out of the original accounts. Two sequences of the biblical narrative often so treated are the life of Adam and Eve on earth after the Fall with the events leading up to the Flood, and the early life of Christ. A somewhat different kind of elaboration – or *amplificatio* as the medieval theorists called the technique – is to take a given minor incident and build up the characters and details. One of the best-known episodes in this group is the story of the linen cloth in which Joseph of Arimathea wrapped the body of the crucified Christ for his burial (see Mark 15: 43–6). A whole literature has grown up round this reference, which in the Middle Ages became confused with the legend of the 'Veronica', the cloth with which a kindly woman wiped Christ's face during the Way of the Cross and on which the imprint of the Holy Face remained. Recent books and documentaries on the Holy Shroud of Turin (which was displayed in France between 1357 and 1535, when it was transferred to Turin) have revived interest in this very complex tissue of stories which occur in one form or another in almost every passion, whether narrative or dramatic.[2] The play of *Sainte Venice* (or Veronica) was composed in the late fifteenth century, and the miracle-working cloth also played an important role in the plays of the *Vengeance of Christ* (*Vengeance Jésus-Christ*), the story of the sack of Jerusalem by Vespasian in AD70, seen in the Middle Ages as an act of revenge by the Roman emperor for the crucifixion. There is even a play which appears to refer directly to the Turin Shroud, for the *Semur Passion* from Burgundy, copied in 1485, contains a speech by Mary Magdalene in which she displays the shroud to her fellow-Maries and the audience: 'She takes the shroud and displays it: "The pain is visible on his shroud that the felons made him bear. Ten thousand and five hundred drops, more if one would count them all, of his blood with which he was wet when bound to the whipping-post, for his body was broken in many places" ' (*Semur Passion*, 9121–7). The play was written at Semur-en-Auxois at a time when the shroud was being displayed in both Burgundy and Champagne and attracting many pilgrims, so the author may well have had the relic in mind when composing his resurrection scene.

An ever-increasing interest in the humanity of Christ and his life on earth, coupled with growing devotion to the Virgin Mary, led to changes in their representation in art and literature in the twelfth and thirteenth centuries. The stylised hieratic figures of Romanesque art were replaced by the more natural and human sculptures of the Gothic age; while works like the *Golden Legend* (*Legenda Aurea*) by Jacobus de Voragine, or the *Meditations* attributed to St Bonaventure, introduced countless pious and devotional legends into the biblical narrative, highlighting the stories with vivid personal details as the gilding and coloured paint emphasised the faces and figures on the portals and capitals of the churches.

Both writers and artists laid great emphasis on the linking of the two Testaments, the Old and the New. Sometimes they followed the theologians who had created a multi-layered exegesis of the Bible with certain Old Testament events being seen as 'types' or 'figures' of incidents in the New: the announcement of the birth of Isaac to Abraham and Sarah (Genesis 18: 1–15) prefigures the annunciation; Jonah escaping from the whale's belly, or Daniel from the lions' den, were types of the resurrection, and so on. A different kind of link was provided by legends like those of the Holy Rood in which the wood of the cross is grown from a pip, core or stem of the forbidden fruit. These legends were very widely diffused in all parts of Europe in Latin and many vernaculars, including French. In the version found in the thirteenth-century Andrius manuscript – a compilation of stories of the Fall and its consequences – there is an interesting reflection of the medieval belief in the importance of written authority. Seth is told to write the story of his father's life on tablets of stone and of clay, so that if God judges the world by flood the tablets of stone will survive, and if by fire, the tablets of clay. After the Flood, we are told, the tablets were found but the people of that age could not decipher them. Only Solomon can read them and God explains them to him: 'Thus this matter was known to Solomon who passed it on to those who came after him' (*The Penitence of Adam*, p. 85). The Andrius Manuscript (which also contains a number of romances) was written about 1280, and this incident reflects the growing stress on the written, rather than the oral, transmission of information and tradition typical of the period.

Biblical, apocryphal or typological, the stories are narrated with a wealth of descriptive detail of people and places: Sidonie, the shroud-seller, washes herself all over and dresses carefully before going out to sell her cloth (*Minstrels' Passion*, 3252–62). Such personal and realistic treatment was necessary because the writers of these religious narratives knew they were competing with the writers of romances and other profane stories. Like the historical figures of Charlemagne or Arthur, the biblical characters wear medieval clothes and live essentially European lives: Herod and Pilate are contemporary lords, and the shepherds, often shown with their wives and sweethearts eating, drinking, dancing and merrymaking, belong to the same recognisable tradition as Robin and Marion (see p. 98 above), or the shepherd boys who befriend Nicolette (see p. 100). The gifts they give to the infant Christ are medieval ones – a ball or spoon, a hat or whistle. These might be of any period, but not the fine wooden calendar which shows the days and months given by one of the shepherds in Greban's *Passion* (5498–508).

The skill of the medieval dramatists in making the remote stained-glass figures real to their audiences is not limited to their own time, as the many modern and successful productions of the English cycles has amply proved. French plays, with the exception of the Anglo-Norman *Adam*, have had fewer modern productions, partly because of their length, partly because some of the best-known ones are rather formal and stylised with little of the popular earthy humour of their English counterparts, more like the *Oberammergau Passion* than the *Second Shepherds' Play*.

Biblical narratives and plays made regular use of medieval speech patterns and customs – the plays also used contemporary costume – but like the *chansons de geste* and the romances these tales remained essentially 'historical'. Large numbers of stories, however, portrayed the scriptural characters and the saints intervening directly in medieval life, miraculously helping their devotees and confounding the unbelievers. Outstanding among them are the stories in which Our Lady acts as mediator between the sinner and the increasingly remote persons of the Trinity; in the later Middle Ages the cult of the Virgin was one of the most powerful social and cultural influences in an increasingly divided Christendom.

(b)   *Mother and Maiden*

Medieval attitudes to women were usually extreme, the absolute subservience of the lover to his lady in the literature of *fin'amor* contrasting with the implicit anti-feminism of the *fabliau* and farce and the outspoken criticisms of a Jean de Meung or a Matheolus. However, women were not without their defenders, as can be seen in the rare poem of *The Goodness of Women* (*Du Bonté des Femmes*) written by an Englishman in the thirteenth century. The author uses mainly well-known arguments in defence of women: they are made from clean bone rather than dirty earth like man, 'who has to remove the filth from his face and shave himself and cut his hair every fifteen days' (*Bonté*, 77–80). Women can bear children without the help of man, as can be seen from the example of the Virgin Mary. No man can do this: 'God made of woman his mother, he did not make a man his father' (*Bonté*, 1172–3). It is wrong to blame Eve for Adam's sin: if he had been a wise man he would have forbidden Eve to eat the apple, and as she was subject to him she would have paid no heed to the serpent's bad advice. Anyway, it is no defence in law to say another person advised you to commit a crime! Although he is not original in his basic arguments, the author is certainly unusual in his treatment of the subject and in particular of the relationship between Adam and Eve. He is entirely conventional, however, in his praise and exaltation of the Virgin Mary: 'Would you like to know why? Her son is such a powerful king that he has all kings under his command. Has woman then not got great power who can call so great a king her son? And since by right of Nature a son should obey his mother then it appears, though I do not say so, that woman has God in her power!' (*Bonté*, 182–91).

The role of the Virgin Mary in the redemption was the supreme act of woman; her willing submission to the word of God redeemed the disobedience of Eve even for the latter's most severe critics. 'For though woman was the first to sin, a woman afterwards restored us. . . . But if Eve worked great folly, holy Mary repaired and corrected this fault' (*L'Advocacie Notre-Dame*, S. 4). Because of her obedience, the Virgin was qualified to act as advocate for man and especially for woman against the devil.

The cult of the Virgin was encouraged by many great churchmen – first of all, in France, by St Bernard of Clairvaux – and from the twelfth century onwards her importance in the life and literature of the medieval world increased steadily. One consequence of this interest was the elaboration of her role in the New Testament, with legends of her conception, birth and childhood being included in the Latin and vernacular versions of the Bible, while her actions during the ministry and passion of Christ were stressed more and more, especially in the dramatic versions of the crucifixion where an extended lament or *planctus* became part of the tradition in both Latin and French plays. Philippe de Mézières (see p. 219 below), who was instrumental in popularising the new *Feast of the Presentation of the Virgin in the Temple* in the fourteenth century, composed a lengthy Latin play on the subject which was performed in 1372; in the great passion plays of the fifteenth century the role of the Virgin was second only to that of Christ in length and importance, with the relationship of mother and son being

stressed in such scenes as the last meeting before the passion in
Michel's play:

Virgin:	Let it at least then be your lot
	To die a swift and easy death.
Christ:	I shall die in bitter pain.
Virgin:	Not in shame and villainy?
Christ:	Yes, in great ignominy.
Virgin:	May it take place far away?
Christ:	No, in the midst of all my friends.
Virgin:	In darkness then, I beg of you.
Christ:	Rather at the stroke of noon.
Virgin:	Die then as becomes a king.
Christ:	I shall die between two thieves.
Virgin:	Let it be secret, out of sight.
Christ:	It will be on a cross most high.

(Michel's *Passion*, 16675–87)

The most significant examples of Marian literature, however, are not those in which she is held up as an example of
humility and pity, but rather the so-called *Miracles of the Virgin*,
the numerous stories set in the post-gospel period in which the
Virgin saves her devotees from every peril of body and soul. By
the end of the Middle Ages she is not so much an example to be
followed as a powerful intercessor, a real friend at court. Scores
of such stories are extant. Many of them were translated from
Latin into French in a huge collection by Gautier de Coinci in
the late twelfth century, and another major group are the
dramatised versions of the fourteenth century also known as the
Miracles de la Vierge. Epic, romance, *fabliau* or farce, every kind
of story is found in these collections, whose only common
denominator is the Virgin herself in the role of *dea ex machina*.
They include characters from all levels of society, as well as
historical figures like Robert the Devil, or saints such as St
Guilhem-le-désert (otherwise known as the epic hero William,
Count of Orange).

The pictures of contemporary life are often very vivid. In one
Miracle, a woman who has just given birth to her first child is
encouraged by her attendant to have a bath: 'I'm sure it will do
you a lot of good; so get in' (*Miracle of the Child Restored to Life*,
584–5). The lady does so and then asks to hold her baby in her

arms, before sending the attendant next door to ask her neighbour to come and see her. Left alone in the bath (the husband has gone off on a pilgrimage of thanksgiving to a shrine of the Virgin), the wife falls asleep and drops the child in the water and drowns it. She is condemned to be burnt but saved by the action of the Virgin who restores the child to life. Another woman saved by the Virgin had murdered her son-in-law because he was trying to seduce her. The local judge visits the house to see the corpse and certify the death: 'Uncover the bier for me quickly and unstitch speedily part of his shroud so that I can see him as far as the thigh so as to be the more certain. I will make my attestation before he is buried. . . . Uncover his face for me, completely, so I can see his throat and chest. . . . Hey there! Seize the mother, the daughter and the father. They cannot deny that it looks as if he has been murdered. It's obvious. See how black his throat is. Someone, whoever it may be, has strangled him' (*Miracle of a Woman whom Our Lady Saved from being Burned*, 578–84; 593–600; this is probably the first example in French of a detective story on the stage). The mother-in-law admits her guilt and is condemned to death but in acknowledgement of her repentance, the Virgin intervenes and her life is spared. She spends the rest of her days doing penance in a nunnery.

In all the miracles, narrative or dramatic, as well as the many prayers and meditations addressed to her, the Virgin apparently has unlimited power: her Son refuses her nothing as a devil wryly notices: 'We're fools to have applied to God in this affair – he's always against us. Doesn't dare do anything else because of his mother. If he did anything against her he'd get a beating when he went home' (*Miracle of the Child Vowed to the Devil*, 1380–5).

Only at the Last Judgement is the Virgin no longer able to help. In the most elaborate French Judgement play, from the Rouergue in Southern France, many groups appear to be judged – the unmerciful rulers, corrupt lawyers, false pastors, even, most unusually, the devils themselves. Lucifer ironically decides to appeal to Our Lady, who now appears and in a very long speech pleads for mercy for everyone. Her appeal is rejected. It is too late (*Jugement Général*, 6710–820). However, God does promise that those who repented before they died will be pardoned, and his attitude to his mother is less harsh in this play than in the German *Last Judgement* play of 1467 where he says firmly:

> Sit down again there in your place!
> In my heart no mercy is.
> (*Last Judgement*, ed. Mone, I, p. 299)

(c)   *Lives and Miracles of the Saints*

The pre-eminence of the Virgin Mary in medieval literature in no way precluded the composition of a very extensive literature on the other saints, some hundred different men and women being celebrated in the extant narrative and dramatic works in French. The popularity of individual saints fluctuates interestingly over the centuries though certain ones, such as St Nicholas, remain constantly in favour – at least with the dramatists.

There are certain obvious choices among both the narrative and dramatic vernacular saints' lives: the apostles and early martyrs, including St Denis, have major roles in a number of plays, among them the great *Acts of the Apostles* performed at Bourges in 1536. St Margaret of Antioch and St Catherine of Alexandria are the most popular of the female saints after the Virgin and Mary Magdalene, and of the scores of other saints thus commemorated the principal stress, at least in the field of drama, is on the French saints. St Martin of Tours is the subject of no less than three different plays and his best-known action, dividing his cloak with a beggar, is vividly portrayed on stage: 'You shall have the greater share of the cloak I am wearing; therefore in order to divide it so that your flesh shall no longer be naked, take one end of it so that it divides. Take it willingly, for the love of God' (*Mystère de Saint Martin*, 1582–8). The cloak had been given to St Martin in the previous scene by his father to protect him 'from the rain and the wind' (1490).

St Remigius, the patron of Rheims, 'by whom France was brought to God' (*Vie de Saint Rémi*, 29) was the subject of a verse life composed in the thirteenth century from the Latin *Acta*, and distinguished by the exceptionally flat and unpoetic language in which it is presented: only the regularity of the rhyme scheme alerts us to the fact that the work is in verse not prose, whereas the twelfth-century *Life of St Gilles*, whose shrine at Gard in Provence was a major place of pilgrimage, is as lively and vivid as any *chanson de geste*: 'He looked out to sea and saw a ship in danger pursued by the tempest and constantly covered by the waves that were both high and deep, for the sea was all stirred up, rolling and roaring like a mad thing' (*Vie de St Gilles*, 776–82).

Perhaps the most interesting French saints' lives for the modern reader are those written by near contemporaries: St Louis, whose biography by Joinville has already been mentioned (see p. 131 above), is also the subject of two different medieval plays, while the *Life of St Thomas à Becket* was composed by Guernes de Pont-Sainte-Maxence shortly after the canonisation of Thomas in 1173. Guernes relates how he went to Canterbury to collect eye-witness details for his work, completed it there and read it to pilgrims at the tomb of Chaucer's 'holy blissful martyr':

No romance as good as this was ever made or found. It was made and completed at Canterbury and not a single word is in it that is not the truth. The verse form is a five-rhyme stanza. My language is good for I was born in France. . . . Here Guernes the clerk from le Pont ends his sermon of the martyr, St Thomas, and his death. He often reads it at the noble man's tomb.   (*Vie de St Thomas Becket*, 6161–5, 6156–8)

A short verse epilogue tells us that Thomas's sister, the abbess of Barking, gave him a palfrey and accoutrements: 'even the spurs were not omitted'. This suggests that the abbess may have commissioned the poem though it is not certain.

The reference to the pilgrims at the tomb of the martyr is a useful reminder of the role of the pilgrimage in the cult of saints in the Middle Ages. Many an obscure or minor saint probably only achieved the honour of a vernacular life (they all had Latin ones of necessity) as part of a publicity campaign to attract the 'passing trade' of travellers on their way to the great shrines: St Germer, for example, whose church at Fly is not very far from the important church of St Benoît-sur-Loire.

Not all saints' lives were written for the pilgrims, of course, or even for general edification. There are a few which were designed only for the community to which the saint belonged, such as the *Life of St Beatrice of Ornacieux*, written by a fellow Carthusian nun, Marguerite of Oingt, not without a touch of criticism for the excesses of Beatrice's mortifications: 'During this period of penance, because of her great fear of being deceived by the devil she gave herself to practices which were sometimes lacking in moderation. But she undertook them from great fear and fervour and Our Lord every time put all back in good order' (*Vie de Sainte Béatrix d'Ornacieux*, p. 46; see p. 171 below).

Narrative, and especially dramatic, lives were often written for a confraternity or guild in honour of their patron saint; for example, the *Mystery of Saint Venice* (or Veronica) was composed for the guild of Master Gardeners of Paris, whose principal patron was the little-known St Fiacre, the hero of two medieval plays but only remembered today for the horse-drawn vehicles which bear his name because they used to ply for hire outside the church of St Fiacre in Paris. The extent to which these patron saints of guilds or individual Christians were becoming stereotypes of an almost magical protective power rather than examples of real people who had achieved the goal (Heaven) to which all Christians should be striving, is indicated by the fact that in the two plays on St Fiacre the saint is respectively described as being the son of the king of Scotland (which he was not) and the son of a wealthy Irish lord (which he may have been). With the Church torn apart by schism and nationalistic politics, many of the saints ceased to be examples to be followed and became personal protective deities under whose aegis the states, cities, groups or families might find refuge from the troubles of this world and the next.

Literature of Repentance

> I am lost beyond redemption.
> I have sinned against my lord
> And can never win his pardon.
> (*Adam*, 341–3)

The sin of Adam, original sin, was atoned for by the redemptive act of Christ, but man's will was still weak and he frequently succumbed to the triple temptations of the world, the flesh and the devil, and could only be cleansed from these sins, actual sin, by the sacrament of penance which involved three stages: contrition, confession and amendment.[3] To bring man to the first stage, repentance, was the primary duty of the Church, and one of its most effective weapons in this struggle with the devil was the homily or sermon.

The oldest extant vernacular sermons are twelfth-century French translations of the sermons of St Bernard of Clairvaux, founder of the Cistercian movement and a major figure in the religious life of Europe in the early part of that century. Some other fathers of the Church, especially St Gregory, were also translated into French, and a number of rhymed sermons are extant which were specially composed in the vernacular so that 'those who had no grammar might not be in doubt' (Guischart, *Sermon*, 8). Gautier de Coinci, writing to a community of nuns on the theme of chastity, stresses that he is sending them a written text as a present: 'Thus I send them and present to them this fair book and these pages which will speak better than any page or messenger or runner' (*Chastée as Nonains*, 10–13).

The moral teaching in these sermons, and the use of illustrative anecdotes or *exempla*, are very close to the didactic literature discussed in the previous chapter, but there is an important difference: the clergy could also threaten. And they did, especially in the persons of the friars – the Order of Preachers or Dominicans and the Franciscans – whose founders envisaged them primarily as itinerant preachers. The series of sermons for different Sundays and feast days in the Church's year, composed by the fathers or by secular clergy like Maurice of Sully, Bishop of Paris in the twelfth century, and copied, translated and quoted by many writers, are very different from the revivalist-meeting hell-fire style of sermon pronounced by the friars; broadly speaking the fathers preached about God, the friars against man.

Series of sermons for the penitential seasons of Advent and Lent, delivered in major churches all over France from the thirteenth century onwards, used every device of allusion, example and anecdote to attract and hold the audience's attention. Many such sermons have survived in Latin trans-

cripts, often with extracts in French and lists of words glossed
for the use of the preacher, and there are also a number of late
medieval Latin guides to preachers which contain detailed
analyses of the structure of these sermons, and suggestions for
phrases, *exempla* and allusions to illustrate the biblical texts.
Thus the story of the pearl of great price (Matthew 13: 45) is
used as an excuse to criticise the dishonest merchants who keep
their spices on damp floors so they will weigh heavier and
enable them to make a bigger profit. The *Carême*, or lenten
sermons, were, like the passion plays, seen as an enjoyable
social occasion, and the large, mixed audiences had clearly not
all come to be edified, to judge by the preachers' attacks on the
women, over-dressed and over made-up, using the church for a
rendezvous with their lovers, or the young men with their
falcons and hounds, which they insisted on bringing into the
sacred precincts: 'O sinner, wretched youth, degenerate son,
you have before your eyes the gibbet on which is hanged your
father and your master and you are laughing and joking and
going on your way to the banquet of the thirty thousand devils'
(Maillard, *Carême de Nantes*, Sermon 44).[4] A vivid contemporary picture of the attitude to these sermons is to be found in a
passion play where Mary Magdalene, hearing from her friends
about the new preacher, Jesus, cross-questions them about his
appearance:

M: Is he very handsome to look at?
A: He is tall and straight, wise, controlled, constant and
       cold.
M: Well made?
G: Best in the world.
M: What sort of face?
T: Long and round.
M: How old?
A: Thirty-two years old.
M: Hair and beard?
G: Long and pleasing, slightly waving and coloured.
M: And of what shade?
G: Slightly golden.
M: Complexion?
A: Red and brown.

M: The eyes?
T: Bright as a fair moon.
M: The hands?
G: Beautiful, long and clean.

(Michel's *Passion*, 10465–77)

The scene continues for a considerable time as Mary Magdalene wants to know also what he is wearing, how he speaks and so on. She then performs a special toilet before going to hear this exciting new preacher. This whole sequence of scenes, usually known as the 'worldliness' of the Magdalene with emphasis on her appearance and behaviour, stresses the immediacy of the event for the audience and brings home to them the reality of the sermon which she hears Jesus pronounce. Sermons are an integral feature of the passion plays both at the beginning of the spectacle, to put the audience in the right mood, and also in the course of the action, where Jesus or John the Baptist have long speeches in which, with many modern details, they urge repentance on their audience or obedience to the commandments of Moses. Thus the commandment not to kill means also not to take from a man what is his due: 'for if he has poor children and small and has not got a sheaf of barley you could not better cut his throat than to refuse to give him what is his due' (*Semur Passion*, 3533–6). You shall not covet your neighbour's ox nor his ass, 'nor his cat or dog' either (*Semur Passion*, 3555).

Some didactic writers used extensive quotations from the fathers and the Scriptures to support their exhortations and give authority to their recipe for a good life. The *Mirror of Ladies* (*Miroir des Dames*), a work written, as the name implies, for women but without being either adulatory or antagonistic, contains an interesting section on the need for self-examination and quotes the twelfth-century spiritual writer, Hugh of St Victor, on the best way of setting about this necessary preparation for repentance and confession:

He says: you must look into your heart and analyse yourself carefully [*subtillement*]. Consider whence you come and whither you are going, how you live and what you do, what you leave undone and how much, what is profitable to you and what you are lacking . . . and when you have thus discovered the whole state of the inner man, not only what he is but what he should be, by this knowledge you can be raised up and taken up to the true knowledge of God the Creator.   (*Mirror*, p. 88)

An unusual chapter in this work is that which deals with 'the sufferings peculiar to the feminine sex', which are those brought upon women by the sins of Eve. There is a vivid description of the ills of pregnancy: 'When a woman has conceived her face becomes pale, her belly swells, she walks heavily, her body is weighed down, her actions are weakened, her sleep diminished, her heart is troubled, sad and pensive, her appetite changeable' (*Mirror*, p. 110). Having brought his reader – the work was originally written for Jeanne de France, the wife of Philip the Fair – to a proper appreciation of her lowly estate as sinful *woman*, the author then gives sound advice to the *queen*: let her act so that her estate will be honoured by her virtues rather than her rank be an adornment to her (*Mirror*, p. 112).

Both in the sermons proper and in the moral treatises there is considerable use of imagery and personification. In *The God-given Talent* (*Le Besant de Dieu*) the author explains that his only talent is eloquence and he used to 'write fables and tales and versify in the Romance tongue' (*Talent*, 80–1). But realising this was a sin, and also that his only way of earning a living to keep his wife and children was his poems, he decided the best thing to do was to compose 'suitable verses in which one could find example and good matter, to hate and despise the world and to serve our lord' (*Talent*, 154–7). Perhaps because he had been a writer of tales and fables, Guillaume uses a particularly high proportion of *exempla* in his 'sermon', taking a series of biblical parables as the starting-points for his moralising, and also introducing a skilfully developed allegory of the contrast between the City of Pride and the Castle of Maidens. In the former, the guest receives very poor attention from the children of Pride: 'Filth [*ordure*] brings their tablecloths and lays them on their knees or on their cloaks [cf. the *vilain* who spread his cloak on the ground before laying the cloth to eat the partridges, see *The Tale of the Partridges*, p. 88]. Avarice brings their bread, and as she comes and goes she hides as much as she can away in her lap or her bosom' (*Talent*, 1907–12). This is a great contrast to the fair treatment received by everyone who comes to the Castle of Maidens, for there 'Charity sits on the high dais and her daughters serve there most courteously. . . . Honour and Joy and Courtesy and Sobriety, who is neither too sleepy nor too slow, these four who have much skill in this, supervise the tables when food is served and have very courteous helpers who together do this service' (1871–3, 1847–53). Guillaume sums up his work by urging his readers to leave the City of Pride and enter the Castle of Maidens; to join the virtuous in the parables: work in the vineyard and go to the marriage feast; above all, like the Prodigal Son, they should repent and go to their father and confess their sins: 'For every sinner who repents there is more joy in Heaven than for ninety-nine just men who have no need of repentance' (3665–end).

Some of the verse sermons are the work of professional preachers such as the Franciscan Nicholas of Bozon, whose nine verse *Sermons* make use of many of the traditional themes already mentioned. Sermon Six is on chattering in church and the general misbehaviour of women: 'And then the housewife complains to her neighbours, Jill and Joan, that she has lost her little pigs through her neighbour's wickedness and one replies: "and through my neighbours' wives' faults I've lost my hens." ' (Bozon, VI, 32–8). Another sermon criticises dancing on Sundays while a third warns of the need to prepare for death. Bozon also wrote a number of *Moral Tales* (*Contes Moralisés*) which were another popular form of admonitory literature.

In their desire to convert and instruct, some writers went much further in their use of secular material. Ovid's *Metamorphoses* was given a gloss, or explanation of the moral sense of the stories, in the fourteenth century (the *Ovide moralisé*), and there were several different versions of a moralised *Renart* (see p. 107 above). Occasionally, even a work that was already an allegory was reinterpreted, the most celebrated example being Clément Marot's moralisation of the *Romance of the Rose* in the sixteenth century. Not all writers of allegory reused old material, however. Some created their own and one of the most original, coherent, attractive, and shortest, is the *Bird Mass* (*Messe des Oiseaux*), written by Jean de Condé early in the fourteenth century. He dreams that in a pleasant place he sees a great tree where Venus on a high seat presides over the mass said by the nightingale with other birds taking individual roles: 'the blackbird read the gospel – never in country or town did I hear singing so melodious, agreeable and sweet' (*Bird Mass*, 189–91). The music is interrupted by the dissonant voice of the cuckoo who is forcibly expelled by the other birds. The parrot preaches the sermon and the priest celebrates, holding up a red rose instead of a host. After the mass there is a law-suit between the canonesses and the nuns on the right way to love, and Venus pronounces her verdict: 'After God and Nature I have power over all creatures . . . by the authority given me by Nature herself' (957–8, 963–4). So far there is nothing at all to suggest that this is not a work on the nature of courtly love, comparable to the first part of the *Romance of the Rose*. The apparent burlesque of the mass is merely part of the allegory and quite inoffensive, as we discover when we come to the last part of the text, where Jean de Condé explains his work: 'You have heard good jokes [*risées*] and things disguised from which one can take example and learn much of value' (1219–22). Although the author declares it would take too long to gloss the whole work he does give a fair amount of explanation. For example, he claims that he used the image of the rose for the consecrated host because 'the rose is prized above all other flowers for its colour, scent and grace' (1324–6). Nevertheless the sacrament surpasses it a hundredfold, for it is 'heavenly work, by the high Godhead and the Holy Trinity which is truly contained in the Body of God' (1330–3). Having made clear that his poem is a religious allegory, Jean de Condé explains he has 'cast his poem in such a form that it may please both wise men and fools: the wise may take example from it and the fools may find pleasure in it' (1495–9). Worldly love is but a dream but the love of God will last for ever. This emphasis on God's love and forgiveness is found even more in the literature designed to encourage personal piety and devotion and the enrichment of the individual Christian's spiritual life.

Literature of Piety and Devotion

Not all spiritual writings were condemnatory and penitential.

There were also plenty of more encouraging texts in vernacular, ranging from prayers in homage to Christ or the Virgin Mary, many of them in verse, to meditations on such subjects as the passion, the joys and sorrows of Mary, or lives of saints. Several thousand such devotional works have survived as well as a range of vernacular writings of a more explicitly didactic nature.

The need for instruction manuals for the laity was emphasised in the thirteenth century following the decree of the Lateran Council of 1215 requiring annual confession by every Christian, and the subsequent decrees which insisted that laymen be instructed in the rudiments of the faith. Some of these texts are more or less direct translations from Latin originals, such as Peter of Peckham's *Light for Laymen* (*Lumière as Lais*), a verse rendition of parts of the *Elucidarium* by Honorius of Autun interspersed with extracts from other writers, and arranged according to the scholastic format in a series of numbered divisions and sub-divisions; for example

> 'Book V, The Sacraments', 'Section IV, The Eucharist', Question 7: how the body of Christ can be present everywhere it is instituted. Numerous masses are celebrated simultaneously in different parts of the world, so how can the body of Jesus Christ be everywhere at once? There would be no merit in belief if we could understand everything, but consider that the sun can be reflected in a hundred thousand mirrors at the same time.   (*Lumière*, IV, p. 106)

Peter of Peckham wrote in French, he tells us, because that is 'understandable by laymen' and it is for them he is writing (*Lumière*, IV, p. 71), but some translators admit that, even in French, philosophical and theological texts are difficult to understand and indeed to translate, as Jean de Meung explains in the dedication to Philip the Fair of his prose translation of Boethius's *Consolation of Philosophy*, one of the most popular works from Classical antiquity:

> And since you have told me, and I take your words for commands, that I should take the whole sense of the author without following the Latin words too literally, I have used my modest best to do as your graciousness has commanded.

And I beg all those who will see this work to pardon me if they think that I have gone too far away from the author's words or have sometimes put in too little, for if I had rendered the Latin word for word into French the book would have been too obscure for the layman, and a clerk, even if he understood Latin, could not easily grasp the Latin from the French.   (*Boethius*, IV, p. 276)

Jean de Meung stresses elsewhere in this dedication that he has translated it 'although I know that you understand Latin well, but nevertheless it is much easier to understand it in French than in Latin' (*Boethius*, IV, p. 276).[5] Not all the translations of Boethius are in prose, and one of the verse translators explicitly condemns the use of prose: 'it seems to me a crude method since this great work is a high and noble mystery'; he claims the author he is criticising lacks accuracy as well, leaving out or inserting matter in many places (*Boethius*, IV, p. 290). Since there were at least a dozen different translations of Boethius in medieval French, it is unlikely the critic was referring to Jean de Meung's text here.

The dialogue form used by Boethius was a popular one with didactic writers, being convenient for the author and more attractive to the reader than the rigid format of the *Light for Laymen*. One of the original compilations which uses Latin material without being in any way a translation of a particular work is the *Dialogue of the Father and his Son* (*C'est dou pere qui son filz enseigne et dou filz qui u pere demande ce que il ne set*) in which the son asks questions on many aspects of belief and practice which his father answers as best he can. The whole tone of the work is easy and natural. When the son asks about the Trinity, the father comments that that is the greatest mystery in the faith; nevertheless he tries to explain using a well-known image: 'the sun has three properties, heat, brightness and substance, yet it is not three suns but one.' He then explains the relationship of the Son with the Father as being like the brightness of the sun born of its substance. His son is still not satisfied: 'I believe as you have taught me, that one must believe without knowing the reason for everything, nevertheless if you would give me a little of the reason and explanation of this I would be happier' (*Dialogue*, IV, pp. 56–7).

This work is imaginary but we do have at least one text genuinely composed by a father for his son, the *Instructions* (*Enseignement*) of St Louis, composed for his son, Philip the Bold. The numerous surviving texts, testimony of the medieval popularity of the royal advice, are mostly vernacular retranslations of the Latin version of the original collection of teachings translated by the king's confessor, Geoffrey, on the order of Pope Gregory X. The *Instructions* were one of the pieces of evidence used in the process of canonisation in 1297. The king's *Instructions* include specifically royal advice on the importance of only raising just taxes or trying to avoid war, together with more generally applicable advice on avoiding extravagance and being faithful in the observance of religious duties. A short *Instruction* to his daughter, Isabelle, has also survived in which the king again warns against extravagance: 'It seems to me a good thing that you should not have too large a collection of dresses at one time, nor of jewels. . . . Take care that your outfits [*atours*] are never excessive. Always incline to the less rather than the more' (*Instructions*, IV, p. 45).

It was apparently the royal saint's custom to encourage discussion of theological and spiritual matters among his immediate followers, and Joinville his biographer (see p. 131 above, composed an explanation and illustration of the Creed (*Credo*) in which each of the twelve articles (traditionally, though not here, ascribed to the twelve apostles – one article each) is illustrated by figures and prophecies from the Old Testament or the Gospels. Joinville explains that his *Creed* was composed while he was with St Louis in Acre during the winter of 1250/1.

Probably the most celebrated manual of religious instruction is *The King's Compendium* (*La Somme le Roy*) composed for Philip the Bold by Brother Lorens in 1279. The large number of surviving manuscripts of both the French text and the English translation attest to the continuing popularity of the work, which contains analyses and commentaries on the Lord's Prayer, the Creed and the Seven Sacraments, as well as many other 'sevens', as indicated in the description of the garden of the virtues in which the seven trees are the virtues, the seven springs the gifts of the Holy Spirit, 'and the seven maidens who draw water from these seven springs are the seven petitions of the *Pater Noster* which pray for the seven gifts of the Holy Spirit' (*Somme*, f. 69vo).[6] Brother Lorens used many different sources for his work, both Latin and French, and much of the material in the *Compendium* is also found in the *Mirror of the World* (*Mirouer du Monde*), another popular and much-copied work. Some of the most original and vivid descriptions are found in the section on the seven sins, common to both *Compendium* and *Mirror*, in which the sins are each sub-divided many times. Thus under Avarice are found analyses of the seven different kinds of usurers as well as various types of merchants, including taverners who make the drinks froth in the glasses so as to serve less, or the public scriveners who show good writing on their samples to get the job and then write badly (*Compendium*, iv, p. 162). Under the sin of Gluttony there are two dialogues, one between the man and his stomach and another between the stomach and the purse, and other lively exclamations: ' "Lady throat you're killing me, I'm so full I shall burst", says the stomach but the throat merely replies: "Even if you burst I'm not going to miss out on this dish" ' (*Compendium*, iv, p. 166). The most complete attack on greed is probably the morality play of the *Condemnation of Feasting* (*Condamnation de Banquet*), in which the gluttonous body is assailed by personified illnesses.

A very different kind of mirror is that also known as *The Sunday Gospels* (*Evangile des Domnees*) or *Mirror* in which the author provides an exegesis on the proper gospels for the different Sundays and feast days. (The 'propers' of a feast were those peculiar to the occasion, in contrast to the 'commons' which were regular parts of the mass: *Agnus Dei*, Creed, and so on.) Robert has a long explanation of his use of the title *Mirror* for his work: 'The mirror is to show man how to adorn himself; this one teaches the true adornment of virtues. The bright mirrors of the world show women how to deck themselves so that they shall be more desirable when they are beautifully adorned; and this one shows the beauty which Jesus truly loves and makes souls shape themselves so that God shall truly desire them' (*Evangile*, 165–76). But although Robert warns and exhorts his readers, he does so quite gently, providing them with an allegorical commentary on the scriptural texts that is interesting, illustrated with lively examples and above all practical. He is aware, too, of the problems posed by linguistic

ignorance when faced with strange language in the Scriptures:
'What is the use of learning the names if one cannot understand
the meanings? For it is of little value to know the names if one
does not know the exegesis. They are all names in Greek which
is virtually unknown to the French' (*Evangile*, 11662–7; Robert
is here talking about the angels and their Nine Orders).
However, he does not merely explain the meanings, he reminds
his hearers that it is no use understanding the names if you do
not 'make an effort to join their company and dwell with them
here in this life' (*Evangile*, 11719–21).

Though rich in prayers and meditations, commentaries and
the medieval equivalent of the Bible Reading Fellowship Notes,
French devotional literature includes little of the visionary,
ecstatic, mystical writing which became common especially in
Northern Europe in the later Middle Ages with the work of
such writers as Brigid of Sweden or Julian of Norwich. Such
writing is not completely unknown in France, however, as can
be seen from the *Speculum* or *Mirror* of Marguerite d'Oingt, the
Carthusian nun who wrote the life of St Beatrice of Ornacieux
(see p. 160 above). Marguerite appears to have been a genuine
contemplative mystic to judge by the Latin *Meditations* and the
vernacular *Mirror* (*Speculum*) in which, for the benefit of her
confessor and spiritual director, she describes in the third
person, in cool, precise language, her visions of Christ and his
passion: 'This glorious Body was so noble and so transparent
that one could clearly see the soul within. This Body was so
noble that one could see oneself in it more clearly than in a
mirror. This Body was so beautiful that one could see in it the
angels and saints as if they were painted there' (*Speculum*, S. 24).
Marguerite's controlled and disciplined reporting of her mystic
experiences belong with the main stream of French medieval
devotional writers for whom even the ecstasies of the visionary
were subject to the rules of obedience and the teachings of
the Church. The price of failure in this respect was high.
Marguerite Porete of Hainault, whose *Mirror of Simple Souls*
(*Miroir des simples Ames*) was widely disseminated in Latin and
English translations, was broken on the wheel in Paris in
1310 for heresy because she claimed that Love was superior to
Reason, and especially that the love-inspired souls were the
real, superior, Holy Church: 'Now tell me, said Love, O Holy

Church inferior to the Holy Church, what do you think of these souls who are thus commended and praised more than you, who do everything by the advice of Reason?' (*Mirror*, S. 43).

The mystic, like the preacher and the moralist, the hagiographer and the passion writer, used symbolic language often of a very visual kind, a practice deriving directly from the parables in the gospels or the allegories of the pauline epistles, as well as the example of numerous Greek and Latin fathers of the Church. Not surprisingly, therefore, a substantial corpus of fully allegorical literature, exemplary, admonitory and devotional was composed in French between the twelfth and sixteenth centuries.

Allegories of Salvation: Guillaume de Deguilleville

GUILLAUME de Deguilleville wrote three verse *Pilgrimages* which, with the *Romance of the Rose* and the prose *Quest of the Holy Grail*, make up the trinity of medieval French allegorical literature.[7]

Composed in the first half of the fourteenth century, when Deguilleville was a monk in the Cistercian house at Chaalis, near Senlis, in northern France, the three long allegorical poems, the *Pilgrimage of Human Life* (*Pèlerinage de Vie Humaine*), the *Pilgrimage of the Soul* (*Pèlerinage de l'Ame*) and *Pilgrimage of Jesus Christ* (*Pèlerinage de Jésus-Christ*) were very successful in their own day, especially the first, which was retold in Latin and French prose versions in the fifteenth century, while English translations of both verse and prose texts were being copied even as late as the seventeenth. Unfortunately for Deguilleville, the inventive detail of his allegory and his fluent but undistinguished style have not stood up to the test of time and the challenge of other works on the same subjects by writers greater than he. The *Pilgrimage of Jesus Christ* cannot compete with the dramatic richness of the passion plays, nor the *Pilgrimage of Human life* with the searing simplicity of Bunyan's *Pilgrim's Progress*, while the *Pilgrimage of the Soul* pales into insignificance beside the poetic genius of the undisputed masterpiece of medieval vision literature, Dante's *Divine Comedy*.

The *Pilgrimage of Human Life* is not just another sermon or moral treatise; it is an allegorical autobiography. Unlike Bunyan's Christian, Deguilleville's Pilgrim is also the narrator and the dreamer, as the Lover is both in the *Romance of the Rose*. It is his own spiritual progress he describes from his first meeting with God's Grace (*GraceDieu*) who leads him to baptism. Afraid to pass through the thorns of penitence, the Pilgrim suffers attacks from many horrific monsters, the seven deadly sins, who are vividly portrayed: Avarice has six hands, 'all for taking, none for giving' and a hump, property, the same hump that prevents the camel going through the eye of the needle and the rich man from entering Heaven (*Human Life*, 9389–90, 10124–34). Eventually, tired of the troubles and dangers of the world, the Pilgrim seeks refuge in the ship of religion and enters the castle of Cîteaux. In the first version of the text, composed in 1331, there is only a general description of the monastery and his profession when the prioress Obedience binds him and gags him 'like a dog on a leash' (13044). Then, a long time after, come Illness and Old Age. In the second, ampler version written twenty years later,[8] the author inserts here an account of a visit made by the Pilgrim to other 'castles' where he finds either corrupt religious, who have forgotten charity, or else true monks harassed by external enemies, from pirates (a genuine hazard of life in the fourteenth century) to corrupt administrators, including the king and the Pope.

The description of the horrors of Sickness and Old Age is very vivid. Old Age reminds him that 'I am she whom you never thought to see when you were with Youth. "She's a long way off," you said, "and moves slowly. She cannot hurry with her feet of lead – I have time to enjoy myself"'. Now I tell you that truly I have feet of lead and go slowly, but bit by bit one can go a long way.' The Pilgrim tries to reject the two figures but is told they will be with him for ever now till Death comes in person. He gradually becomes weaker and is confined to bed in the Infirmary, and then at last, 'suddenly with a start I saw an old woman who had climbed up on to my bed, which frightened me very much and scared me so that I could not speak to her nor ask her anything. She had a sickle in her hand and carried a wooden coffin, and had already put one of her feet on my chest to crush me' (13419–28). *GraceDieu* returns and explains to the Pilgrim that this is Death, the common lot of all, men or women, and she calls on the Pilgrim to prepare for his end since he is at the wicket and the gate which he saw in the mirror long ago. This refers to the reflection of the Holy City which he had been shown 'in a glass darkly' at his baptism. At the last moment, as Death's sickle separates his soul from his body, 'I heard the monastery bell ring for matins as was usual' (13496–8). He wakes up, sweating and much disturbed by his dream which he writes down so that others may learn from it as well as he.

Guillaume's allegory is essentially visual, sometimes almost surrealist in its plethora of significant detail and literal interpretations: thus the well of repentance is an eye from which flow the tears of contrition. Like the *Romance of the Rose*, the text was usually illustrated, and a recurring series of illuminations and later woodcuts represent some of the strange personified abstractions. Although his allegorical moralising can be over-elaborate, especially in the second, enlarged edition of the *Pilgrimage*, there are also vivid, natural and even humorous scenes, such as the Pilgrim's fear of the water of baptism because he can't swim (419–22), and especially the sequence when *GraceDieu* arms him with all the protective armour he needs, including the helmet of Attemprance which has narrow eyelets so no arrow can pass through and wound the wearer to death (4093–6; cf. the arrows of love, p. 74 above). The Pilgrim has no sooner got it all on than he has to remove it.

These arms burden me so much that I cannot walk in them. I shall either have to stay here or take them off. The helmet, above all, is such an impediment that I am deaf and blind and dumbfounded. I see nothing that pleases me and cannot hear what I want to. I can smell nothing, which is a great torment. Then the awful gorget – curse it! – restricts me so by the throat that I think I'm being strangled, and it constricts me so I cannot talk freely nor swallow anything that delights me or is pleasing to my body.   (4523–42)

GraceDieu rebukes him for putting her to the trouble of asking

for the armour 'when you either cannot or will not wear it!'
(4603–6).

A very different attitude to the preparation of the Pilgrim is
displayed in the other allegory of salvation, the *Pilgrimage of
Jesus Christ*, which is a mixture of biblical narrative and
symbolic invention. It opens with the Debate in Heaven and
God's decision to redeem man, after which Christ is armed as
the Pilgrim (*Jesus Christ*, 960–81). Then follows one of Deguilleville's most beautiful visual descriptions, an extended
metaphor of the moment of incarnation developed from
Augustine's simile of the sun passing through glass.

> I saw a very great marvel which must not be forgotten: the
> Virgin without changing her fair fashion appeared like
> crystal in which there was nothing high or low which was not
> quite transparent and as truly diaphanous as clear glass, the
> purest that could be found, and therein the king settled
> himself like the sun, set in the midst in such a way that he
> glowed within her and illumined her. No lantern ever glowed
> from the candle burning within it as brightly as the sun
> which glowed in her.   (*Jesus Christ*, 1345–62)

After comparing this vision with that in the Book of Revelation
of the crowned Virgin with the moon beneath her feet
(Revelation, 12:1), Deguilleville continues: 'Quite soon afterwards I saw how this sun covered himself in a fine cloth, white,
pure and bleached which he found within the Virgin, under
which he veiled his great brightness, so that I saw him clearly in
the form of a human body. . . . He was small and like a child
and spoke to his angels outside' (443–56).

The scenes of Christ's life on earth and his passion are
interspersed with moralisation and commentaries, sometimes
in the form of dialogues, such as the one in which Joseph
explains to Ignorance the reasons for the flight into Egypt and
why Christ allowed the other children to be killed in his place
(3300–570). Deguilleville's style is strongly oral in all his works
and a very high proportion of the poems are in direct speech,
the *Pilgrimage of Jesus Christ* having a particularly dramatic
quality as befits material that was frequently used in plays.

There is also a play of part of the *Human Life*, dramatised by
the simple expedient of cutting out the 'he said' or 'she said',

even at the expense of the scansion, and putting the speaker's name instead at the beginning of the speeches. The result is a fairly conventional morality-play on the nature of the Eucharist and the proper way to approach it – virtually indistinguishable from any other of the numerous morality-plays of the later Middle Ages (see p. 192 below), with the personified faults and foibles, vices and virtues, battling it out on stage in an endless dramatic psychomachia.

One such play, preserved like the Deguilleville dramatisation in a manuscript collection of plays composed by and for the ladies of the convent at Huy, near Liège, is also derived from an allegorical poem, the *Mirror of Life and Death* (*Miroir de Vie et de Mort*).[9] Here the reader or spectator is reminded of the inevitability of death and its sequel, the judgement, which will determine whether the soul will go to Hell or to Heaven: 'Listen now anyone, man or woman, who wants to have a fine stone placed over a body which soon rots in the ground . . . as if his soul were still there. Every man and woman gapes at it and says it's well made, and then they go away from there and make no other prayer for the soul. Many people believe that the soul is nothing else but air' (*Miroir*, S. 515). Then, so that others shall not lack warning, Robert tells of his dream of the tree of sin 'in Romance so that the layman may take example from it' (655–6).

> Great grief is this to us but worse will come!
> We shall be led to Hell, as I believe,
> Nor pain nor torment will be lacking there.
> *(Adam, 546–8)*

Heaven and Hell

SINCE death for the Christian is merely the first of the four last things to be followed by judgement and then Hell or Heaven, it is not surprising that the Middle Ages, with its preoccupation with concrete description and the personification of the abstract, created a plethora of visions of Heaven and Hell in words, music, art and sculpture. Although indisputably the greatest, Dante was neither the first nor the last writer to describe the fate of souls in the hereafter.

Hell was not difficult to represent in an age that believed firmly in the tortures of the damned and was only too familiar with the execution of the living: burning, hanging, breaking on the wheel were common spectacles and well attended by respectable citizens. Hell is therefore as easily comprehended but worse, a spectacle of tangible horror, pain, cacophony and stench, the acme of awfulness.

Numerous descriptions of the torments of Hell are extant in medieval French, some of them intercalated into other works like Judas's brief but vivid explanation to St Brendan of the two Hells: 'No one else has more than one of them but I, the wretched one, have both. One is high up and one low down and the salt sea divides them. . . . The one above is more painful and the one below more horrible, the first in the air is hot and sweating, the one below is cold and stinking' (*Voyage of St Brendan*, 1337–40, 1343–6). One of the most widely used interpolations is the account of Hell given by Lazarus after his raising. In the passion plays this is often included as part of the action, and the warning is thereby made particularly effective. In the *Ste-Geneviève Passion* the speech is a hundred lines long as Lazarus relates the individual torments to specific sins: 'Those who have sinned by hatred have serpents in their company; and those who have performed works of envy, I assure you, the dragon often gnaws their heart and bowels and toads hang from their ears' (*Passion*, 838–44). Lazarus's account is obviously far easier to represent on the stage than the type of Hell described by Judas, and there are extant descriptions of stage structures of Hell which fit very well the former's picture of mobile horrors – serpents, toads and other loathsome creatures:

After this infernal crew came a Hell, fourteen feet long and eight wide, in the form of a rock on which was constructed a tower, continually blazing and shooting out flames, in which Lucifer appeared. . . . He ceaselessly vomited flames, held in his hands various serpents or vipers which moved or spat fire. At the four corners of the rock were four small towers inside which could be seen souls undergoing various torments. And from the front of the rock there came a great serpent, whistling and spitting fire from throat, nostrils and eyes. And on every part of the rock there clambered and climbed all kinds of serpents and great toads.[10]

The many narrative visions of Hell often cast their description in the form of a journey through the infernal regions with various guides. La Motte's *Vision of Hell* (*Voie d'Enfer*) opens with the poet expressing a sudden desire to visit Hell and being offered an immediate escort by Murder and Despair, in whose company he spends a night with each of the seven deadly sins in turn. A more original touch to this type of journey is given in Raoul De Houdenc's twelfth-century *Vision of Hell* (*Songe d'Enfer*) for on his way he lodges at Vile Tavern where he meets Hazard; in a scene which foreshadows the *Jeu de la Feuillée* (see p. 99 above). Raoul discusses with Hazard and Mischance various mutual friends: Hazard asks Raoul for news of Michel de Treilles and tells him in return about Girart de Troies. This method of anchoring the vision in daily reality is not followed up, however, by the actual introduction of these real people. Instead, Raoul goes on to Hell where he is made welcome at the banquet of the sinners, which includes fine fat usurers, larded with other men's money, while the gamey flavour and smell of the old wrinkled whores with their skins like donkeys' hides is much appreciated by some diabolical gourmets, though others prefer the great dish of roast heretics with Paris sauce: 'A sauce of fire with a final dash of damnation. In this sauce I have described, all hot and smoking they were served at the Table of Hell on an iron spit in front of the King' (Raoul, *Vision*, 495–501).

Neither in play nor in poem do we find the devils portrayed as insignificant, though they are often funny. The *Semur Passion* includes a Cook in the hellish crew, *Coquus Inferni*, while the morality of *Bien Avisé, Mal Avisé* (*Well-advised, Ill-advised*) contains the following direction: 'Note that Hell should be arranged like the kitchen in the house of a lord' (*Comédie*, p. 81).[11] Many texts give names, often Classical, and individual identities to the inhabitants of Hell. There is much cruelty and viciousness in these devils but little grandeur: only the devil who tempts Adam in the Anglo-Norman play can begin to rank among Milton's 'grand infernal peers'.

The place of torment is only one of the four regions of Hell according to most medieval commentators, the others being Limbo, where the souls of the Old Testament righteous awaited the coming of Christ; Purgatory, where the penitent are purged of the sins they had confessed but not done penance for; and the place of the unbaptised children (*Ste-Geneviève Passion*, 892–914). Guillaume de Deguilleville compares the layers of Hell to a nut with the Pit of Hell in the centre as the kernel; then the skin, Limbo (which for him is the place of the unbaptised children, forever debarred from the Vision of God); next the shell, the region of Purgatory; and around that a sort of halo, Abraham's Bosom, the place of the redeemed Old Testament righteous, the outer husk (*Soul*, 3593–752). Lazarus in the *Passion* is, of course, speaking of the regions of Hell in the period before the redemption and Deguilleville after it.

Deguilleville's *Pilgrimage of the Soul* is the second of his works and describes the fate of the Pilgrim after death. The Soul comes first to the place of judgement before the heavenly tribunal presided over by St Michael, such as can be seen depicted in many sculptured portrayals of the judgement on the tympana of church doorways, for example the church of St Foy at Conques in southern France. Deguilleville elaborates the scene, introducing Justice, Reason and Truth as prosecuting counsel, though the most damning witness against the Pilgrim is his own conscience (*Synderesis*). Even when St Benedict, founder of his monastic order, adds his merits to the right-hand pan, the Soul sees the scales of justice tipped against him until Mercy arrives with God's own testimony in writing: the grace of the redemption is sufficient to redress the balance and the Soul is saved from the Hell of the unrepentant, though he must still pass through the fire of Purgatory before he can enter the Heavenly City. His sins are bound on his back in a bundle (reminding us of Christian's burden in Bunyan) and then he takes his place in the fire till all the sin shall be burnt away. The doctrine of the cleansing fire of Purgatory is put forward by St Augustine in the *City of God* and developed by many subsequent writers. The most important aspect of the doctrine is that it is a penance undergone willingly by the soul to prepare it for its future glory, not a punishment reluctantly accepted.[12]

A well-known medieval description of Purgatory is that

given in the early Latin text of the *Vision of St Patrick's Purgatory*. A certain island in Lough Derg in Western Ireland was traditionally the entrance to the underworld which could be visited by those who were prepared and strong enough to confront the perils of the journey: a sort of ultimate pilgrimage. This Latin text was first translated into French by Marie de France: 'for I desire to help many people to profit by this and mend their ways, to serve and fear God more' (*Patrick's Purgatory*, 17–20).

Unlike Dante's great description in the *Purgatorio*, the Irish Purgatory is indistinguishable from Hell in the types and horror of the torments described. The only difference is that the former are not eternal and can be eased by the prayers and alms of the living. Finally, if he resists the attacks of the devils during his tour of the torments, the pilgrim–explorer crosses a narrow bridge over the Pit of Hell and finds his way to the bliss of the Earthly Paradise en route for the Celestial City.

Deguilleville is the only French writer to break away from this traditional picture of Purgatory and his Soul has some very different experiences. He is first set in the fire, where he is comforted by the presence of his guardian angel who never leaves him and answers all the questions he asks about the region they are in. Although the Soul is suffering greatly from the fire, as he tells us, there are no other torments and from time to time Prayer arrives with boxes of ointment, the prayers of the living, which are cooling balm to the burning pilgrim. Towards the end of his thousand years of purgation the Pilgrim Soul, still wrapped in flame, is taken by the angel on a visit to other regions, passing through physical obstacles with the ease of Scrooge and the Spirit of Christmas. He sees souls doing penance in the place of their sin and talks to some of them, passes near the Pit which allows the opportunity for a brief description of the horrors of Hell, and at one point comes to the place where his own body is awaiting the last trumpet. In a scene of high comedy the Soul and Body argue vehemently as to who is responsible for the pains they are having to suffer, till they are stopped by the angel: ' "What's this?" he said, "Have you found cause to quarrel already? It's time to stop this arguing between you two for it is not helpful for your salvation." Then my body lay down again at once and didn't say another word.' At last the Pilgrim's sins are all burnt away and the angel tells him he can now pass into Heaven (*Soul*, 4331–48).

Heaven is a place of perfect beauty, appealing to all the senses, so that it is usually portrayed as filled with flowers and fine colours, harmonious music and sweet smells. The Heaven of the passion plays required rich hangings, a throne for God, music and often a wheel or circle of artificial angels behind the throne. Deguilleville has an original variant on the theme of the wheel and the heavenly host, for the Soul sees a great series of concentric, many-coloured, brilliant circles revolving through the zodiac and learns it is the calendar of saints. Every day is a festival in Heaven but some are more gloriously celebrated than others. One of the most interesting he describes is the feast of the conception of the Virgin, 'when she was planted and cleansed of the sin of her line' (*Soul*, 9851–2). The doctrine of the immaculate conception was only declared dogma in 1854 after centuries of argument. In the Middle Ages the idea that Mary was conceived without original sin, though popular, was not accepted by many of the theologians including St Bernard and Thomas Aquinas. Its importance in Deguilleville's *Pilgrimage of the Soul* is described as being because it is the first step towards the birth of Christ and the redemption.

As there has been no harmony in Heaven since the Fall of Man, to celebrate it worthily the angels decide to take music lessons: 'Let us all go to the music schools to learn harmony and rhythm' (9867–9). Cherubim approves but suggests that they cannot do much with voices only: 'But instruments in which you have to blow or touch them to make them work – we could do very little without them' (9883–6). Lacking these necessary adjuncts of heavenly harmony, some of the angels proceed to Limbo where they notify the waiting patriarchs of the imminence of salvation and also consult David, the harper, on how to make musical instruments. They learn quickly, and the combination of their new skill in making such instruments as they need, coupled with the daily music lessons of the singing angels produces such 'echoes of sound, songs and melodies and sweet harmonies that the whole sky was amazed; having never heard such sound!' (9946–50). Orpheus himself was as nothing in comparison for sound or art.

Not all medieval writers were content merely to portray the marvels of Heaven; they sought also to explore the mysteries of God, and with a boldness which transcends blasphemy they reported the secret counsels of the Holy Trinity. The trial or debate in Heaven and its related theme of the Four Daughters of God derives ultimately from a sermon of St Bernard (*On the Annunciation*, II) in which he introduces the personified virtues from the reference in Psalm 84 (Vulgate numbering), 'Mercy and truth have met each other: justice and peace have kissed' (v. 11). The reconciliation of justice and peace is achieved by the Atonement, as a result of which Man and God are once more 'at one'. The theme of the debate of the virtues, the Daughters of God, representing different attributes of the Godhead, became very popular in literature because it was convenient and enabled writers to present theological arguments in an easily comprehensible way. It was particularly effective in dramatic form and there are numerous versions of the scene in plays from all parts of Europe. In France, two versions developed, one of them being more legalistic and therefore known as the trial in Heaven. Justice rejects Mercy's plea for the redemption of man on the grounds that he is unable to make the necessary legal restitution: he cannot pay the price of his sin, his debt to God. After a long argument (1300 lines in Greban's *Passion*) the virtues, led by Truth, finally refer the question to God the Father: man cannot pay the price, but God could, if he were willing. God reluctantly agrees. This kind of legal argument was apparently acceptable to medieval audiences for it appears in many French plays, but a more obviously attractive version of the scene, the debate, is also found in various forms. In the *Creation and Fall* play of the Old Testament group (*Viel Testament*), God informs Justice and Mercy immediately after the Fall that he intends eventually to redeem man and, when Justice questions this, explains that he will send the oil of mercy to cleanse him and bring him not to Earthly Paradise from which he has been debarred but to the *Paradis Celeste* (1834). The oil of mercy in the medieval legends of the holy cross was the Incarnate Christ.

Another type of debate is that given in the Semur play in which Charity and Hope intercede with God who then explains to them the difficulty which faces him: 'Although I can destroy all and create all I cannot free myself from myself. I who am truth could not lie, for if I lied I would not be God' (*Semur Passion*, 1758–61). This kind of divine self-analysis is a very different thing from the thomistic legalism of the trial scenes, though the result is, of course, essentially the same; God will redeem man by making a new earthly paradise: 'It is the body of the Virgin into which I shall descend' (*Semur Passion*, 1787). God will become the fruit of life which can be given to man and the theme of fruit is developed in the later part of the play as the fruit of life is given to the apostles in the Eucharist. It seems likely that the Semur author took this theme from Deguilleville for in the last, rather incoherent, section of Deguilleville's *Pilgrimage of the Soul*, the theme of the fruit of salvation is elaborated in several ways, culminating in the Pilgrim's seeing two trees – a dead one (the cross) and a living one (the Virgin) whose fruit is taken and hung on the dead tree: 'The apple from the sweet, green apple-tree was hung on the dry tree so high and publicly that from near and far all men of every place and district saw the restitution' (*Soul*, 6344–8). The allegory of the fruit culminates in a scene where St Peter comes from God and gives communion to Adam and Eve: 'And he had the table set down on which were only bread and wine. "Now then," he said, "old father Adam and you old mother Eve, I have come to make you taste a dish, a new food, so that you can judge afterwards which fruit, the old or the new is more worthy and more valuable" ' (*Soul*, 10593–601).

Redeemed by Christ, the first fruit, succoured by the Church which gives him the new fruit, purified by Purgatory, the Pilgrim Soul will await in Heaven the resurrection of the body and the Last Judgement:

And Our Lord Jesus Christ, the son of St Mary, who suffered on the cross and brought us to life from death . . . grant us to live and die in him . . . and if anyone weakens anything in this prophecy may God take from him his place in the book of life and in the holy city as he has said. . . . The grace of our lord Jesus Christ who blesses us with his hand be with us. AMEN. (*French Apocalypse*, 4522–3, 4530, 4485–7, 4491–3)

7. A Stage is All the World

> The dog who preferred the reflection of his bone in the water to the bone itself, though from a practical point of view he made a lamentable mistake, was aesthetically justified.
>
> (Havelock Ellis)

THEATRE is the least literary and most social of all the verbal arts. The poet or story-teller (unless he is working in an oral tradition) completes his work and the reader is then merely the recipient of his creation; but a play is not really complete until it is performed and the performance requires both actors and spectators, for without an audience there can be no real theatre.[1] Drama is therefore essentially a group activity and the two *milieux* in which it flourished in the Middle Ages were the civic and religious communities, the city and the church.

Play texts in French are to be found in the twelfth century and Latin drama already in the eleventh, but the golden age of early drama was the fifteenth century where it provided the richest harvest of the autumn of medieval literature. Evidence for performance is widespread and the bulk of surviving texts enormous: some million lines of religious drama and several hundred plays in the categories loosely described as secular – farces, moralities and *sotties*. The two classes of drama can be considered separately since they were composed and performed mostly by different groups of people, though like the romance and the *fabliau* they shared a common readership, a common audience.

Staging the Past: Biblical and Saints' Plays

RELIGIOUS drama takes its subject-matter from the past, the Bible or the lives of saints, only a few miracle plays having a contemporary setting. Like the epics and the romances, these

184

plays bring the past to life for their audiences by a judicious blend of historical detail and contemporary manners. The use of accurate period costume on the stage does not begin to appear until the eighteenth century, with the tentative audaciousness of Voltaire and Diderot, and the use of everyday costume is the more significant in plays performed by amateurs in their home community. The Jews who condemn Christ, or the Romans who torture the saints, are indistinguishable in appearance from the neighbours, friends and kinsmen of the spectators who thus find themselves involved in the action in a more intense and significant way, especially when there are no proscenium arch and footlights to separate stage and auditorium.

These biblical plays had another hold on their audiences, for they were closely linked with the liturgy from which they sprang. The Latin sung drama, which burgeoned in the jubilant atmosphere of Easter Day and Christmas and has survived in hundreds of manuscripts from all over Europe, was as much an expression of joy and praise as the bells and music, incense and vestments of these solemn feasts. Music drama, be it the *Visit to the Sepulchre*, the *Daniel* plays or Wagner's *Ring*, depends on the audience knowing the story, but not all theatre is operatic in its assumptions, relying on sound and sight, music and mime to convey its meaning direct to the receptive senses. The liturgy included preaching as well as prayer, learning as well as adoration, and to put over logical or theological arguments required a spoken not a sung text, and the use of the vernacular for the benefit of those who had no *clergie*. French spoken drama developed side by side with Latin sung drama, supplementing and eventually surpassing, but never entirely superseding it.

With certain exceptions which have been mentioned already (see p. 94 above), vernacular drama has left few traces before the fourteenth century in the form of either texts or records of performance, nor is there a great deal even then: only the first short passion plays, the *Palatinus* and *Autun Passions* and the *Day of Judgement* (*Jour du Jugement*) and, above all, a group of forty *Miracles of the Virgin* (*Miracles de la Vierge*) preserved in a single manuscript collection, known to have been written and performed for and possibly by the Goldsmiths' Guild in Paris between 1330–90 (see p. 156 above).

Producing a play even with amateurs needs some kind of organisation within which to work and medieval religious plays were staged by one of three kinds of community: a religious confraternity like the Brotherhood of the Passion (*Confrérie de la Passion*), a trade guild such as the Goldsmiths or the Shoemakers, or a civic community, like Mons or Romans or Seurre.

(a)   *Guilds and Fraternities: the Brotherhood of the Passion*

When in 1401, King Charles VI gave letters-patent to the Paris Brotherhood of the Passion he was confirming and legalising an already active and well-known group of actors. There are records of performances in and around Paris for many years before the charter, including one piece of indirect evidence of the hazards of medieval stage production: in 1380, during the performance of a passion play, a cannon went off prematurely and inaccurately and the burning wad struck the assistant machinist who subsequently died from his injuries. The text of the royal exoneration which freed the machinist from any criminal blame in this matter includes a reference to the use of cannon at the crucifixion: 'as it is the custom to do at the said plays each year in Paris' (see *The Staging of Religious Drama in Europe in the Later Middle Ages*, p. 191).

The kind of regular annual performance suggested by this document was rare in France except for the performance of saints' plays by the trade guilds, whose right to stage a play on their own patron saint was not abrogated by the monopoly granted to the Brotherhood of the Passion. Although a considerable number of such plays have survived we have few details about the organisation and mode of presentation of what were often essentially private performances with restricted audiences.

The groups that performed publicly, like the Brotherhood of the Passion, were the religious fraternities whose members were largely drawn from the merchant and artisan classes and which, like the *Confrérie des Jongleurs et Bourgeois d'Arras* (see p. 94 above), combined spiritual and social benefits for their members, like modern benevolent societies or masonic lodges.

Such societies abounded in the Middle Ages all over Europe in scores of towns and under as many names. Nor did the title of the group limit the range of their performances: the many 'Brotherhoods of the Passion' might stage saints' plays or even secular ones, while a passion play might be mounted by any confraternity. The great passion play of Lucerne was under the control of the Brotherhood of the Coronation, while the Company of the Bannerbearers of Saint Lucy was responsible for the annual passion play staged in the Colosseum in Rome from 1460 to 1540 (see *Staging, passim*).

When the Paris Brotherhood of the Passion received the royal charter in 1401 they already possessed a headquarters in the church of La Trinité, and they proceeded to convert the adjoining hospital into a theatre where they presented plays for the next century or more. In 1539 they moved to the Hôtel de Flandres, and when that was demolished in 1545 they took over and refurbished the Hôtel de Bourgogne. But their time was running out, and when they applied in August 1548 for permission to restart their performances in their new theatre they were allowed to do so but only on condition that they did not play 'the mystery of the Passion of our Lord nor any sacred mystery on pain of immediate fine' (Petit de Julleville, *Les Mystères*, I, p. 129). It was the death knell of the group, which had derived fame and finance from playing the biblical plays, and although they struggled on against all odds for another century, they were unable to compete with the new professional groups, first from Italy and then from other parts of France, who performed the now popular Classical tragedies and comedies in the theatre of the *Confrérie de la Passion*. When the Brotherhood was finally disbanded by Louis XIV in 1676, Molière was already dead, Corneille had retired from the theatre and Racine was about to present his last great secular tragedy: *Phèdre* was first performed in 1677.

Despite its importance as France's first regular theatre company, the Brotherhood of the Passion's activities in the fifteenth century are virtually undocumented. It is possible that the collection of plays in the Ste-Geneviève manuscript, including a Creation, Passion and Resurrection with a number of saints' plays, represents an early repertoire of the Brotherhood (the manuscript is from Paris and the plays were composed in the late fourteenth to early fifteenth century), but such a link is only speculation. The best known of the Brotherhood's performances are the last ones, the *Acts of the Apostles* in 1540 and the *Old Testament* in 1541. The former used a revised version of the text prepared for the great production in Bourges in 1536 (see p. 158 above). It is an immense play of some 62,000 lines and using 500 performers, so the Brotherhood made a great 'cry et proclamation publique' to announce their performance and recruit actors. The *Acts* were immensely successful and played on Sundays and holidays for several months in 1540 but when the group wanted to stage the *Old Testament*, another huge undertaking, the following year they were allowed to do so only under strict limitations. They might only play on certain days and at certain times and the price of admission was also fixed, at 2 *sous* per person; they had to ensure there was no uproar or scandal and, in addition, 'because the people will be distracted from divine service and this will diminish the alms giving, they shall pay to the poor the sum of one thousand pounds' (*Mystères*, I, p. 425; see p. 198 below). It says much for the financial soundness of the company and the numbers of spectators they could count on attracting that they paid the money and went ahead with the performance.

Although they had a permanent theatre and charged admission, neither the Paris confraternity nor any of the other groups who staged plays in the provinces were professional; only minstrels (*jongleurs*) and musicians were professionally organised in the Middle Ages. These acting groups were very similar to the modern English phenomenon of the amateur dramatic society, with a core of members performing plays at regular intervals but retaining their normal professions and jobs. The admission charges financed the production, not the performers. Plays so staged are recorded in many towns in France right through the fifteenth and sixteenth centuries and there is also some evidence of touring by the Paris Brotherhood to nearby towns like Rouen. However, outside Paris the large-scale productions were normally a special occasion, such as a modern arts festival, and the preparations and performance were organised by the civic authorities rather than any one group or individual.

(b)   '*To comb and mirror, 18d.*': *the Civic Plays*

In contrast to the general absence of details on the staging of the
guild and confraternity plays, we have the text and detailed
accounts for the production of the play of the *Three Martyrs*
(*Trois Doms*) in Romans in 1509, and the accounts and
producer's copies of the *Mystery of the Passion* performed at Mons
in 1501, as well as much information of a more fragmentary
kind from other towns.

Most civic plays were multi-day occasions: like Wagner's
Ring, Shakespeare's *Henry VI* or a Test Match, they occupied
several consecutive days or a series of Sundays and feast days.
Each play or scene was performed once only on a purpose-built
stage which allowed simultaneous presentation of an unspeci-
fied number of locations. The stage or *hourd* and the stands for
the audience were constructed of wood by the local carpenters
(a number of contracts have survived) and many other trades
were also involved: boatmen provided the huge, flat-bottomed
ferry which represented the Sea of Galilee at Mons and the
small skiff which floated on the waters amidst the sheepskin
waves: 'item, for five sheepskins to make the waves, 29*s*' (*Mons
Passion*, p. 531); glove-makers sold baskets of leather scraps to
be boiled down for glue; iron-workers forged the Jaws of Hell
and the machinery to lift Christ up to the top of the Mount of
the Transfiguration. Most actors provided their own clothes,
but the drapers and tailors were paid for the material and
making-up of the robe of special white *treille* (a silk/wool
mixture) worn by the Transfigured Christ. The sewing thread
cost 9*d*.

Members of these same guilds of tailors and carpenters,
iron-workers or glove-makers also acted in the plays, together
with other townsfolk, clergy and even a few women, and formed
an important part of the audience. At Romans the carpenters
had a free box as part of their fee for making the *hourd*, and the
Romans boxes were particularly sophisticated, with individual lockable doors, a guard-rail to prevent the children
falling out and privies at each end of the access gallery (*Staging*,
p. 62). These large-scale plays with enormous casts attracted
equally large audiences, whose refusal to listen quietly is
reflected in many prologues and opening speeches. 'But take

care whatever happens not to make an uproar . . . and if anyone is bored or annoyed by our play I advise him to go away and leave the others in peace' (*Mystères*, I, p. 247). Sometimes the tone was more cajoling, as in the *Play of the Martyrs* (*Cycle des Premiers Martyrs*) where, after the *Ave Maria*, the Prologue continues: 'Good people, listen a little, quietly, without making a fuss. You'll have less trouble, be assured, if you consent to be silent a while than if you jostle one another or make an uproar or disturbance. Now sit down and listen and you'll hear what I am trying to say' (*Martyrs*, 11–18). When all else failed the producer had one trump card: stage noise. 'Let the daughter of the Canaanite begin the day raving like one possessed of the devil until there is decent silence' (Michel's *Passion*, p. 107). The potential risk of trouble with these huge audiences is indirectly reflected at Mons where the council agreed not to admit children under ten, the old and infirm, and pregnant women (*Mons Passion*, p. 591). A full day's perform- ance might last from morning (at Mons the audience was not allowed in until nine o'clock) to early evening, with a break at noon to allow cast and audience to have dinner, sometimes in the stands as at the *Play of St Louis*: 'For the players want to rest a bit and refesh themselves with a drink, it's the best way; and within half an hour we'll begin again . . . for we shall not be very long, so let no one leave his place for you will only have to wait a short time' (*St Louis*, p. 83). At Mons, on the other hand, the cast all ate at the various local inns in groups, so the break must have been much longer: 'After dinner we'll continue' (*Mons Passion*, p. 35).

These civic plays were thus very much a community effort involving the whole town. Once the initial decision had been taken, the town council would often appoint a group of senior townsmen (*echevins*) to supervise the overall arrangements, while an experienced director (*régisseur*) might be brought in from outside the district to oversee the details of the perform- ance, and especially to organise the special effects – fireworks and cannons, trap-doors, machinery and décors, those of Heaven and Hell requiring particular attention. The Hell's Mouth at Mons needed sixteen men to work the effects: cannon, thunder-machine, opening and closing the Jaws, and so on.

Obviously these elaborate productions were very expensive and money was needed for the preparations. This might be provided by the town, the local church, or wealthy, pious individuals. Sometimes the actors contributed a fixed sum beforehand in exchange for a share in the hypothetical profits. The *Mons Passion*, which took eight days to perform, cost £2281. 18s. 6d. while the income from the admission charges and selling off the timber and scenery afterwards amounted to only £1338. 4s. 4d. The substantial loss was met by the town. Romans, on the other hand, with a more modest three-day play but having also less appeal to the surrounding area than the Mons players, made a loss of nearly a thousand florins (a florin was worth 12s.). The use of £.s.d. as money of account was widespread in France in the later Middle Ages, the pound in question being either the *livre parisis* or the *livre tournois* (see p. 196 below; in the fifteenth century the pound sterling was worth about £7–£10 *tournois*).[2]

The careful detail of play-accounts means that a great deal of economic information can be derived from them as they are invariably dated and include wages for skilled and unskilled workers and the cost of basic foodstuffs, since meat and bread were used for meals on the stage and itemised, as in these few examples from Mons: carpenters and painters are paid 8s. *per diem*; a plasterer with his boy gets 12s.; a guard at the town gate, 2s. 6d (he was standing in for one of the actors). A man with a horse and cart was paid 18d. per journey. The cost of living is indicated by such entries as 5s. a measure (1/2 gallon) of wine; 20s. a barrel for beer and 16s. for a roast lamb. A shoulder and breast of roast mutton cost 12s. Bread is not quantified but ranges from 4s. to 10s. per day on the stage for meals in the play (and once for the children in Heaven!), the five loaves for the miracle of the feeding of the five thousand cost 1s. each (as did the white, flat bread-cakes for Melchisedech – see Genesis 14:18), while the two fishes, together with the other fish, carp and pike for the stage banquet of Herod and the meal at Simon the Leper's house, together cost 32s. All the meals that day were fish because it was Friday, a fast day.

Although the economics of the plays were important to the medieval impresarios, a financial loss did not imply a dramatic or civic failure. The influx of visitors to the town, the presence of important dignitaries, full employment of the tradesmen for many months beforehand: all these advantages were also appreciated as well as the outstanding 'invisible asset' of the civic religious drama, the spiritual benefits that accrued to the organisers, players and audience alike, for the passion play was the mirror of the sufferings of Christ: 'and so that you may look in it and humbly reflect on it we bring before your eyes as best we may, corporeally, played out by men this devout mirror. If you are wise you'll look in it, for everyman sees his image there, and who looks well at himself, well sees himself' (Greban's *Passion*, 19952–9).

Staging the Present: Moralities, Farces and *Sotties*

THE great passion plays with their unities of eternity, infinity and the history of man belong with the megaliths, the Bayeux Tapestry and stained-glass windows, the *Divine Comedy* and Arthurian romance, *Summa Theologica* and Gothic cathedrals, the macrocosm of the medieval genius; but under the huge legs of this cultural colossus the petty men of the farces, moralities and *sotties* peep about their microcosm of miniatures, marginalia and misericords.

The secular drama, treating of the contemporary world, the *saeculum*, comprised three main types of play: the morality, the farce and the *sottie*, which appear at first sight to be easily distinguishable. The morality presented personified abstractions or allegories, 'for instruction in manners' (Sibilet, *Art Poétique*, in *Comédie*, p. 50), while the farce, like its narrative ancestor the *fabliau*, portrayed scenes and characters from contemporary society: 'and there should be cause for mirth in every line' (Delaudun, *Art Poétique*, in *Comédie*, p. 67). The *sottie* is a peculiarly French type of play performed by actors wearing the headgear of fools (*sots*), the traditional long-eared cap of the jester: 'It is called a *sottie* in France because the *sots* enact the great follies of men of great renown or petty men in polished language on the stage' (Bouchet, *Epistre Morale*, p. 13). All three genres were performed by the societies and groups which abounded in towns in medieval France.

(a)   *The King of the 'Basoche' and the Prince of Fools*

The two best-known groups of players of the huge surviving repertory of secular drama were the *Basoche* and the *Enfants-sans-Souci*. The *Basoche* (from the Latin *basilica*: royal hall of justice) was the name given in the fifteenth century to the association of law-clerks attached to one or other of the great legal/administrative centres of Paris or any large town. In Paris the *Basoche* was formed of the clerks from the *Parlement de Paris* (the supreme court of justice, but not a law-making body) while the clerks of the Châtelet, the centre for law-enforcement in Paris, were referred to as the Little *Basoche*. A third group, the clerks of the Treasury (*Chambre des Comptes*) were organised into the *Empire de Galilée* but rarely performed plays. The two *Basoches* were highly organised, like most medieval confraternities, with the king and his ministers having total control over the activities of the group. They had certain fixed days each year for their guild activities, the *Basoche* itself meeting at Epiphany, early in May and especially in July when they had a great procession or *montre* of costumed groups each under their appointed leader. The *Basoche* of the Châtelet had their procession on Shrove Tuesday right through until the eighteenth century. The earliest document concerning the *Basoches* to mention plays dates only from 1442, but it is in the form of an act of the *Parlement* condemning the actors to several days in prison for having disobeyed the order forbidding them to perform plays. It is thus certain that such performances were known before this date. A little more information comes from an edict of 1476 forbidding them to 'perform farces or moralities, publicly or otherwise, on the first of May without permission and a licence' (*Comédiens*, p. 101).

These continual attacks by the authorities are not surprising when we consider the surviving texts of these plays, for the *Basoche* were invariably satirical and their targets varied from their own legal profession to the more dangerous quarries of the royal family or the Church. They flourished above all in the reign of Louis XII (1498–1515) for the king, whose nickname was the Father of his People, was prepared to tolerate their attacks provided they were not too impudent about the royal person and avoided satire about the queen, Anne of Brittany.

As a contemporary author put it: 'the king, Louis XII, wanted them to perform them [plays] in Paris and said that by these plays he learnt of many faults which were hidden from him by over-cautious advisers' (Bouchet, *Epistre Morale*, p. 13).

Jean Bouchet, like many other respectable citizens of the fifteenth and sixteenth centuries, was a former *basochien*, and there seems to have existed an extensive 'old-boy network' of these writers. Bouchet, for example, composed an epistle to the *Roy de la Bazoche de Bourdeaulx* in which he reminds him of his duties as king to 'declare by grave tragedy, rude satire and feigned comedy the good of the good and the evil of the wicked' (*Epistre familière*, XLII). It seems unlikely, however, that the *Basoche* in Bordeaux was any more inclined than its counterpart in Paris to deal in grave tragedy: rude satire was their common mode of performance, and many of the moralities and *sotties* they performed, as well as the farces, were crude in their humour and cruel in their criticism.

The groups known as *Enfants-sans-Souci* (or some similar name in other towns) were rather different from the *basochiens* in their origins and formation, having no professional link binding them to each other, nor any specific axe to grind. They drew their membership mainly from the middle and upper middle classes (many *basochiens* were also *sots*), and the only common denominator seems to have been their youth. They were, however, formally organised, recognised societies ruled by the *Prince des Sots* (Prince of Fools) and *Mère Sotte* (Mother Fool). Like the *basochiens*, they presented plays on a wide range of subjects, in the three major modes of farce, *sottie* or morality.

Both in Paris and the provinces between 1400 and 1550 numerous 'joyous societies' (*sociétés joyeuses*) were formed in addition to the two major groups so far considered. These societies, like the *puys* (the literary societies, see p. 94 above), linked groups of citizens informally for the purpose of enjoying themselves and on occasion giving entertainment to others. Even less formal groups seem to have combined in some towns for the purpose of putting on plays and taking part in competitions. At Draguignan in 1462 and at Toulon in 1494 a number of townsfolk including churchmen, professional men and tradesmen joined themselves together by contract to present a play, agreeing to rehearse and perform at the arranged times without fail, 'and anyone who is not at the rehearsal at the prearranged time and place must pay a penny [*gros*] each time to be put into the common fund of the society' (*Répertoire*, p. 338). Such contracts were not uncommon for the big, civic mysteries, as at Valenciennes in 1547 (*Staging*, p. 41). The towns of northern France seem to have been the most interested in competitions and there are many references from Lille, Béthune and St-Omer, for example, to groups being rewarded by their native town for bringing glory to it by winning prizes at such a contest.[3] In Arras in 1431 the *Puy* organised a *concours* to which Cambrai, Douai and Valenciennes sent entries: 'They performed plays, and prizes were given for the best actors as well as the best poets' (*Répertoire*, pp. 328–9). These performers were possibly of a superior class to the group from St-Omer under Jehan Descamps, or Wastelet, a barber, who several times took part in such contests. In 1444 Wastelet was given 25*s*. from the town's funds *en courtoisie*, while in 1462 the same Jehan Descamps and several of his friends went to the town of Aire, 'and there over four days they performed in the evenings several morality plays and performed so well and skilfully that they received the first prize and one or two others'. They were given £12 towards their expenses on that occasion (*Mystères à Saint-Omer*, p. 362).

A very wide range of dramatic and semi-dramatic performances are recorded from the later Middle Ages, ranging from mock sermons to full-scale passions and saints' plays, and with few exceptions the actors are amateurs. Professional status might be claimed for the *farceurs* who performed at weddings and were paid, as the minstrels were on such occasions. 'When the wedding day approaches you must . . . hire the minstrels and the *farceurs*', says the poem 'Evils of Marriage', adding that the day after the festivities 'the cook will come, the minstrels, the taverner, the *farceurs* and the caterers to get their wages' (*Comédiens*, pp. 330–1). We can also attribute official standing to the players who formed part of some royal and noble households from the late fourteenth century. These entertainers had the same status and role as the minstrels (*Comédiens*, p. 325) but the vast majority of medieval players were amateurs with other jobs and professions. They might be merely an *ad hoc* group from the 'towns and villages' enacting scenes (*hystoires*) from the passion story during a series of Lenten sermons – as at Laval in 1507, 'with curtains of cloth of gold and silk'. When it was time to draw back the curtains the preacher altered his usual text, and instead of singing *veritatis*, he sang 'There, sirs you may see' (*ostendatis*: it seems probable the *hystoires* were in fact tableaux; *Mystères*, I, p. 203).

Many of the big religious processions, especially those for Corpus Christi, were enriched by the inclusion of set-pieces either at stations along the route or on floats that formed part of the *cortège* accompanying the Blessed Sacrament. Many descriptions of these have survived, especially from Draguignan where they go back to 1437 when a florin was given to the organiser of the play which 'he is accustomed to put on for the Feast of Corpus Christi, and which he cannot do without a subsidy' (*Mystères*, I, p. 208). More interesting, perhaps, are the records from Béthune, where the annual Corpus Christi procession was organised by the trade guilds like the English Corpus Christi plays. However, there seems no reason to think that the floats with biblical scenes allocated to different groups, described in the records for 1549, were other than tableaux or at most mimes (*Mystères*, I, p. 212).[4] The strictly religious processions naturally inspired only religious plays and tableaux, but processions were also organised for more secular, civic and national occasions. The raising of the Siege of Orleans by the English in 1429 was celebrated by an annual procession on 8 May which was sometimes supplemented by stages bearing tableaux of an appropriate kind: in 1439 Jehan Hilaire was paid for the purchase of a standard and banner to be used in the representation of the attack on the Tourelles when they were recaptured from the English, 'seven *livres tournois* which are worth in Paris 112 *sous parisis*' (*Mystères*, I, p. 192). This is a rare example of the rate of exchange being given and indicates clearly the difference that might operate between the local monetary systems. The rate of 16*s. parisis* to 20*s. tournois* was constant throughout the period.

By far the commonest secular occasions for presenting plays, mimes or dumb-shows, however, were the Solemn Entries of king, emperor or other royal personage. These occasions were always as gorgeous and elaborate as the town could afford: in

1455 the Duke of Burgundy was greeted in Arras with a series of stages representing the story of Gideon in mime, 'living people who did not speak or do anything except make the gestures of the story'. It was reputed to have cost the town a thousand gold crowns (*Mystères*, II, p. 194). Indeed at Montélimar in 1513 the corporation decided they could not afford to stage the Passion during the forthcoming visit of Louis XII as they had no money to pay for the stages or the effects (*Mystères*, II, p. 204). Often the subject-matter of these entries would be a mixture of biblical and Classical subjects or allegories. When Charles VIII entered Abbeville in 1493 he was shown a series of tableaux illustrating the different phrases of the hymn *Ave maris stella* in honour of the Virgin Mary, the final tableau being a Paradise with the Trinity 'splendidly placed in front of a bright sun which turned continuously' (*Mystères*, II, p. 200).

Some of the most detailed records for the Royal Entries survive from Paris. The sovereign would ride on horseback through the streets where different groups, *basochiens*, *confréries* or tradesmen would present their offering in the form of a tableau, mime or short allegorical speech. Traditionally the *Confrérie de la Passion* had their 'stand' outside the Hospice of La Trinité where they had their theatre and they usually presented a biblical scene. For the ten-year-old Henry VI of France and England in 1431 there was 'on stages the mystery from the Conception of Our Lady as far as Joseph taking her into Egypt . . . and the stages stretched from a short distance past the church of Saint Sauveur as far as the end of the rue d'Ernetal' (*Mystères*, II, p. 190). But the *Confrérie de la Passion* was not the only group to have a regular location; the *Enfants-sans-Souci* under the guidance of their *Mère Sotte*, Pierre Gringore, presented tableaux outside the Châtelet at many Royal Entries between 1500 and 1520. Gringore and a carpenter named Jean Marchand collaborated on the presentation, for which they were paid by the city. The usual fee was £100, for building the stages and *composer les mystères*, which probably means arranging the subjects and characters in the tableaux, as well as writing the words for the singers who formed part of the presentation, at least in 1514 where their receipt mentions they had 'had the scaffolds made, composed the mysteries, the clothes of the characters, hired tapestries, paid the singers, minstrels and other persons who took part in the mysteries which had to be prepared for the entry of the queen at the gate of the Châtelet in Paris' (*Mystères*, II, p. 205; the queen was Mary of England who was married to the old Louis XII a few months before his death).

The collaboration between the *Confrérie de la Passion*, the *Basoche* and the *Enfants-sans-Souci* in such public celebrations may have been involuntary but the three groups had a good working relationship, as can be seen from the fact that from about 1440 onwards the *Enfants* or the *basochiens* regularly put on farces at La Trinité on days when the *Confrérie* were not performing. It was the secular plays of this kind that they were allowed to continue presenting after the ban on religious drama in 1548. With satire by the *Basoche* at the Palais de Justice, and farces at La Trinité by the *Enfants-sans-Souci*, the burden of holding the mirror up to Nature in the years before the professional comedians from Italy invaded the French capital was laid squarely on the shoulders of the King of the *Basoche* and the Prince of Fools.

(b)   *The Mirror of Folly*

Despite differences of form, secular drama had a common core of subject-matter, a common function. Safeguarded (to a limited extent only) by their comic mask and jester's cocks-comb, the players demonstrated that 'It is a folly second to none to try to put the world to rights' (Molière, *Misanthrope*, I. i). But the folly that Molière's reasonable man rejected was a sacred charge to the *basochiens* and the *Enfants*, a rallying cry to the *sots* and *sottes*. Both morality plays and *sotties* employ personified abstractions as their characters, and the tradition of political satire and outspoken criticism of the Establishment was the strength and ultimately the downfall of these plays. Louis XII's successor, Francis I, was much less liberal in his attitude to these performances, and in 1516 three *joueurs de farces* were taken before the king at Amboise in chains for having played farces in Paris suggesting that 'Mère Sotte ruled the court and was taxing, robbing and pillaging everyone. Being informed of this, the king and the regent were very angry.' The luckless players were imprisoned but later given a pardon when the queen entered Paris (*Journal d'un Bourgeois de Paris*, in *Comédiens*, pp. 114–5). The situation was worse in the towns of the Burgundian Netherlands which, by the middle of the sixteenth century, found themselves under the rule of Catholic Spain with a risk of being accused of heresy if their plays were found to contain any matter critical of the Church.

Satire is a genre that makes great demands on author and audience alike, for to be effective it must not only be topical but apt and preferably witty. Since it is topical it is also ephemeral and many of the *sotties* and moralities that have survived in print could not now stand exposure to an audience. Most of the moralities are merely tedious brief histories; none of them is of the stature of an *Everyman* or even a *Mankind*. But a few of the *sotties* have a sufficiently timeless body under the fashionable dress of the day to be at least understood and, given an up-dated outfit, enjoyed today. Such a one is the *sottie* of *Le Monde, Abus et les Sots* in which *Abus* summons his followers: *Sot-Dissolu*, dressed as a churchman; *Sot-Glorieux*, a soldier; *Sot-Corrompu*, a judge; *Sot-Trompeur*, a merchant; *Sot-Ignorant*, popular stupidity; and *Sotte-Folle*, the woman. Together they mock and reject Old World and under the guidance of their proud Lucifer set to work 'to make all things new' in an act of diabolical creation. Unable to agree, they finally settle on Chaos for their foundations and then each builds one pillar; *Sot-Dissolu* rejects Devotion and Prayer in favour of Simony and Apostasy for his building-stones; *Sot-Corrompu* cannot find a place for Justice and Equity but makes use of Corruption and Ambition; while *Sot-Trompeur* makes good use of a chunk of Usury and False Measure; *Sot-Glorieux* brings instead of Nobility and Generosity, Cowardice and Meanness (the latter with a passing reference to the economy dear to Louis XII). Many of these ideas are still relevant today and with a judicious substitution of contemporary references for the more outmoded terms, the *sottie* has been performed successfully in recent years by the University of Liège.[5] Having completed the task, the *sots* make advances to *Sotte-Folle*, in the course of which they knock down the pillars of their frail construction. The *sots* flee and the *Vieux Monde* is left to moralise in the ruins of their Brave New World.

The author of this *sottie* is unknown and it has been described as both too good and too bad to have been the work of the most important actor/author of the genre, Pierre Gringore, who wrote a play of *St Louis* for the Guild of Carpenters and Masons in Paris and a number of other poems and plays, particularly a triple bill of *sottie*, morality and farce performed in the *Halles* in Paris on Shrove Tuesday, 1512, by the *Enfants-sans-Souci* with Gringore himself as *Mère Sotte*. The *sottie* is the most substantial of the three, and is simply called the play of the *Prince des Sots et Mère Sotte*, its subject being the quarrel between the King of France, represented by the *Prince des Sots* and the Pope (Julius II) portrayed by *Mère Sotte*. It is probable that the play was commissioned by Louis XII who wanted to whip up popular support for his effort to depose the Pope who had broken his alliance with France. The play opens with a discussion by three *sots* on the political situation, with stress on the wisdom and desire for peace of the Prince. Lords and prelates join the debate, their burlesque names continuing the almost allegorical parallel between the kingdom of the *Prince des Sots* and the kingdom of France. The Prince himself appears and also *Sotte-Commune*, the common people who want nothing better than to have peace at any cost so they can get their harvest in. Writing for an urban and elitist audience, Gringore has no hesitation in making the rural commons into a figure of fun. Finally, Mother Church enters, defending the actions of her leader, the Pope, but she is rapidly unfrocked and revealed as being – *Mère Sotte!*

> *Prince*: Is it truly the church?
> *Commune*: I don't know, she's raving.
> *Sot I*: Perhaps it's *Mère Sotte* who has put on the robe of the church? [*she is unfrocked*] . . .
> *Prince*: Advise me now what I should do? I do not want to harm the church . . .
> *Commune*: Let everyone take heed to this, it is not holy Mother Church who wars against us, truly it is just our own *Mère Sotte*. (Gringore, i, pp. 240–3)

In the morality which follows the characters are no longer *sots* but personified abstractions, though the theme is still the same. The French People try to convince the Italian People that they have been deceived by the Obstinate Man (the Pope again). Eventually they are convinced, and the two peoples draw the Obstinate Man's attention to the vision of Divine Punishment, 'sitting in a throne high in the air,' but he will only listen to his boon companions, Hypocrisy and Simony. Eventually his Demerits come in person to accuse him and all other hypocritical clergy, as well as corrupt judges and greedy merchants, and the morality ends with the usual warning of the need 'to cry God mercy for Divine Punishment threatens us' (Gringore, I, p. 269).

The farce which terminated Gringore's triple bill is a straightforward humorous tale of marital conflict. The old husband complains to his overlord about the behaviour of his young wife with her two servants, Doing and Saying (*Faire* and *Dire*). The lord gives judgement for the wife and rejects the husband's claim to appeal: 'It will be disallowed, and it will always be decided without contradiction that for women actions speak louder than words' (Gringore, I, p. 286).

In the farce, as in all three plays, Gringore makes constant use of puns and word-play, frequently of a crude, even obscene, variety. The whole farce turns on such a double meaning, for the basis of the wife's case to the overlord is that her vineyard is being allowed to lie fallow and needs to be regularly dug over. Nor are the farce characters any more real than the *sots* or the personifications: they are mere types with no attempt at individualisation or psychological detail. Farce, like the *fabliau*, concentrates on action, tricks and jokes. It is a comedy of manners and slapstick, parody and satire – verbal, visual humour leading to a 'dissolute laugh' (Sibilet, *Comédie*, p. 66).

The use of the farce as a savoury stuffing (*farcir* means to stuff poultry or game) is not limited to secular drama. When the performance of Andrieu de la Vigne's *Mystery of St Martin* at Seurre in 1496 was delayed by heavy rain, the audience were entertained by the *Farce of The Miller, his Wife and the Priest* and then sent home with a promise that the mystery play would be performed the next day. Meanwhile the whole cast went in procession to the church of St Martin to pray for fine weather – which they got. The farce was also the work of Andrieu, a former *basochien*, and includes a scene in which the priest hears the confession of the dying man while making love to his penitent's wife. Hardly an edifying prologue to a saint's play!

The mixture of genres, serious and comic – an integral part of medieval drama in France as in England – was one of the reasons for the rejection of medieval dramatic forms in the sixteenth and seventeenth centuries when the Classical tradition of separate tragedies and comedies became the standard theatrical practice and dominated the French theatre to the extent that Voltaire, writing in the eighteenth century, could criticise Shakespeare, 'a powerful rich genius . . . without a spark of good taste or the least knowledge of the rules', for having written 'his monstrous farces which are called tragedies' (*Lettres Philosophiques: On Tragedy*). But there was one notable exception to the universal damnation of farce, one play among the multitude that the critics were prepared to save from the everlasting bonfire, the play of which Tressan in the eighteenth-century *Encyclopédie* simply said it 'would be a credit to Molière' (*Encyclopédie*, XI, *article*: Parade). The play was the *Farce of Master Peter Pathelin* (*Maistre Pierre Pathelin*).

(c) *Back to these Sheep: the 'Farce of Pathelin'*

The authorship of this masterpiece which found favour even with the writers of the Renaissance is unknown though this prestigious crown has been awarded at various times to a number of major writers from Jean de Meung to Pierre Gringore. It was probably composed sometime in the second half of the fifteenth century, and the oldest extant edition dates from 1486. Pathelin, like many other play-texts, has survived only in print, not in manuscript, and at least six editions are known from before 1501.

The play is much longer than the 500 lines recommended for farces by Gracien du Pont in 1539: 'farces and *soties* five hundred, moralities a thousand or twelve hundred lines at most' (*Comédie*, pp. 65–6). Indeed Pathelin even exceeds the allowance for moralities, being more than 1500 lines long, or about one and a half hours playing time; Molière's *Misanthrope* is only some 1800 lines.

The plot of Pathelin is fairly complex, involving a double trick played by the lawyer Pathelin on his friend and dupe, the draper Guillaume. Having purchased six ells of fine cloth to make himself a gown, Pathelin persuades the draper to come and collect the money from his house and dine with him as well. But when the draper duly turns up to get his dinner and his money he finds Pathelin in bed, sick and delirious, raving in several different languages with his wife swearing he has not been out all day. Balked of his money the draper is forced to leave for he has a court case coming up: his shepherd, he claims, has been stealing his sheep. Pathelin is asked to defend the errant shepherd and advises his client to answer nothing but 'Baa' to all and any questions. The last third of the play is the scene in the court when Guillaume, seeing Pathelin on his feet and in perfect health, immediately starts demanding his money, to the confusion of the judge who is there to try a case of sheep-stealing. So arises the famous appeal: 'But let's get back to these sheep [*Revenons à ces moutons*]', which has become proverbial. Guillaume becomes incoherent with rage and frustration, for Pathelin denies everything and the shepherd only bleats. The judge dismisses the draper and the case. Finally Pathelin is left with his client and demands his fee, but all he gets, in his turn, is 'Baa'.

It is tempting to see in *Pathelin* with its details of medieval life in shop and home and courtroom a true comedy of social manners, but the realism is, in fact, more apparent than genuine, for the draper would have been most unlikely to own sheep or sell cloth made from his own wool – trade demarcation was very strict in the Middle Ages. Indeed in *Pathelin*, as in the majority of farces and *fabliaux*, the comedy depends on our being distanced from the characters – not as a modern audience is removed from these plays by the passage of five centuries, but as a medieval crowd is separated by the creation of a situation whose realism is like the false two-storey façade of the houses in a Western, concealing the simple log cabin behind. It looks like the town they know and live in, but there is none of the supreme naturalism of the fourth-wall box-set of modern situation-comedy.

The characters have sufficient truth in them to hold our interest without invoking our sympathies; the unfortunate draper has the tragic flaw of all comic butts: stupidity – not the moral or political folly of the targets of the *sotties* and morality plays but human weakness and fallibility. It is a measure of the truth of the play that we rejoice at the end when Pathelin himself, an endearing Renart-like rogue, is outwitted by the simple inarticulate shepherd in a battle using Pathelin's own choice of weapons: words.

The humour of the farce usually depends on folly, stupidity and weakness. It is unheroic and pessimistic. Whatever may be going to happen in the hereafter, present society is full of tricksters and dupes, unfaithful wives and dishonest servants, husbands helpless to avoid the cuckold's horns, dishonest merchants and a clergy whose hypocrisy is only equalled by its lechery. It is a society such that the spectator, in the words of the most famous theatrical barber of all time, 'hastens to laugh at everything for fear of being obliged to weep at it' (*Barber of Seville*, I.ii) – a world in which, as the twentieth-century comic Max Wall puts it, 'All the sadness of life comes out in the comedy.'

Reality and Illusion

THE theatre is 'a mirror that concentrates, that far from weakening the coloured rays takes them up and condenses them . . . everything that exists in the world, in history, in life, in man can and should be reflected in it' (Victor Hugo, *Préface de Cromwell*). The mirror of the theatre is more than any other art the reflection of an illusion. The suspension of disbelief is essential to any worthwhile theatrical experience. But the nature of the reality of which the theatre reflects the illusion, and the manner of creating the illusion, have varied considerably through the centuries.

The key to the illusion of reality in the theatre is in the staging of the play, and we have little information about the method of performance of the secular drama. From the few records and the internal evidence of the texts themselves we can deduce that the farces probably had settings and costumes appropriate to the characters, while the reality of the *sotties* and the moralities depended almost entirely on the truth of the topical situation being satirised or the human foible being criticised. In the political morality of the *Council of Basle* (*Concil de Basle*) in 1434, the characters are all abstractions and the only clue we have to their appearance is that they are dressed as women since they greet each other as 'Dame'. The reality of this play depends entirely on the use of actual contemporary events and their personification as Heresy, Church, Council or Reform.

A very different mirror is provided by the great plays – the saints' lives and the biblical drama – for we have very detailed accounts of how they were staged and from this evidence we can deduce something of the medieval attitude to theatrical reality. The fundamental truth of the subject-matter is attested for actors and audience alike by the authority of the sources: the Bible, including apocryphal writings, and the Latin lives of the saints. In counterpoint to this historical validity, which later centuries found in the Classical myths or historical events, medieval producers created a contemporary reality for the representation and re-enactment of these moments of time.

Three kinds of reality can be distinguished in the plays: an attempt to express the ineffable godhead, an illusion of naturalism, and the truly miraculous.

Something has already been said in the previous chapter about the presentation of the Trinity on the stage. The use of personified attributes of God, especially the Four Daughters, and the creation of a Heaven of beauty in music, flowers and fine materials went a good way towards satisfying the need to portray in anthropomorphic form the supreme being and creator. Since Christian drama, like Christianity itself, is strongly Christocentric, the reality of the Incarnation could be presented without too much difficulty. Most interesting of the details of staging are those which show us how certain special effects were achieved. Thus the Transfiguration of Christ was staged with the maximum of brightness in the Revello *Passion* (which is based on French staging traditions): 'When Jesus is on the mountain let there be a polished bowl which makes the brightness of the sun striking the bowl reflect on Jesus and towards his disciples . . . and if the sun is not shining let there be torches and some other lights' (*Staging*, p. 114). This reference reminds us that all the big plays in France for which we have information were performed in daylight, out of doors, with no elaborate lighting available. A special effect like that at Revello would be all the more striking therefore. Sometimes very simple devices could be effective. In Michel's *Passion*, the Transfiguration relies entirely on the language for its brightness: 'His clothes have changed colour. They are so white that I have never seen anything so white, not even snow – they glow with such marvellous light' (9408–11). But the baptism of Christ has the direction: 'Note that the speech by God the Father can be pronounced audibly and effectively by three voices, a high one above, a counter-high and a counter-bass, well-matched, and the whole of the following speech can be spoken in this harmony' (Michel's *Passion*, p. 26).

At the other end of the supernatural spectrum, the devils used fireworks and cannon to create their illusions of Hell, sometimes with dangerous consequences for the performers, such as the actor at Seurre whose belt of fireworks accidentally caught light 'so that he was badly burned. But he was so swiftly succoured, stripped and reclothed that without giving any sign of pain he came and played his part' (*Staging*, p. 261). For an audience that believed in devils and angels, the appearance of these supernatural beings on stage was no more difficult to accept than any other human character, the only difference being that the producers took the opportunity to create particularly effective spectacles at these points in the play.

Magnificence was a realistic effect when portraying the princes of this world and no one denied the right of these characters to appear in silks and velvets, pearls and gold, but it was a different matter when the actors portraying more humble roles insisted on wearing silks for the apostles! Since most French plays required actors to provide their own costumes this could be a difficulty and Jean Bouchet, writing to the inhabitants of Issoudun who were preparing to stage the Passion in 1535, reminds them that they should 'assign your roles to people of the right ages and do not use borrowed costumes (even if they are of gold) unless they are appropriate to the characters being portrayed. It is not good that learned doctors, pharisees or councillors should be dressed the same as Pilate' (*Epistre Familiere*, p. xcii). Apart from the costumes, however, little attempt was made to portray realistically the ordinary setting of the scenes in the world. Fixed locations or mansions might be reused from one day to the next. At Mons the house of Adam became the house of Mary and Joseph by a simple change of label: 'To Sir Jehan Portier, priest, for having made

. . . ninety-eight notices in large letters of the places on the stage
– 48s.' The pins to attach them to the mansions cost 3s. (*Staging*,
p. 80).

A different kind of reality is invoked in the matter of stage
meals. The entries at Mons make it clear that they were always
real food and therefore probably actually consumed. Roast
meat and bread are the commonest items, with an interesting
reference to fish for the banquet at which Salome dances – the
date of the entry shows it was a Friday so that even on the stage
the actors must not break the fasting rule (see p. 191 above).
More difficult is the situation when the present rule of the
Church comes into conflict with the known biblical data, as in
the presentation of the Last Supper at Mons. Here the meal
must include the Paschal Lamb, as well as the bitter herbs
(usually represented by lettuce) and the unleavened bread for
which a communion wafer was often used, though at Mons they
specify rather *fouaces blanches*, a fine white-flour breadcake. The
Mons accounts duly record the sum of 16s. for the roast lamb
'for God to keep his paschal meal', but they also have an entry
for 'another lamb, of paste, covered with roast fish eaten on the
stage at the said paschal meal instead of the other because of
Saturday' (*Staging*, p. 126). The interesting point here is not the
use of a fake lamb made of fish, since Saturday like Friday was a
fast day, but the presence of a genuine roast lamb as well. Since
it is impossible that the director should have been unaware of
the problem in advance, the real lamb must be included
because it is an integral part of the biblical reality and could not
be omitted.

The Last Supper also raises the whole problem endemic to
the plays of the portrayal of miracles and supranatural
happenings on stage. The use of machinery for such marvels as
the Ascension or Simon Magus's diabolically-assisted flight is
fairly straightforward. It is the miracles, like the changing of
water into wine, that needed to be presented with great care
since they are too easy to do on the stage, and to be convincing
the producers sometimes resorted to the conjuror's trick of
inviting the audience to taste the wine after the miracle had
been enacted.[6] Death and resurrection were also difficult to stage
convincingly for an audience that expected realism and had
come a long way from the laconic stage-directions of the *Play of*

St Nicholas: 'Now the pagans kill all the Christians' (see p. 95 above). Battles were carefully choreographed, with plenty of dead bodies; and scenes of torture and murder, the mainstay of so many saints' plays, were presented with much gory detail (*Staging*, pp. 101–10). Trapdoors in the stage enabled the living character to disappear conveniently while his dummy substitute was being torn apart by live horses. Very few fake animals were used in France except for the talking ass ridden by Balaam – even the fish at the Creation were alive, but we have unfortunately no record of how they performed.

The peculiar contribution of France to the drama of the later Middle Ages was not the cosmic dimensions – the Lucerne *Passion* and the English cycle plays, though shorter, are conceived on the same all-embracing scale; nor was it the spectacle – in Florence the flying-machinery was designed by Brunelleschi; it was the illusions and feigned realities, the *secrets* and *feintes* which were unequalled in the theatre of any other country. The list of *feintes* required for the performance of the *Acts of the Apostles* in Bourges in 1536, twenty-three printed pages long, covers every type of stage-property from a camp-bed to a singing dog, from fire-breathing dragons to a ship-wreckable boat; a large number of entries in the Mons accounts deal with items for the *secret* of the Flood: barrels of water in high places, ropes and pulleys, timber, masking clouds and a trapdoor in the turf-covered stage for the drowned and the flood-water to escape through to the undercroft where ditches carried off the overflow.

But the incredible range, variety and ingenuity of these illusions should not blind us to their essentially utilitarian purpose: they are sugar on the pill, not icing on the cake. The function of every aspect of French medieval theatre, mystery or morality, fools'-play or farce, was the restoration of order and measure to the moral and political chaos of the created world. A woodcut on the title-page of Gringore's play of the *Prince des Sots, Mère Sotte et les Sots* says it all. *Mère Sotte* and two companions, in their fools' garb and asses'-ears head-dresses are framed by a scroll bearing the motto shared by Gringore and *Mère Sotte*: *Tout par raison. Raison par tout. Par tout raison* (Everything by reason. Reason in all things. Everywhere reason).

8. Inside, Outside: Man in Society

Searching for me I wander through a hall of mirrors.
(Leonard Nimoy)

THE outbreak of the Hundred Years War between France and England in 1340 marked a turning-point in the cultural as well as the political history of France. The great flowering of vernacular literature and Gothic art in the twelfth and thirteenth centuries was in full bloom by the beginning of the fourteenth century, with some genres, especially the narrative ones of epic and romance, already overblown. For the next two centuries, the exploits of Arthur or Charlemagne and their followers, or the antics of Renart and his fellows, amplified or abridged, continued or selected, are endlessly retold but only rarely revitalised. In the late fifteenth century, with few exceptions, the only versions of these ever-popular tales available to the contemporary reading public are preserved in prose and pickled in print: pleasing to the palate, perhaps, but as remote from the original poems as tinned pineapple from fresh.

Other genres, such as lyric and didactic poetry and drama, were more fortunate. In a world at war it is the fate of literature to become escapism, propaganda or instruction. The personal lyricism of earlier centuries was continued and developed in the work of Machaut and his successors, while the growing importance of the bourgeoisie and the increasing demand for vernacular literature made the lot of the populariser and encyclopaedist happier than that of most of his fellow-countrymen. Drama began to insist more and more on the moral need for reform in personal behaviour and public institutions, while the preachers in the pulpits added their voices to the general cry of misery and despair. For war was not the only scourge of fourteenth-century France: close behind the crowned rider on his white steed there followed the other three apocalyptic horsemen, red and black and pale, harbingers of slaughter, famine and plague. The *Jacquerie*, or peasants' revolt, the Black Death, the famine-producing natural disasters were compounded by internecine strife which culminated in open warfare between the Armagnacs, led by Louis of Orleans, brother of Charles VI, and the Burgundians under the king's cousin, John the Fearless (see below, p. 235). These accumulated disasters created in France a situation unequalled in its calamitous horror since the barbarian invasions which accompanied and precipitated the downfall of the Roman Empire.

It is hardly surprising, therefore, that a high proportion of the texts produced during this troubled age were polemical or didactic, mouthpieces for contemporary criticism and concern. But a more creative and personal literature also flowered among the ruins and many of the finest works of medieval drama and lyric poetry were composed in the cities and courts of fifteenth-century France.

Mirror of France: the Hundred Years War

A NOTABLE feature of late medieval literature is the shift of interest from the creation to the creator. Writers become more important as individuals. We know their names, their lives and their personalities, not because they cease to hide behind the mask of anonymity, allegory or fiction, but because their feelings, culture and even daily routine become the openly acknowledged material from which their works are made, reflecting the society in which they live in the magnifying mirrors of personal experience. This common approach to the creative process links together three otherwise very different poets who span the period of the Hundred Years War: Guillaume de Machaut, Eustache Deschamps and Alain Chartier. All were educated men, writing in Latin as well as French; all were at the centre of affairs, closely connected with the policy-making factions of capital and court, and all in their works reflect the dichotomy between the horrors of war and disaster and the continuing daily life of prince and prelate, poet and peasant.

Earliest of the three, Machaut was not just a poet but an outstanding musician, the greatest composer of his age; for this reason much of his work cannot be fairly judged except in performance. In the prologue to the *Poem of the Orchard* (*Dit du Vergier*), one of his last works, Machaut describes how Nature sent him three of her children, sense, rhetoric and music, to give him practical assistance in writing a new poem of love. This association of Nature and Art, personal inspiration and cultured craftsmanship, is typical of the lyric poetry of the period, especially the love poems, and is also found in the wider range of didactic, epic or satirical writings for which verse was still a common medium, though prose was also increasingly popular for serious matters. Metrical variety had hitherto only really been important in the lyrics of the troubadours and *trouvères*, narrative and didactic writers contenting themselves with a more or less skilled handling of the ubiquitous octosyllabic rhyming couplet. Machaut and his successors wrote lyric, dramatic and didactic poetry in a rich variety of verse forms: *ballade, chant royal, virelay* and *rondeau*.

This emphasis on form and structure, found also in the decorated (*rayonnant*) and then flamboyant styles of later Gothic art, is echoed in the content of the poems where elaborate imagery, stylised concepts and logically developed legal arguments adorn or bedizen the natural thoughts and feelings of the poets. Machaut's love poems are elegant, refined and courtly, the poet and his lady delicately performing the prescribed steps of the amorous *carole*, not against the chequered background in red and gold and blue of the early Gothic manuscript illuminations, but in a world of gardens and formalised landscapes where 'there was no place nor path which was not sewn with tiny flowers, white and yellow and scarlet or some other strange colour' (Machaut, *Oeuvres*, I, p. 14). The *Remedy of Fortune* (*Remède de Fortune*), one of Machaut's most important and typical works, presents a series of dialogues between the Lover, the Lady and Hope, with songs in seven different musical forms set like jewels at intervals in the narrative (Machaut, *Oeuvres*, II, pp. 1–157; the music for the songs is included in the manuscript).

Machaut was the most important of the late fourteenth-century poets but not the only one to write of love in a courtly setting. Froissart, better known for his *Chronicles*, was a considerable poet also. His lyrics are often enlivened with a wry humour at his own expense, while his pastoral setting includes a number of shepherds and shepherdesses who are lineal descendants of these described by Adam de la Halle or the author of *Aucassin and Nicolette* (see p. 98 above). Sometimes they discuss the contemporary situation, arguing whether the French can control the 'pride of Bruges and Ghent', or going to Westminster to watch the procession of 'him who bears the lily' (Froissart, *Lyric Poetry*, p. 179). In another *pastourelle*, a father and mother who have been helping their son to gain an education refuse to give him food until he has related 'to your father and to me some true story or some fable'. The child complies with the story of Jason and the Golden Fleece, 'the golden sheep which is very well known', and the mother concedes, 'you are a very adequate clerk' (Froissart, *Lyric Poetry*, pp. 177–8). One of the most personal and original of all the lyrics is that in which Froissart describes those things which 'to see or hear them lifts up my heart'. In his list, which foreshadows Rupert Brooke's 'These I have loved', Froissart includes the sight of vineyards and the sound of wine being poured from the bottle, wearing fine clothes, games and dances during the long evenings in chambers lit by many candles, and at bedtime, spiced wines 'to sleep better' (*Lyric Poetry*, pp. 231–2).

The tradition of courtly lyric poetry in a rural, pastoral setting persisted into the fifteenth century but with significant changes. Alain Chartier, writing his *Book of the Four Ladies* (*Livre des Quatre Dames*) in 1416, describes in conventional terms the poet setting out one spring morning when the birds are singing and the flowers are blooming. He meditates on his love for his lady at length but then meets four weeping ladies who ask him to judge their debate: which of them is the most unfortunate? This kind of discussion was a commonplace of courtly literature from the twelfth century onwards but there is one major innovation here. All the ladies have lost their lovers at the Battle of Agincourt. One was killed and the second taken prisoner. The third lady claims her fate is worse as she does not know what has happened to her lover: he is merely 'missing'. The fourth lady introduces a note of grim reality into the discussion, for her lover was one of 'the cowardly rascals that ran from the battle' (*Henry V*, iv.vii). When the lady laments the

shame this action has brought to her and all of France, we hear
not only the voice of Brangane bewailing her shame in having
bestowed her love unworthily (Thomas, *Tristan*, 1420–4),
but Alain Chartier, Frenchman, lamenting the plight of his
native land: 'He fled when he should have fought . . . unwound-
ed, whole, he came back from there' (Chartier, *Poetical Works*,
p. 288).

Awareness of the social and political perils of the age was not
the prerogative of the fifteenth-century writers. Machaut
himself, the least *engagé* of poets, describes vividly the horrors of
the Black Death and the wars of the mid-fourteenth century:
'for the air which had been clean and fresh was foul and vile,
dark and black, ugly, stinking, troubled and polluted . . . all
men were affected by it; sickly and pale, they had swellings and
great boils from which they died, and to put it briefly they
scarcely dared to venture out or to speak to one another at
close quarters' (Machaut, *Oeuvres*, i, p. 148). Like all his
fellow-poets, Machaut wrote a variety of works, from a *chanson
de geste* commemorating the *Capture of Alexandria* by Pierre de
Lusignan, king of Cyprus, to a *Consolation for a Friend* (*Confort
d'Ami*), written for his patron Charles the Bad, king of Navarre,
while he was in prison. The latter work is divided into two
parts, the consolation proper being primarily religious in tone –
Machaut was a canon of Rheims Cathedral and a genuinely
devout man – while the second section is a moral treatise of the
kind already common in the thirteenth and early fourteenth
centuries, on the proper duties and behaviour of princes and
the nobility. This theme is constantly reiterated throughout the
period, from the *Breviary of Nobles* (*Bréviaire des Nobles*) in which
Alain Chartier recommends the virtues of honesty, cleanness,
generosity and fidelity among others, to the *Mirror of Noble Men
of France* (*Miroer des Nobles Hommes de France*) by the Burgundian
chronicler and historian Georges Chastellain in 1457 (see also
Christine de Pisan, below, p. 226).

Less elevated than Machaut and more mundane in his
concerns was his pupil and successor, Eustache Deschamps, a
much inferior poet technically but a shrewd observer of the
world around him and with a gift for humorous description and
portraiture which foreshadows the picture of Rome in the
Regrets of Du Bellay, two centuries later. Whereas Machaut and

Chartier were learned clerks, cathedral canons and, in the latter case, a royal secretary, Deschamps held more domestic, administrative positions at court and in the service of the great nobles of the day. The realities of life 'behind the scenes' is vividly portrayed in poems where he insists, for example, that he never does his turn of duty at court in the winter months, because of the cold: 'for at that time there are frosts and snow, rain and winds in great confusion; then the king goes to hunt the boar and the staff in attendance blow on their hands, each keeps his belly well wrapped up, swinging his arms to keep the cold at bay . . . the little pages weep with cold in the woods, no longer able to hold the bridles' (Deschamps, IV, p. 301).

Deschamps hated travelling as much as he loved Paris: 'Nothing can be compared with Paris' (I, p. 301). He is particularly acid about the food in foreign parts: 'Lice, fleas, stench and swine — that's the essence of Bohemia; bread, smoked fish and cold weather, black pepper, leeks and rotten cabbage, smoked meats, hard and black . . . drinking sour and bitter beer, sleeping badly in darkness and filthy straw . . . that's the essence of Bohemia' (Deschamps, VII, p. 90). In another poem he describes humorously an inn where, whatever sauce he asks for, he always gets mustard (Deschamps, IV, p. 29).

Deschamps's output was enormous and varied, with information for the social historian in every line. One of his most entertaining works is a play of the *Four Offices in the Royal Household* (*Dit des Quatre Offices de l'Ostel du Roy . . . a Jouer par Personnaiges*) in which the four offices, Buttery (*Eschançonnerie*), Pantry (*Panneterie*), Cookery (*Cuisine*) and Saucery (*Sausserie*), debate the relative importance of their contributions to life: wine, bread, cooked food and sauces. Each is portrayed as a female of formidable, comic proportions. Cookery, for example, is greeted by Pantry with the query: 'Who are you with your pot and ladle, carrying a bellows so big it looks like a trumpet?' (Deschamps, VII, p. 183); while Cookery in turn tells Saucery to 'Go grind yourself in your own pestle and mortar!' (p. 188). The case that each of these four ladies puts forward tells us a good deal about the domestic economy of the period in a great household, as well as being very funny; for example, Buttery's account of Cookery's filthy habits with the food being handled

by a man who is 'barefoot, vile, dirty and foul with not a gar-
ment on him worth two *sous tournois*', while another scratches
his head or his arse while handling raw food. 'By such people
the king himself is served' (Deschamps, VII, p. 185). Not
surprisingly, the four ladies come to blows in the end but are
finally reconciled by the majordomo: 'It seems to me it would
be sensible for you four to be friends and not fight each other
any more, for there has never been a time, past or present when
you did not need each other' (VII, p. 191). They accept his
ruling and the *Dit* ends with a song.

Like most of his contemporaries, Deschamps wrote on a
variety of subjects and in didactic as well as humorous or
personal modes. An example of his more serious work is the *Art
of Writing Poetry* (*Art de Dictier*) composed in prose in 1392. It is
the first such treatise to be written in French and consists of two
sections. In the first part, Deschamps describes the Seven
Liberal Arts and their particular uses and concludes with
Music, the 'medicine' of all the others, for 'the hearts and spirits
of those who, toiling at the said arts in thought, imagination
or physical labour, have become wearied and heavy, are
restored and medicined and thereafter more able to study and
labour at the other six arts aforementioned' (Deschamps, VII,
p. 269). After this elevated preamble, Deschamps divides
music into two kinds: artificial, i.e. created by instruments, and
natural, i.e. made by the human voice and words. His concern
is with the second, especially words, and he proceeds to analyse
the alphabet with details of the sound values of every vowel and
consonant, after which he gives rules for the composition of
various verse forms, such as *ballades*, *virelays* and *rondeaux*, with
examples of each form, though he advises those who cannot
remember the complex structural rules for a *lai* to find one to
copy for 'they are very common and it would take too much
space to write it all out in this booklet' (VII, p. 288).

Deschamps's mixture of practical instruction and examples
is typical of the large number of manuals of instruction that
proliferated in the fourteenth century on every aspect of social
life. Some are entirely practical, such as the *Book of Crafts* (*Livre
des Mestiers*) written in Bruges in about 1360 as a phrase-book
for the inhabitants of the area who needed to be bi-lingual in
French and Flemish. The first part of this valuable teaching-aid

includes greetings and general preliminary material, followed by lists of useful words including fruit, trees and the principal feasts of the Church. The compiler of this remarkably modern-seeming little book then provides an alphabet of names with descriptions of the different crafts, such as 'Beatrice the washerwoman will come here after dinner, so give her these linen sheets and she will wash them' (p. 28). Or 'Garniers the cauldron-maker sells cauldrons and other things that I have listed in another chapter' (p. 34). Sometimes the material is arranged in short dialogues: 'If you are buying cloth then ask: "How much is an ell of this cloth, a half-ell or a quarter?" Ask for mixed cloth, red, green or black. . . . "Tell me what I must pay." "Sir, you will pay twelve groats a yard if you please." "Lady, that is not good sense: for that price I should want to have good scarlet!" ' (pp. 15–16).

The need for written text-books of all aspects of daily life stresses the increased complexity of existence and the improved levels of literacy among the middle and upper classes. The wife of the *Goodman of Paris* (*Menagier de Paris*) was only fifteen but he compiled a detailed written book of household management for her which he obviously knew she could read. It contains both moral and practical instruction and includes sections on cooking, gardening, the care of animals, especially horses and hawks, and hiring servants. Much of his material is derived from specialised treatises in Latin, some of which were being translated into French at this date, while new, original works on chess and hunting in particular became very popular. Just as the Goodman starts by giving his wife religious instruction, so many of the specialist works also include moralisations of the basic material. The most elaborate of these are probably the *Books of King Method and Queen Reason* (*Livres du Roy Modus et de la Reine Ratio*). The first book is a detailed analysis on hunting and the correct Method (*Modus*) and Reason (*Ratio*) for doing things – *Book of Pleasures* (*Livre des Deduits*) – and it is followed by a very elaborate allegory called the *Dream of the Plague* (*Songe de Pestillence*) in which the same monarchs become involved in a great combat between God on one hand and the World and the Flesh, corrupted by the Devil, on the other. There are many vivid scenes of contemporary life in the complex *Dream*, such as the picture of the women rushing to help their husbands in battle:

> Then you would hear women shouting, 'Alas, wretched women, shall we let our husbands be killed? By God's flesh we'll go and die with our husbands or else protect them.' Then you would have seen the women tucking up their skirts and tying up their heads in cloths . . . and they went to fight in great array, and when they came to the battle they struck the first they found with distaffs, flesh-hooks, choppers, pestles and all they had brought with them. (*Modus et Ratio*, II, p. 168)

The increasingly serious treatment of the state of France in the didactic works of the fourteenth century, reflecting the worsening situation between France and England in the Hundred Years War and the Great Schism, is also seen in specialist works like Honoré Bonet's great treatise on the laws of warfare, *The Tree of Battles* (*L'Arbre des Batailles*) composed in 1387. Bonet tells us he was moved to write his book by his vision of the mourning Tree which symbolised the Church, torn by schism. (Deschamps, too, had composed a *Complaint of the Church* in Latin, and then translated it into French at the command of his patron, the Duke of Burgundy, in 1393.) Bonet is most concerned with the legal questions raised by the schism and the prolonged war between the two nations. Thus the University of Paris was under the direct authority of the Pope, so that English students attending it were not subject to arrest as members of the 'enemy'. But supposing, says Bonet, one of them fell ill and his English father wanted to come to Paris and visit him? Would he be legally subject to imprisonment and ransom? (Bonet, pt 4, ch. LXXXVIII). The cool analytic presentation of Bonet's *Tree* emphasises the appalling situations he is discussing, and the hopelessness of the plight of France is stressed in the pessimistic answer to the question, 'Whether it is possible in the nature of things that the world should be at peace?', to which the author responds: 'I reply that it can by no means be so. . . . But I do not say that God could not bring peace everywhere or that if all men were wise and good it would be impossible for them to live in peace' (pt 3, ch. II).

Bonet's conclusion that peace is impossible since most men are not wise but fools underlies the bitter treatment of the three estates in Alain Chartier's prose dialogue *Four Angry Voices* (*Le Quadrilogue Invectif*), written in 1422 in the shadow of the French defeat at Agincourt and the Treaty of Troyes. The voices are those of France and the three estates: chivalry, clergy and people. The situation of France is desperate. She is torn by fighting between the English and Burgundians on one side under Henry V's brother, John, Duke of Bedford, regent of France for the child-king Henry VI) and the royal house of France on the other under the Dauphin, son of Charles VI but disinherited by the Treaty of Troyes (1420). France upbraids her countrymen for their idleness and sloth in accepting and even welcoming the English domination which God has permitted to punish them for their sins. The degradation of the country is figured by Chartier in terms of the rich mantle of France adorned with jewels and coats of arms at the top, letters and figures of science and learning in the middle, and animals, fruits and flowers at the lowest part, the whole being torn, dirty, tattered and rent so that 'in many places the land could be seen naked, the seeds and trees uprooted, cast aside and hanging in shreds so that no order could be seen there nor any harvest hoped for' (*Four Voices*, p. 8). In this state, where 'vineyards, fallows, meads and hedges, defective in their natures, grow to wildness' (*Henry V*, v.ii), France exhorts her estates to courage, a quality she finds more common in the accursed English than in the French who need it most desperately. But the estates, thus challenged are not prepared to accept her criticism. For chivalry, the knight points out that though it is true that many noblemen have failed in their duty in war and siege, yet many others have done well but got no thanks or praise for it. The people lament the rapacity of the nobles and their own weakness; the Church admits some of the charges of corruption levelled at her but blames the lack of discipline in the nobles for the fate of the country. Ultimately the buck is passed for the last time: the fault lies, says chivalry, with the leaders, the unwise and unscrupulous councillors: for 'the security of the prince and the safety of the state depend on loyal advisers, and it is there that we shall find the basis of all our difficulties and the solution of our debate' (*Four Voices*, p. 64).

Machaut is the most musical of the poets, Deschamps the most humorous and Chartier the bitterest. All write love poetry which reflects the elegance of contemporary aristocratic society and the courtly revival of the fourteenth century, at a time when Petrarch in Italy was already composing the sonnets which would become the models for the love poems of the sixteenth century. But behind the glitter and the brittle gaiety, the setting becomes increasingly naturalistic, even in works that are not overtly critical or moralistic, like the manuscript illuminations of the great fifteenth-century books of hours, where the familiar architecture of Paris or the castle of Saumur frames the seasonal activities of the peasants or the pastimes of the lords.

Allegories of State: the *Old Pilgrim's Dream*

THE poets could describe and criticise the state of France and the life of the people but they had no power to enforce change, or even to suggest practical ways of bringing about the peace and prosperity that everyone desired. Few of the men who had such power were also writers, but among those few the most substantial and independent is Philippe de Mézières. Like his namesake, Philip of Novara, Philippe had spent his life in positions of authority, primarily in the Eastern Mediterranean where he was Chancellor of Cyprus for several years. He was instrumental in introducing into France the new Feast of the Presentation of the Virgin Mary in the Temple, and was always deeply committed to the spread and enriching of Christianity. So urgent was his feeling of the need to revitalise the Church, especially in the Holy Land, that he began in 1347 to try to obtain support for the founding of a new order of the Chivalry of the Passion (*La Chevalerie de la Passion de Jésus-Christ*) which he described in a work first written down in 1368. This attempt to establish the new military order proving unsuccessful, he undertook a more ambitious literary project and composed the *Old Pilgrim's Dream* (*Songe du Vieil Pèlerin*) in 1389 for the youthful King Charles VI in whom the ageing Philippe saw a last hope for the survival of Christian Europe, hailing him as the young Moses who might lead France to peace, justice and a religious revival.

The *Dream*, as its name suggests, is an allegory, and Philippe several times refers in it to the allegories of the 'good monk of Chaalis' and once to the *Pilgrimage of the Soul* by name (*Dream*, I, p. 572), but there is no direct influence of Deguilleville on the *Dream*, which is essentially political and national in its concerns. In his dream the old Pilgrim narrates the visit to Earth of the Queen, Truth, with her attendant virtues, Mercy, Peace and Justice – a new variation on the Trial in Heaven theme – who come to judge the quality of the coinage in different lands, cities and kingdoms. The *besant* or talent in each place is tried in the alchemist's fire, and also examined to see if it bears the hallmark of Christianity, the Tau. The form of the allegory makes it possible for Philippe to describe many different countries, including parts of the Near East, with precise details of customs and behaviour which are probably based on personal observation rather than mere travellers' tales. In Rome, Genoa and Avignon, Truth's court questions leading figures of the day about the schism which had currently divided Western Christendom, and Philippe allows himself a scathing denunciation of the sins of mankind which have made this division in the Church possible and prolonged. In England, the flying court of enquiry has an interview with the king, Richard II, allegorised (as all the characters are) as the Young White Boar Crowned. Truth's attitude to the Young Boar himself is not unfriendly, and she reserves her criticisms mainly for the kinsmen of the white Boar, the Black Boars, the uncles of Richard, especially John of Gaunt.

At length, having sought good currency in all parts of Europe without success, Truth's court arrived in France and 'finally found themselves near the good city of Paris' (*Dream*, I, p. 405). Book Two of the *Dream* includes Truth's meeting with representatives of the estates who, in Philippe's world, are four hierarchies, the usual third estate being divided into two parts, with the legal fraternity promoted to a superior position to the rest. Each estate is discussed in turn, starting with the lowest, the fourth hierarchy, whose representative is a man who has been in turn a wealthy citizen, a merchant, a craftsman and a labourer, each down-grading being the result of war, disaster and his own sins. He draws an appalling picture of the conditions of the French people in the aftermath of Crécy and

Poitiers, the Black Death and the *Jacquerie*: 'In France the Slave, when we have paid all the taxes imposed on us and with great trouble and difficulty satisfied the officers who behave towards us like ravening wolves, the little that is left to us is taken by our own soldiers and their pillagers without pity or satisfaction' (*Dream*, I, p. 456).

So far, Philippe's picture of misery and degradation has been entirely negative, but with the other three hierarchies his attitude begins to change. He condemns the corruption of justice and taxation but also recommends specific improvements, drawing on the example of other lands, especially the justice of Milan and the financial system of the Venetians. When talking of the army he lays down numerous and precise regulations for the proper behaviour of commanding officers and the ordering of all things military. A new allegory is now introduced, the Ship of State, described in much, almost finicky, detail: 'The Ship Gracious had three levels, to be understood as the three estates of the kingdom of France, the clergy, the nobles and the people. . . . In the middle of the Ship was a great tree, a cypress, called the mast which perfumed the whole ship. By this mast which is high and straight and without which the ship cannot proceed, is to be understood the holy catholic faith in the kingdom of France' (*Dream*, I, p. 555).

Not content with his double allegory, Philippe introduces several more, concurrently with his basic theme of the inquisition of Truth. From Deguilleville he borrows the allegory of the statue of Nebuchadnezzar: 'and to abridge the figure, which is rather prolix the handmaiden recites one example from the statue of King Nebuchadnezzar' (*Dream*, I, p. 572; cf. *Pilgrimage of the Soul*, 7205–8619). The description of the statue as representing the different groups who make up the body politic, from the king at the head to the hands and feet (the labourers) is a variation on a very widely used Classical and medieval figure (see Christine de Pisan, *Book of the Body Politic*, below, p. 227).

In the third book of his long and complex *Dream*, Philippe uses a new allegory of a chess-board as the basis for detailed advice to the new king, first on his behaviour in personal matters, then in relation to his immediate circle, and thirdly in his relationship with his people. In matters of personal behaviour, Philippe shows himself as something of a puritan.

The king is given a new series of tables of the law – an elaboration of the allegorical representation of the young king as Moses receiving instruction and commandments from God – which include a serious attack on blasphemy and the taking of God's name in vain. Deschamps also criticised this apparently wide-spread habit of swearing in a number of *ballades* in which he particularly condemned the custom of swearing by parts of the body of God: 'May he be damned and lost who shall break the body of God in pieces, it is forbidden to dismember it for the sake of God who was transfigured' (Deschamps, I, p. 276).

Philippe advises the king to follow the example of his ancestor, St Louis, and be temperate in all things, to rise early in the morning so as to have time for divine service, and to go to bed in good time. 'When you have been up half the night, or two thirds of it, and had only three or four hours sleep how can you perform your royal duties?' (*Dream*, II, p. 207). The king is to be allowed a game or two of tennis, but not too much and only in private. Only on special occasions should he indulge in tournaments, and then only breaking four or five lances. Dancing is permissible, again in moderation and not at midnight. All dice and games of chance are forbidden. (St Louis had tried to outlaw them for the whole of France but with little success it would seem, since there was in Paris at the end of Louis's reign a special trade guild for dice-makers, 'that is to say makers of dice for backgammon . . . of bone, ivory and horn and any other material or metal' – *Arts et Métiers*, p. 181).[1] Hunting, too, should be indulged in only in moderation, and Philippe recommends instead a game of skill with bows and arrows popular with the Great Khan.

Queen Truth turns eventually to the question of the king's reading and particularly condemns fiction: 'You should take care not to delight in apocryphal writings, and especially those books and romances which are filled with nonsensical matters and attract the reader to things that are foolish, vain and sinful, like the books of the foolish deeds of Lancelot' (*Dream*, II, p. 221). The best book is, of course, the Bible, and for preference it should be read in Latin 'as you have some grounding in learning . . . for the Holy Scripture, written and dictated by the saints in Latin and then translated into French, does not give the same substance in the streams as from the original source. . . . For there are in Holy Scripture certain words, and many of them, which read in Latin pierce the heart with great devotion, but translated into French, they appear in the common tongue tasteless and unpleasing' (*Dream*, II, p. 223–4). This attitude to Latin, which is not limited to the Bible, is particularly interesting when addressed to the son of Charles V, who had encouraged the translations into French of many works. Among these were the *Ethics* of Aristotle, translated by Nicholas of Oresme and highly recommended to young Moses as fitting for a king's reading. Another of Charles V's projects was the translation of Augustine's *City of God*, which Truth commends as well as the *Polycraticus* by John of Salisbury.

Having detailed minutely the right and wrong way to live for the young king, Truth moves on to matters of court and diplomatic behaviour including the hiring of servants and attendants and the advisability of having the total of the royal debts presented to the monarch every two months, so he can be constantly aware of the need to reduce them. Philippe suggests a cunning way of making money-lending legal for Christians so the Jews can be removed from their position of power, and then passes on to matters outside of France and expounds a method of reaching a peaceful settlement with England. At length the exposition of the different squares of the chess-board is complete, and Truth sums up by quoting St Gregory, 'who in his homilies said that good meat taken in small quantities is eaten more willingly and with better appetite than if the said meat is served in too large quantities' (*Dream*, II, p. 430). She has, therefore, given the king small portions and brief statements, since the king is only young and not well disposed to read long writings. (The analysis of the chess-board allegory is more than a hundred folios in the manuscripts.)

Philippe's final section touches on the matter closest to his heart, the founding of the new military order of the *Chivalry of the Passion* which, when peace has been established in Europe, will spearhead a new crusade to free the Holy Land again and reunite the divided Christian kingdoms. His plans, though more positive than any others of the time, were no more successful than the laments of Machaut, the satire of Deschamps or the invective of Chartier. After the temporary cessation of hostilities which followed the victories of Du Guesclin in 1370–80, and the marriage of Richard II with Isabelle of France in 1396, the war flared up again, and France was locked again in Hell to lament her sins until 1429, when, as the playwright puts it, God harkened to the pleas of the Virgin Mary and the saints of Orleans, Evortius and Aignan, and prepared to deliver the captive:

> Michael, my angel, hearken to me: I want to send you with a message to restore the disorder of France, that noble kingdom. You shall go on a journey to Barois and do as I instruct you. Near a little village called Domrémy, in the land and lordship of Vaucouleurs, you will find without seeking further, a noble maiden. . . . You will tell her that I have sent to tell her that in her shall be my strength . . . and by her the English will be defeated. (*Play of the Siege of Orleans*, p. 271)

After this Annunciation to Joan follow lively scenes of the raising of the siege. The play was written very shortly after the events described.

Even earlier was the account of the victories of the Maid of Orleans (but not her capture and death), composed, appropriately, by a woman, the Venetian-born but French-wedded and widowed Christine de Pisan, who broke a silence of eleven years to write her last work, the *Poem of Joan of Arc* (*Dictié de Jeanne d'Arc*) in 1430. 'For the valour of all the noble men of the past cannot equal that of this girl, who has succeeded in driving out our enemies. It is the work of God who guides her and has given her courage greater than a man's' (*Joan of Arc*, S. xxvi).

One and All Alone: Christine de Pisan[2]

'A widow, alone and dressed in black': that was how Christine de Pisan described herself in one of her early poems, and the theme of loneliness and isolation is reiterated many times, especially in one of the *Ballades*, where every line but one begins with the word 'Alone' (*Seulette*). Nor is this the result of neglect by others. 'I am alone and want to be alone' because my 'sweet friend' has left me. It was when she was left a widow at twenty-five with three small children that Christine turned to writing as a profession, since her husband had left her no other resource: 'For it is the custom for married men not to tell and explain their affairs to their wives, which often turns out badly, as I know by experience, and is not sensible when women are not foolish but prudent and good managers' (*Vision*, p. 154). The description she gives here in the *Vision* (*L'Avison*) written in 1405, more than fifteen years after the event, reveals a very different woman from the desolate, lonely widow in black of the lyrics. Christine herself portrays this change in attitude in an allegory, in the longest and in many ways most important of her works, the poem of the *Mutation of Fortune* (*Mutacion de Fortune*), composed between 1401 and 1404. The first section of this very long encyclopaedic history of the world describes in terms of an allegorical voyage her married life and the death of her husband, swept overboard by a storm: 'Then a sudden rushing wind arose, a whirlwind twisted like a gimlet, which came and struck the ship and snatched up our good captain with such force that it carried him far off into the sea. Then I wanted to die!' (*Mutation*, 1234–40). The ship, left masterless, was in peril of being wrecked, but she was too weak and ignorant to do more than lie on the deck and hope for death till Fortune had pity on her and helped her in her great distress: 'But the help was marvellous . . . for she touched me all over my body, handling each limb as I well recall and holding it in her hands; then she left me' (*Mutation*, 1319, 1327–30). As a result Christine finds herself changed, her fear leaves her, her body becomes stronger and swifter, her voice more powerful. 'I found I had a strong bold heart, which much surprised me, but I realised I had truly become a man. . . . As you hear, I am still a man and have been more than thirteen years, but I would three times rather be a woman as I was' (1359–61, 1395–9).

Man or woman, Christine was a successful and prolific writer, composing, she herself tells us, fifteen principal works, not counting other separate little pieces (*Vision*, p. 164). Her father had given her a good education, against her mother's will, and she made the most of her learning. A talented poet and able to describe her imaginary allegorical figures with some vividness, she is nevertheless at her best as a moralist and historian. The second section of the *Mutation of Fortune* contains a description of Fortune's Castle and the ways that lead to its heights, among which is a path which can only be used after defeating the dragon of Cadmus. Thereafter it is a paradise, 'so agreeable and so pleasing, so delightful and so easy, so sweet-smelling and so pretty that there is no sadness, however great, that is not forgotten by the one who walks there. . . . Briefly, what shall I say of it? It seemed a terrestrial paradise. . . . It is called the path of Great Learning [*grant science*]' (*Mutation*, 3199–203, 3223–4, 3237).

The stories with which she illustrates her work, from history, myth and legend, Bible and Classical texts, clearly indicate Christine's wide reading and excellent memory. Her style is discursive and she favours, in prose, a very Latinate convoluted sentence-structure which makes her works opaque, while her allegories are rarely as well structured as she claims, petering out in a morass of detail. Apart from her works in defence of women, which will be considered separately (see p. 228 below), she wrote a variety of different kinds of treatises, including a life of Charles V (*Le Livre des Fais et Bonnes Moeurs du Sage Roy Charles V*), commissioned by Philip the Bold, Duke of Burgundy, and intended to be both a commemoration of the former king and an example to the Dauphin. Christine was very interested in matters of government and law, as can be seen especially in her adaptation of John of Salisbury's *Polycraticus*, the *Book of the Body Politic* (*Livre du Corps de Policie*) in which she also made extensive use of the *Memorable Needs and Words* of Valerius Maximus. Her erudition was extensive rather than profound, but she had a knack of welding together numerous borrowings and quotations from mainly Classical and Italian sources. She was also a devout woman with good knowledge of the Bible, as she showed in her *Seven Allegorised Psalms* (*Sept Psaumes Allégorisés*) or the 'Consolation' she wrote for Mary of Berry, *The Prison of Human Life* (*La Prison de Vie Humaine*). Inevitably, she wrote on peace, her *Book of Peace* (*Livre de Paix*) being one of the many such works spawned by the troubled times.

More unexpectedly, perhaps, she also wrote on war, her book of *The Feats of Arms and of Chivalry* (*Les Fais d'Armes et de Chevalerie*) being one of her most successful at the time. Her principal source was a Latin treatise on military matters, the *De Re Militari* by Vegetius, which was extremely popular and frequently mined for allusion and quotation by fifteenth-century writers. It is ironical that it was first translated into French in 1284, by Christine's *bête noire*, Jean de Meung, as *L'Art de Chevalerie*. Christine herself, however, worked from the fourteenth-century translation by that prolific vulgariser, Jean de Vignay. She also made considerable, though unacknowledged, use of Bonet's *Tree of Battles* (see p. 217 above).

Christine's love of argument and debate, her insistence on the governing power of reason, stressed particularly in the *Body Politic*, her many references to Classical authors, and her consistently didactic and moralising approach to her material, all mark her out as typical of her age, which produced more literature of information and instruction than any preceding century. The political situation made every writer keenly aware of the society in which he lived, and involved him, willy-nilly, in the task of trying to hold together the crumbling civilisation and culture of which he was a part. Christine was no exception. Unlike her fellow authoress, Marie de France, who lived in an age of story-telling and psychological analysis, Christine could not create, she could only reshape and retell. She is a teacher, above all, with many of the characteristics of the nineteenth-century women moralists. Marie de France, with a handicap of two hundred years, has survived better than Christine because her works have a more universal appeal and life. Christine was a great woman but only a talented writer; Marie is virtually unknown as a woman but had real creative gifts. Inevitably, it is the works that survive, not the creator: the poet can grant immortality to others but not guarantee it for herself.

Mirror of Women

BOTH as a professional writer and as a woman, it was natural that Christine de Pisan should be involved in the major domestic as opposed to political question of the day: the status and character of women. The long-running *querelle des femmes* became briefly the more specifically literary *querelle de la Rose*, for the comments about women put into the mouth of the Old Woman (*La Vieille*) and Nature in the second part of the *Rose* by Jean de Meung roused the ire even of the theologian Jean Gerson, Chancellor of the University of Paris, who wrote a Latin *Tract against the Romance of the Rose* (*Tractatus contra Romantium de Rosa*) in which he roundly condemned the work which 'attacks everyone, vilifies everyone, condemns everyone without exception' (see John Fox, *The Middle Ages*, p. 273). Christine's first work to attack the *Rose* is her *Epistle to the God of Love*, complaining about the anti-feminism of the Ovidian school of writers, and such criticism was obviously widespread for in the prologue to the *Legend of Good Women*, we find Chaucer putting into the mouth of Cupid a similar condemnation, albeit ironically: 'Thou hast translated the Romance of the Rose, / That is an heresye ageyns my lawe / and makest wyse folk from me withdrawe' (*Legend of Good Women*, Prologue F, 329–31; only fragments of Lorris's *Rose* have survived in Middle English – some may be Chaucer's).

The picture of women painted by Jean de Meung, Matheolus and the many other writers of the anti-feminist school, presented them as incurably lecherous, unfaithful, unreliable and selfish. The point at issue in the *querelle des femmes*, therefore, was not the status of women in society but their moral character. Christine makes this clear in her major work in the defence of women, her *City of Ladies* (*Cité des Dames*), written in prose about 1405, in which she describes her meeting with three ladies, Reason, Justice and Equity, who instruct her to build a city with their help; it will be founded on Reason, measured and constructed by Equity, and crowned with roofs and towers by Justice, who will bring the Queen and many noble ladies to dwell there.

The major part of the work consists of a series of stories and descriptions of the ladies who qualify for admission, grouped by characteristics: fidelity, honesty, chastity and so forth. A large number of the Classical candidates in this catalogue of virtuous women are taken by Christine from Boccaccio's book of *Famous Women* (*De mulieribus claris*),[3] but Christine also uses Ovid's *Metamorphoses* and adds, too, women from the Bible, saints – including of course the Virgin Mary, Queen of the city – and a number of notable female figures from French history such as

Blanche, mother of St Louis, Isabeau of Bavaria, wife of Charles VI, and the Duchess of Orleans, whose husband was Charles's brother. Conspicuous by their absence from this gallery are the heroines of medieval literature, with the exception of Griselda. Iseult is briefly mentioned as a woman faithful even to death, but not, interestingly, for her skill at healing. Medea, on the other hand, 'whom many historical works mention', surpassed and exceeded all women in learning, especially in knowledge of herbs and potions. Sublimely indifferent to the drastic measures to which Medea resorted in her efforts to help her lover, Jason, Christine merely concludes that it was 'thanks to the art of her enchantments that Jason won the Golden Fleece' (*City of Ladies*, p. 69). Christine's omission of examples from Arthurian romances may indicate that their historicity had become suspect by this date, or possibly that the general behaviour of these heroines made them ineligible for a place of such high moral tone as the *City of Ladies*. Philippe de Mézières had already made a similar point when he warned: 'the worldly valour of King Arthur was very great but the history of him and his followers is so full of foolish tales that the historicity [*l'ystoire de luy*] is doubtful' (*Dream of the Old Pilgrim*, II, p. 222).

Christine was far from being the only author to point out the examples of good women in history. Chaucer's *Legend of Good Women* is a contemporary collection of such tales, and Eustache Deschamps drew up a list of Nine Worthy Women (*Neuf Preuses*) who could be matched to the Nine Worthies (*Neuf Preux*; see p. 130 above). Deschamps's Worthy Women are all women of status (*femmes de terre*; Deschamps, I, p. 199), a point echoed by a number of subsequent writers (there is a book of coats of arms of the nine male and nine female Worthies in a fifteenth-century manuscript – Bibl. Nat. ff. 24381). The stress on the rank of a very large number of the good women by all the writers reminds us that the general run of anti-feminist stories treat of women of the less exalted ranks, the wives of merchants, citizens and *vilains*, or members of the religious orders; these are the targets of the *moralistes* and the central characters of the *fabliaux* and farces. Both in these works and in the most notable example of bourgeois literature on the side of the ladies, the book of *The Goodman of Paris* (*Le Menagier de Paris*), it is noticeable that the social standing of women and their freedom of action is considerable and well-established.

The Goodman, writing a treatise on household management and behaviour for his young wife, divides his work into three sections, the first on the salvation of the soul and the husband's comfort, the second on enhancing the well-being of the household, and the third on pleasures and pastimes. In all three sections, the genial, elderly husband quotes stories and examples for his wife, including that of Griselda on which he comments, however, that, 'I have not included it to apply to you nor because I want such obedience from you, for I am not worthy of it, and what's more *I am not a marquis who has married you, a shepherdess*, nor *I am not so mad and arrogant nor so immature* as not to know that it is not my place to put you to such tests' (*Goodman*, p. 72; my italics). This more mellow attitude is also found in another of the Goodman's stories in which he describes a wife who learns of her husband's affair with a poor seamstress. She goes to the girl and gives her clothes and bedding and furnishings, saying that her husband is used to such comforts 'and I would rather that you and I together looked after his health than I should look after him alone when he is sick' (*Goodman*, p. 114). Her actions have the desired effect: the husband repents of his liaison, pays off the seamstress and goes home to his wife. This theme is not new; Marie de France had drawn in *Eliduc* a moving picture of a man who elopes with a girl in England though he has a wife in France. When Eliduc's wife learns what has happened she first of all comforts the girl, then retires into a convent so the couple can be free to marry.[4] Again, this sublime charity has the desired effect: after a year the husband and the second wife also enter religion.

The Goodman's description of the pastimes and pleasures open to his young wife, and the dangers that may befall her in society, was never completed, but we have a number of texts which can fill the gap, most notably the *Mirror of Marriage* (*Miroir de Mariage*) by Deschamps; and the very similar and better known, but anonymous, *Fifteen Joys of Marriage* (*Quinze Joyes de Mariage*), whose sarcastic title is modelled on the celebrated Fifteen Joys of Mary. The French word for husband, *mari*, stresses the parallel and underlines a horrifying picture of the miseries of the married state, with not the faintest spark of light for the wretched husband, caught like a fish in the meshes 'where he will spend his days in misery for ever and pass the rest of his life wretchedly' (*Fifteen Joys*, p. 13). Some of the details of contemporary life are particularly vivid in Deschamps's verse redaction, such as the behaviour of the wife when she is pregnant: 'Now she wants to eat cinders or coal, now she wants cheese or wants lettuce; now she wants her husband to kill a pig for her to eat the spleen; . . . now she wants to see neither woman nor man, now wants to be in society, now sings, now laughs, now enjoys herself, now wants to weep, now makes lament' (Deschamps, IX, p. 126). Much of the humour here is enhanced by the rhymes and rhythms, such as the couplet where the wife now wants 'a puree of *chardons* [thistles], now she wants to go to pardons' (p. 126). Both Deschamps and the *Fifteen Joys* refer to the variety of outside activities which the wives insist on enjoying, including shopping extravagantly for themselves and the household, spending money, going to church and to festivals, and even going on pilgrimage; all these activities were popular with medieval women and they seem to have had no difficulty in undertaking them, even if their methods of getting their own way were not always those condemned by the satirists. Chaucer's Wife of Bath was, of course, a notable pilgrim as was the true-life Margery Kempe, while the German Dominican Felix Fabbri, in the accounts of his two visits to the Holy Land in the fifteenth century, includes stories of a group of women apparently travelling unescorted, who when the party visited the River Jordan 'bathed among the reeds above us with modesty, silence and devotion' (*The Wanderings of Felix Fabbri*, II, p. 19).[5]

Nor was it only as wives that the women of the third estate had status and position. The statutes and regulations of the crafts and trades of Paris, drawn up at the end of the thirteenth century by order of St Louis's indefatigable provost, Etienne Boileau, make it clear that women had equal status with men in many of the guilds. In the Fringe-makers' guild, for example, it is stated that 'if a man is fringe-maker [*crespinier*] and his wife also is fringe-maker [*crespinière*] . . . they can have two apprentices in the above manner' (*Arts et Métiers*, p. 86). The wife of a master craftsman in the silk and velvet guild can 'work, or oversee the work, in this craft during her widowhood' (p. 93). Some guilds are exclusively female in their membership, such as the Makers of Fancy Purses (*Aumonieres Sarrazinoises*) who drew up and subscribed to the *ordonnance* of that guild in March 1299 in the presence of the clerks of the corporation and in the name of all the community of 'mistress-workers' (*mestresses ouvrières*) of the town of Paris and of the Châtelet. Their names are all given, and it is notable that some are identified by their dwelling place: Jehanneite de la Riviere; others by appearance: Haoys the lame; others by their parentage: Sedile, daughter of Richart the supplier; others again by their husband's name: Sedille, wife of Jehan Douyn (pp. 384–5). The situation is summed up in the regulations for the Poulterers' guild (*Poulaillers*) where it is specifically stated that 'a woman who never had a husband can buy herself into the poulterer's trade and be a poulteress as freely as a man in all things' (p. 179). This trade, like several others, was a royal monopoly, and the right to trade had to be bought from the person who had purchased the monopoly from the king and sold the right 'to one for more and another less as it seems good to him' (p. 178).

Since these guild-rights also applied to the children born in wedlock it is obvious that these women had sufficient status and potential independence to be able to drive hard bargains with their husbands. Interestingly, Deschamps is most urgent in his rejection of marriage as a viable way of life for the first two estates, claiming that knights and clerks should not marry because 'none of them can exercise his profession, one of clerkhood, the other of knighthood, and at the same time be in the service of women. . . . Study, I say, and valour . . . is lost in them by such practices and the bond of marriage' (Deschamps, IX, p. 256). Study, in particular, Deschamps finds incompatible with the married state and he also deprecates the loss of learning among knights, comparing his contemporaries unfavourably with their glorious ancestors under Charlemagne, 'where study was good, chivalry was found to be great, powerful and strong; and where study was dead or lost by accident, chivalry in consequence was poor and empty' (Deschamps, IX, pp. 265–6). For Deschamps, then, as for Christine but from a different point of view, the question of learning and knowledge was capital in any consideration of marriage and women.

Christine refers in the *City of Ladies* not only to her own good education, which she owed to her father, but to other learned women of her day. What she was fighting, however, was not a refusal to allow women education because they were unable to profit by it, but a general feeling that they would misuse it. We are still concerned with women's moral qualities, not their intellectual ones. Philip of Novara's recommendation that only women entering religion should be taught to read and write is echoed in spirit, if not in letter, by the Knight of La Tour Landry whose *Book* is a work he had compiled for his daughters, 'to teach them to read French' (*pour apprendre à rommancier*; Knight of the Tour Landry, *Book*, S. 1). The book is in the usual medieval didactic mode of stories with moral comments and many of the *exempla* are from history, chronicles and other well-known collections in the knight's library: 'books of the Bible, that I had, Deeds of Kings and Chronicles of France, of Greece and of England, of many other strange lands' (S. 1).

Perhaps because of his class or because he is writing for very young girls, 'young and small and without understanding' (S. 1), the Knight is very severe and strict in his recommendations and tells horrifying tales of women who were tormented by devils after their death for having plucked their eyebrows or used make-up. They should avoid jousts and dances and even pilgrimages, for there are always slanderers around ready to gossip even about innocent behaviour (p. 57). The violent and cruel fate that often befalls those guilty of little worse than folly is in marked contrast to the more gentle and loving admonitions of the Goodman of Paris, and puts the Knight's *Book* in the class of the severe moral tales for children of the later centuries such as *Strewelpeter* or *The Fairchild Family*.

This prejudice against women's learning spills over into the romances, where heroines may safely be competent to read or write a love letter but no more. Thus the daughter of King Ypomenes, trained in the seven arts, sells herself to the devil in exchange for his help in punishing her brother who has refused her incestuous advances. The brother is to be torn to pieces by dogs and predicts that she will give birth to a monster: 'and because you make me give my flesh to the dogs, this beast will have in its belly hounds that will continually bark in memory . . . of the beasts to which I am thrown'. In due course the monster is born and becomes the celebrated Questing Beast of Arthurian romance (see *The Questing Beast*, p. 30).[6]

Although the study of the arts could be dangerous, many of Christine's contemporaries were interested patrons of letters, and she herself had no apparent difficulty in earning a living by her pen. Nor was it only poets who benefited from the involvement of these cultured members of the aristocracy. There are many references to women as patrons of the drama: the Canonesses of St Waudru regularly gave money towards the staging of religious plays in Mons and had a box for the 1501 passion play, which was also attended by the wife of the bailiff of Hainault, the ducal representative in the province (*Mons Passion*, p. xvi). In Metz in 1468, Dame Catherine Baudoiche had the play of St Catherine of Siena performed at 'her charge and expense'. The role of the saint was taken by a young girl, daughter of a local furrier, 'who did her duty marvellously well to the delight and pleasure of all. Nevertheless the said girl had twenty-three hundred lines in her part, but she knew them all perfectly. And this girl spoke so pitifully and convincingly that she made several people weep and everyone was very pleased' (*Mystères*, II, 32). As a direct result of her performance, the girl married a gentleman, a soldier from Metz, 'who fell in love with her because of the great pleasure he took in her playing'. This seems to be the earliest recorded example in post-Classical times of an actress marrying into the aristocracy. It is also the first but not the only reference to women acting on the stage in France in the fifteenth century: there are several women recorded as performers in the Passion at Mons and Valenciennes, while at Romans in 1509 all the female roles were played by women, including the torturers' tart who was enacted by the wife of a leading citizen. No stigma attached to such amateur involvement in the drama for men or women but female professional entertainers, or *jongleresses*, shared the lowly status of their male colleagues, who were included in the category of vagabonds and wastrels by all respectable members of society.

The young actress's ability to remember such a long role would have particularly endeared her to Christine de Pisan, who prided herself on her Memory, one of the four jewels in the chaplet given to her by her mother, Nature, the other three being Consideration, Discretion and Retentiveness (*Mutation*, 568–640). Christine was a scholar and a teacher, not an entertainer or polemicist. Her collection of tales and the elaborate allegory in which they are enshrined, are presented in reasonable and orderly and truthful form. Unfortunately for her cause and that of her fellow women the opposition possessed stronger weapons – lively stories, vigorous vocabulary, above all the humour and vitality which make for popular literature. It takes a great writer to make goodness as interesting as evil, as is notable in the narrative and dramatic accounts of the life of Christ. Christine with all her learning and desire to reinstate her fellows lacks the literary skills which alone could have given her *City of Ladies* the same status as the *Decameron* or the *Canterbury Tales*. She has neither the acid cynicism of the *Fifteen Joys of Marriage* nor the narrative gifts of the story-tellers in the *Seven Sages of Rome* or the *Cent Nouvelles Nouvelles*, the big collections of tales, many of them showing women in a less than favourable light, that were so popular in the fourteenth and fifteenth centuries. They aimed only to entertain, not to instruct, and as a result have survived the centuries. When she writes as a mourning widow, Christine, too, can still move us and this personal quality is even more marked in the verse of the two greatest poets of the fifteenth century who, through the fortune of war or the misfortune of character, were outside the society in which they lived: Charles d'Orléans and François Villon.

The Poet as Outsider

(a)   *Charles d'Orléans*

Charles d'Orléans was involved in and suffered from the political disorders of the age from early childhood: he was only thirteen years old when in 1407 his father Louis, Duke of Orleans and leader of the Armagnac faction, was assassinated by followers of his cousin and rival, John the Fearless, duke of Burgundy. The new duke of Orleans saw his mother die of grief in 1408, and the following year his wife, Isabelle, widow of Richard II of England, died in childbirth. For several more years Charles struggled to obtain satisfaction from Burgundy for his father's death but without success, and then in 1415 he was wounded in the Battle of Agincourt and captured by the English. He spent the next twenty-five years as a prisoner in England, and during this enforced exile from his native land and exclusion from the society to which he belonged, Charles, like so many others before and since, turned to poetry for consolation.

Charles d'Orléans was an amateur poet in the best sense of the word, writing only what he wished and needed to write, with no axe to grind or patron to please. His whole output is lyrical, personal and essentially aristocratic. Though he was a prisoner and often in straitened circumstances, very few details of his daily life can be gleaned from the large number of poems composed in both French and English during the quarter of a century in which he painfully matured: 'I am a fruit of winter, less tender than summer fruit, and have been put in store to soften my green hardness, set to ripen in the straw of prison' (*Ballade* LXXX).

Nor is there much in his poetry about the war or the political situation in France, though a few poems reveal his frustration and longing for his native land, which inspired an impassioned plea for peace at any price in *Ballade* LXXVI. He appeals in turn to the Virgin Mary, 'queen of Heaven and mistress of the world', to the 'prelates and men of holy life', to the princes and lords, 'kings, dukes, counts, barons filled with nobility, gentlemen of chivalry', to 'people who suffer tyranny . . . loyal merchants', and to the joyous gallants of society 'who want to spend your money graciously'. To all he addresses the same plea: 'Pray for peace, the true treasure of joy'. In 1433 during peace negotiations between France and England, Charles was taken to Dover, expecting to be freed, 'and looked towards the land of France' but the plans did not mature and he was taken back to his prison, having experienced memories of 'the sweet pleasure I used to find in that land'. Disappointed but still hopeful, he 'loaded the ship Hopefulness with all my desires, praying them to cross the sea without delay and to commend

me to France. Now God grant us a good peace without delay'
(*Ballade* LXXV).

But peace was not yet signed and Charles returned, resigned,
to his prison physically and to his private fantasy world
poetically, a world where he could dwell 'in the chamber of my
thoughts well equipped with pleasant comforts; then I counsel
my heart to dwell therein and guard it well against all
disturbing news' (*Ballade* CXIX). Lying in bed in his room, his
heart reads all night 'in the romance of pleasant thoughts', for
his world is peopled by abstractions, many of them drawn from
the *Romance of the Rose*. Surrounded by them, in *ballades* and a
few longer poems he chronicles his love for his lady, Beauty,
whose identity, or even reality, has been much discussed by
scholars.

His whole life is lived in this imaginary society which
becomes strangely real. The forests of Tedious Sadness and
Long Delay are peopled by Loyalty, with his banner unfurled,
or by the *cortège* of more than forty horses of his train, 'not
counting the baggage and the pack animals', as the poet rides
through on his way to the City of Destiny, staying awhile in the
Hostelry of Thought (*Ballade* CV). There are sounds of war as
Burning Desire assails again the dwelling of his heart, with
Greek fire which cannot be put out by all his tears (*Ballade*
XXVI). He plays chess and backgammon with Love, but loses;
declines to ride out maying or join in the pastimes of Saint
Valentine's Day because he is unable to rise from the bed of
Dreary Thought (*Ballade* LXVI); but he welcomes the return of
spring and the end of the cold winter in a rare reference to
physical discomfort: 'Winter makes the fields and trees old,
with beards hoary with snow, and is so cold and harsh and wet
that we have to crouch close to the fire, unable to go out of
doors, like a moulting hawk' (*Ballade* LXXIX).

Eventually Charles was freed, thanks, ironically, to the
efforts of Philip of Burgundy, son of his father's murderer, and
returned to France where he married Mary of Cleves, niece of
Burgundy, and after a brief period of political activity settled
down to another twenty-five years of poetic dream-world
existence, this time at his castle of Blois. There is not much
change in the substance of the poems, though he wrote many

rondeaux instead of his previous favourite form, the *ballade*, but one difference is noticeable: the descriptions are still basically courtly and aristocratic, but now the melancholy shadow-world of the poems written in prison is tinged with life and colour, a sensual reality of texture and scent: the ghost-ship of Good Hope is now a Loire boat on which the duke journeyed from Orleans to Blois, watching the vessels passing him blown by a favourable wind (*Ballade* xcviii). Instead of the colourless forests of Long Delay, where his servants were sent ahead, he describes the outriders of Summer 'who have come to prepare his dwelling and spread his carpets woven of flowers and green. Spreading out the velvet carpet of green grass over the land, Summer's servants have arrived' (*Rondeau* xxx). It is from this last happier period of his life that comes his best-known poem:

> The season has left off his cloak
> Of wind, of coldness and of rain,
> And dressed himself in broidered clothes
> Of gleaming sunshine, bright and clear.
> There is no animal or bird
> But in its own tongue sings or shouts:
> The season has left off his cloak.
>
> The river and the brook and spring
> All bear a lovely livery;
> In silver drops of filigree
> Each one is decked out anew.
> The season has left off his cloak.
>
> (*Rondeau* xxxi)

Life at Blois was not entirely lived in an imaginary world, however. It was an age of drama and poetry competitions in the towns among the *puys* and the *confréries*, and Charles organised many poetry contests at Blois, where the first line and the form of the poem were prescribed. On one occasion the contestants included a young Parisian scholar and poet who, like the duke, was set apart from the society around him, not in this case by blind Fate but by his own temperament and actions. His name was François Villon.

(b)   *François Villon*

Villon's experience on the Wheel of Fortune was almost a mirror-image of his fellow-poet's. The son of poor parents, François was adopted by a Parisian priest, Guillaume de Villon, educated at the Sorbonne and became Master of Arts in 1452. So far, Fortune had smiled on him but in 1455 Villon killed a priest in a brawl and the following year was involved in a robbery and fled from Paris. For the next eight years he was in and out of prison, and in 1463 was condemned to be hanged but the sentence was commuted to banishment from Paris. Nothing is known of his life after that time, nor of his death.

In his poetry Villon, like Charles, stood apart from the society in which he lived, but where the prince created for himself a courtly Garden of Love, the context of Villon's works, the *Legacy* (*Lais*) and the *Testament*, is the tavern-hell of the *fabliaux* and the drama, peopled by types rather than abstractions, warm and colourful where Charles's prison world had been cool and austere. Using the device of a series of mock bequests, Villon introduces the names of friends and enemies as Adam de la Halle or Raoul de Houdenc had done (see p. 178 above) but the names are only labels: there is no life in them. Catherine de Vaucelles, mentioned once in a *ballade*, is no more real than the anonymous 'she' to whom he bequeathed his enshrined heart. Behind the mockery of the legacies – his hair-clippings to the barber, a fine feast to the religious orders: 'Item, I leave to the Mendicants, the Daughters of God and the Beguines, savoury, tasty titbits, flawns and capons and fat hens' (*Legacy*, xxxii) – there is an abyss of emptiness, of fear, old age and death. The Belle Heaulmière laments the passing years: 'I seem to hear her say, "O proud cruel age why have you struck me so soon, . . . taking from me the beauty which gave me great power over clerks and merchants and churchmen" ' (Villon, *Oeuvres*, p. 39); and Villon returns to this theme constantly: 'This world does not last for ever whatever the rich bullies think' and the poor old women who watched the young girls enviously 'ask God why they were born so soon and for what right. Our Lord keeps quiet and silent, for in an argument he'd lose' (Villon, *Oeuvres*, p. 38). In verses like this Villon speaks to the human condition at all times, and there is a hopeless despair in the Heaulmière's lines: 'who shall hold me back, who, from striking myself and killing myself here and now?' This is a bleak picture that Villon paints, like the speeches of Judas in the passion plays or the laments of the Fallen Angels, for unlike the usual pictures of misery in the fifteenth century, it is a world that cannot be amended. Moralists and satirists both fundamentally believe that things could be better if everyone did their duty, but Villon speaks not to, but for, the weak and the sinners: 'I want to talk about myself, poor me' (p. 49).

Although he had no hope of better things in this life, Villon has at least a spark of belief if not hope in the mercy of God hereafter, or so it would appear from the genuine religious feeling he conveys in the *ballade* he wrote as a legacy for his mother: 'Item I give to my poor mother [a poem] in homage to Our Mistress. . . . I have no other castle or fortress where I can find refuge for soul or body when great distress falls on me, nor my mother, wretched woman.' In the *ballade*, 'a prayer to Our Lady', Villon speaks in the last stanza as his mother: 'I am a poor woman and old, ignorant and never learnt to read. I go to my parish church and there I see Paradise, painted with harps and lutes, and a Hell where the damned are boiled; one frightens me, the other makes me glad. Grant me to have the joy, high Goddess to whom all sinners should resort, filled with faith, without hypocrisy or sloth. In this faith I want to live and die' (p. 61).

Although the setting of his poems is the world of thieves, prostitutes and drunkards, Villon's language and imagery reveal his education and poetic gifts. In many poems he recalls heroes and heroines of legends and history, the great men like Charlemagne and Alexander who 'have gone with the wind', or the beautiful and good women who passed 'like the snows of yesteryear'. He neither conceals nor parades his learning: it is a part of him, like the brutal humour or the grim despair. Villon swings to and fro between the lost past and the future he fears, like the hanged men in his last and most moving *ballade*, the *Epitaph*, the poem of the hanged men: only on the gallows does Villon become part of the crowd, one of the group, in whose name he appeals to all men:

Brothers, fellow men, who live after us, do not have your hearts hardened against us, for if you have pity on us, poor wretches, God will more readily have mercy on you. . . . If we call you brothers you should not scorn it, though we are executed by justice. For you know that not all men are born with good sense in them . . . we swing to and fro in the varying wind, in ceaseless movement, the birds have pecked us more full of holes than a sewing thimble. Do not join our brotherhood but pray to God that he will pardon us. (p. 153).

These bleached skeletons, dangling on the gallows, belong with the skull-faced popes and kings of the Dance of Death and the marble-shrouded corpses of the cadaver-tombs. Like the statue of the Tempter on Strasburg Cathedral, the fifteenth century concealed behind its smiling face and elegant robes the crawling snakes and toads of corruption and death. The towns were prosperous, the courts magnificent and the Church ritual of unparalleled splendour, but the upheavals of the fourteenth century had left indelible scars. The vitality of the epics, the ideals of courtesy and chivalry had dwindled to the pale wraiths of Charles d'Orléans's shadow-plays; faith and fervour were replaced by frantic attempts to buy the favour of the Church, not for love of God or man but from fear of death and damnation. The towns that had survived the wars and disasters flourished on the surface, but the dregs of society in the over-crowded slums and stews seethed with impotent resentment or drowned their sorrows and fears in taverns: 'Whoever dies, dies in agony, as he loses breath and wind. His gall bursts on his heart and he sweats, God knows that sweat! There is no one to ease his pain, no child, no brother or sister there would be willing then to take his place' (p. 30). It is not inappropriate that the greatest poet of the fifteenth century, indeed perhaps of the whole medieval period, was a drunken brawler, a thief and a convicted murderer.

Conclusion: the End and the Beginning

THE *Epitaph* was not quite Villon's last poem and he himself not quite the last medieval writer. The delicately barbed irony of *Little John of Saintré* (*Petit Jean de Saintré*) by Villon's contemporary Antoine de la Sale, with his less-than-rose-tinted view of courtly love, was followed by the more robust satire of *John of Paris* (*Jean de Paris*) with its cheerful mockery of the English, and the bawdy, unsubtle but vigorous story-telling of the *Hundred New Tales* (*Cent Nouvelles Nouvelles*). Above all in this fifteenth-century society, where the law governed the health of the body politic as priest and physician cared for the spiritual and physical needs of the individual, legal forms and terminology dominated the literature of the last decades, from the farces and *sotties* of the secular drama to the mock case-histories of Martial d'Auvergne's *Love's Verdict* (*Arrêts d'Amour*) or the satirical poetry of the *basochien* Guillaume Coquillart. But time was running out for the Middle Ages and these writers, like the composers of the great passion plays or the poets of the school of the *Grand Rhétoriqueurs*, exist in a literary no man's land between the end of the Middle Ages – baptised (*in extremis* and in Latin (*media tempestas*) by Giovanni Andrea in 1469 – and the ambivalent, enigmatic sixteenth century which lies like a hinge between the medieval period and the Golden Age of French Classicism.

The Renaissance was not really a moment in time for French culture: it was more a series of convulsive changes in attitudes and ideas, birth pangs of the new world. Neither Renaissance nor Reform could create from nothing; their purpose was renewal rather than novelty, revival and imitation not originality; a reworking and remoulding of pre-existent and often well-used material. When Columbus found the New World he was actually looking for another way to the Old.

This principle of renewal was expressed in literature in many ways. The fool's-cap farces of fifteenth-century France were rejected in favour of the equally conventionalised *commedia dell'arte* masks of the Italian comedians. In the *Defence and*

Illustration of the French Language (1549), Du Bellay and his fellow poets of the Pléiade condemned the *virelays* and *rondeaux* of Machaut's courtly poetry and urged that these 'dainties' (*épiceries*) should be replaced by the sonnet, perfected by Machaut's contemporary, Petrarch, with his equally formalised code of love.

One of the first works to be printed in French was *The Mirror of Human Life* (Lyons, 1477). The title proved something of an omen, and from then on medieval epics and romances, poems and plays streamed off the presses while Caxton's list of publications includes many translations from French literature of the fourteenth and fifteenth centuries.

Like the twelfth century, the sixteenth was an age of change, development and evolution. It was above all a time of youth, reacting vigorously against the culture it had inherited, rejecting the authority of the preceding generation in favour of the fashionable novelties from Italy or the Classical sources of its ancestors.

One man above all epitomises this double-headed Janus activity: François Rabelais. In the five books of his saga of the giants *Gargantua and Pantagruel*, published between 1535 and 1560, he utilises every part of the legacy the Middle Ages had bequeathed to him: the birth and youthful exploits of the hero-prince, Gargantua; his education – moral, physical and intellectual; the horrors of invasion and conquest, with the defence of the 'just' war; the allegorical, ideal community of the Abbey of the Will; the Classical erudition of the philosopher-king, Pantagruel; the crude humour of Panurge; the belly-laugh and sly humour of Brother John; the superabundance of language; the examination of attitudes to women and marriage in *Book Three*, the travels of *Books Four and Five* when the giant and his companions set off on their pilgrimage to the holy place of the oracle; the quest for the Sacred Bottle with its enigmatic one-word challenge: Drink.

However, Rabelais is more, much more, than the sum of his medieval parts, though his roots are firmly in the age when men were 'dwarves mounted on the shoulders of giants so that we can see more and further than they . . . because we are raised and born aloft upon that giant mass' (Bernard of Chartres). For in Rabelais, the giants and men walk side by side, no longer looking only ahead and above but also around and among, talking not of Man but of men; no longer a reflection of the greater world of the macrocosm but making the world itself their mirror. Doctor, priest, mocker and moralist, pragmatist, humanist, preacher and poet, Rabelais presided over the emergence of the new man, reformed from the fragments of medieval thought, reborn of the floodwaters of disaster and the fires of heresy and war.

Appendix I: Genealogical Tables

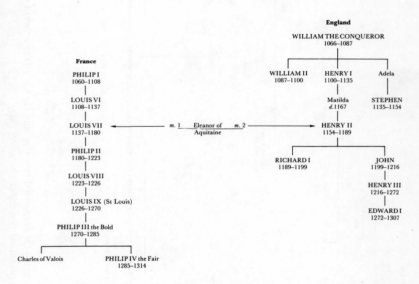

TABLE 1 *Royal Houses of France and England up to the beginning of the Hundred Years War*

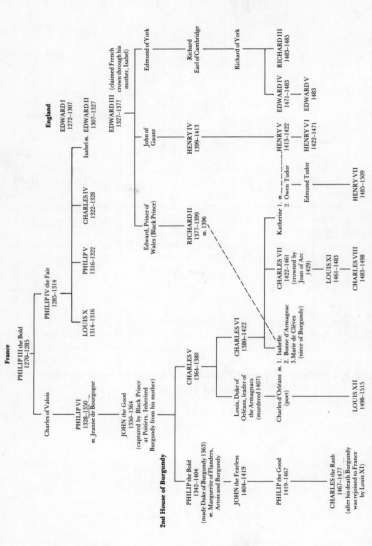

TABLE 2 *England, France and Burgundy during the Hundred Years War and the Civil War between the Armagnacs and the Burgundians (principal characters only)*

Appendix II: Suggestions for Further Reading and Notes

1. INTRODUCTION: THE MIRROR AND THE IMAGE

John Fox, *A Literary History of France*, vol. 1: *The Middle Ages* (London, 1974). The most recent and useful general history of French literature. Fox includes many quotations from texts in both French and English.

P.-Y. Badel, *Introduction à la vie littéraire du moyen âge* (Paris, 1969).

NOTES

1. For the relationship between Latin and the vernacular literature, see E. R. Curtius, *European Literature and the Latin Middle Ages*, trans. Willard Trask, Bollingen Series no. xxxvi (New York, 1952).

2. Lydgate's *Pilgrimage of Human Life*, ed. Furnivall and Locock, Early English Text Society, 1901–4, was translated from the second, expanded version of Guillaume de Deguilleville's *Pèlerinage de Vie Humaine*. The first, shorter redaction, the only French one to be available in a modern edition, does not include the Mirror of Conscience referred to there. See also pp. 172–6.

2. THE FIGHTING COMMUNITY

Gaston Paris, *La vie poétique de Charlemagne* (Paris, 1905, rev. edn).

The Bibliographical Bulletin of the International Rencesvals Society (*BBSR*). This bulletin is published periodically and contains details of all work on the Franco-Spanish epic published in the preceding years. So far fourteen bulletins have appeared since 1958.

Norman Daniel, *Heroes and Saracens: An Interpretation of the 'Chansons de geste'* (Edinburgh, 1984). This study of the Saracens in literature includes brief summaries of some seventy texts (see pp. 328–40).

For Arthurian bibliography see next chapter.

NOTES

1. For the Cycle of the Crusades, built up round the character of Godfrey of Bouillon, see chapter 4.

2. The French word *sage* has a wider range of meanings than the modern English 'wise': it implies also moderation, prudence and commonsense.

3. See *Letters of C. S. Lewis*, ed. W. H. Lewis (London, 1966), pp. 270–1, 279.

4. For the rules of challenge and relationship between life and literature see: R. H. Bloch, 'From Grail Quest to Inquest: the Death of King Arthur and the Birth of France', *Modern Language Review*, 69 (1974), pp. 40–55; and Lynette

247

R. Muir and R. H. Bloch, 'Further Thoughts on the *Mort Artu*', *Modern Language Review*, 71 (1976), pp. 26–30.

    5. For bibliography on pilgrimage, see below, chapter 8, note 5.

    6. See Jean Gimpel, *The Cathedral Builders*, trans. Theresa Waugh (Salisbury, 1983), p. 51.

    7. A less-bigoted attitude to Muslims in the thirteenth century is also indicated by such works as the *Livre de l'eschiele Mahomet*, a translation into French of *Mahomet's Journey to Paradise*, ed. Peter Wunderli, Romanica Helvetica, no. 77 (Berne, 1968). Ramon Lull's *Dialogue of the Gentile and the Three Wise Men*, summarised in E. Langlois, *La Vie en France au moyen âge*, vol. IV: *La Vie spirituelle* (Paris, 1928; rept 1970), consists of a discussion between a Christian, a Muslim and a Jew on the differences between their religions. Many references to medieval texts may be found in the notes to R. Finucane, *Soldiers of the Faith: Crusaders and Moslems at War* (London, 1983). Norman Daniel, *Heroes and Saracens*, considers especially the medieval equation of Saracens with pagans.

3. THE QUEST OF THE SELF

Colin Morris, *The Discovery of the Individual, 1050–1200* (London, 1972).

Roger Boase, *The Origin and Meaning of Courtly Love* (Manchester UP, 1977).

R. S. Loomis (ed.), *Arthurian Literature in the Middle Ages* (Oxford, 1959).

Bibliographical Bulletin of the International Arthurian Society (BBIAS). Published annually since 1948, it contains details of all works on Arthurian material published in the preceding year.

C. E. Pickford and R. W. Last (eds), *The Arthurian Bibliography*, vols I and II (Ipswich, 1981–3).

Eugene Vinaver, *The Rise of Romance* (Oxford, 1971).

NOTES

    1. For outlines of the main theories on the origin of the concept of courtly love see R. Boase, *The Origin and Meaning of Courtly Love*.

    2. See Richard W. Southern, *The Making of the Middle Ages* (London, 1953), ch. v, and C. S. Lewis, *The Allegory of Love* (Oxford, 1936).

    3. The custom of defending a ford or other particular site against all comers was not peculiar to the heroes of romance. It was also practised in real life by knights who wished to earn a reputation for themselves. One of the most notable of the later exponents of this custom was Boucicaut who held the lists for twenty-four days. The *Livre des faits du bon messire Jean Le Maingre, dit Bouciquaut*, ed. Theodore Godefroy (Paris, 1620), was written about 1420 by an anonymous writer but has been attributed to Christine de Pisan (see p. 252, n.2).

    4. I have given a detailed account of the early Grail literature in French because the subject is so frequently and inaccurately treated.

    5. See Lynette Muir, 'Villard de Honnecourt and the Grail', *Bibliographical Bulletin of the International Arthurian Society*, 23 (1971), pp. 137–41.

6. For the iconography of the *Romance of the Rose* and other allegories, see Rosemond Tuve, *Allegorical Imagery: Some Medieval Books and their Posterity* (Princeton UP, 1966).

7. Sources for the lore about weasels and other animals may be found in Beryl Rowland, *Animals with Human Faces: A Guide to Animal Symbolism* (London, 1974).

4.   THE WORLD UPSIDE DOWN

Kenneth Varty, *Reynard the Fox* (Leicester UP, 1967).

Grace Frank, *The Medieval French Drama* (Oxford, 1954).

Jean Dufournet, *Adam de la Halle à la recherche de lui-même ou le jeu dramatique de la Feuillée* (Paris, 1974).

NOTES

1. The game of Kings and Queens is cited by a number of authors in the thirteenth and fourteenth centuries. See Mathilde Laigle, *Le Livre des Trois Vertus de Christine de Pisan et son milieu historique et littéraire* (Paris, 1912), ch. VI. It seems to have been a sort of question-and-answer game with the speaker sworn to tell the truth.

2. Examples of women disguising themselves as men are also found in the saints' plays. In the *Mystère de St Adrien*, for example, the saints' wives dress up as men in order to visit their imprisoned husbands.

5.   MACROCOSM AND MICROCOSM

E. Langlois, *La Vie en France au moyen âge*, 4 vols (Paris, 1927; rept 1970). The four volumes of Langlois' study cover a vast range of French literature, much of it still unedited fifty years later. Volume 2: *D'apres les moralistes du temps* and volume 3: *La Connaissance de la nature et du monde* have been particularly useful in this chapter.

C. S. Lewis, *The Discarded Image* (Oxford, 1964).

E. M. W. Tillyard, *The Elizabethan World Picture* (London, 1943). These last two books provide valuable source material for the continuing traditions of the world-image in medieval times.

NOTES

1. The four things 'long' are neck, leg, hoof and tail; the four things 'broad': chest, croup, mouth and nostril; and the four things 'short': paston, back, ears and tail-bone (Br. Lib. Additional MS 16, 563, fo. 75 verso). See also William H. Hulme, 'A Probable Source for Some of the Lore of Fitzherbert's *Book of Husbandry*', *Modern Philology*, 6 (Chicago, 1908).

2. Details of the various medieval versions of the *Voyage of St Brendan* and of the Celtic *immrama* may be found in the critical apparatus of *The Anglo-Norman Voyage of St Brendan* by Benedeit, ed. Ian Short and Brian Merrilees (Manchester UP, 1979).

3. There are a number of versions of the Alexander romance in medieval French. I have used that by Alexandre de Paris in vol. II of the edition in the Elliott Monograph Series (Princeton UP, 1937).

4. Useful sources of iconographical material can be found in the following books: D. D. R. Owen, *The Legend of Roland: A Pageant of the Middle Ages* (Oxford, 1973); Elizabeth Jenkins, *The Mystery of King Arthur* (London, 1975); Kenneth Varty, *Reynard the Fox* (Leicester, 1967); Gertrud Schiller, *Iconography of Christian Art*, trans. Janet Seligman, 2 vols (London, 1971).

5. Emile Mâle, *The Gothic Image* (London, 1961). (New translations of Mâle's three books on *Religous Art in France* are being published in the Bollingen Series, no. XC, Princeton UP, 1984.)

6.   THE CITY AND THE PILGRIM

S. Berger, *La Bible française au moyen-âge: Etude sur les plus anciennes versions de la Bible écrites en prose de langue d'oil* (Paris, 1884).

Jean Bonnard, *Les Traductions de la Bible en vers français au moyen-âge* (Paris, 1884).

A. Lecoy de la Marche, *La Chaire française au moyen-âge* (Paris, 1886).

E. Langlois, *La Vie en France au moyen âge*, vol. IV: *La Vie spirituelle* (Paris, 1928; rept 1970).

C. A. Robson, *Cambridge History of the Bible*, vol. II: *Vernacular Scriptures in France* (Cambridge, 1969).

NOTES

1. S. Berger, *La Bible française au moyen-âge* (Paris, 1884), p. 28.

2. Ian Wilson, *The Turin Shroud* (London, 1978). See also L. R. Muir, 'The Holy Shroud in Medieval Literature', *Sindon* (Turin, 1982), pp. 23–36.

3. J. C. Payen, *Le Motif du repentir dans la littérature française médiévale*, Publications Romanes et Françaises, no. 98 (Geneva, 1967).

4. This collection of sermons was printed in 1506 and probably preached in the 1460s. Only the last phrase of the quotation is in French.

5. Ramon Lull stated that he was going to present his book *D'Amiche Amat* to the king in Latin and to the queen in French (E. Langlois, *La Vie en France au moyen âge*, vol. IV: *La Vie spirituelle* (Paris, 1928) p. 337). Philippe de Mézières also assumed the king would have a knowledge of Latin (see p. 222). The lack of Latin for the ladies is attested in the seventeenth century, also, by Corneille who in the Preface of his play *Pompée* declares he has given two extracts about Pompey in Latin 'lest my translation cause them to lose too much of their power and elegance. The ladies will get someone to translate them for them' – *Au lecteur*, P. Corneille, *Théâtre complet*, vol. II (Paris, 1942).

6. The *Somme le roy* is unpublished and I have quoted mainly from the outline in Langlois, *La Vie spirituelle*. A few pages have been printed in *The Parisian Miniaturist, Honoré*, ed. Eric G. Millar, Faber Library of Illuminated Manuscripts (London, 1959), Plates 3–8.

7. For these allegories see R. Tuve, *Allegorical Imagery*.

8. See ch. 1 n. 2.

9. Gustave Cohen, *Mystères et Moralités du MS 617 de Chantilly*. The plays were composed and copied by 'Sueur Katherine Bourlet'. It is significant that one of the two Nativity plays in the manuscript includes roles for St Anne and the Virgin's sisters who all go to visit the mother and baby. Such additional women's roles in a play composed for a convent are unique in French drama.

10. Bourges, in *The Staging of Religious Drama in Europe in the later Middle Ages*, ed. Meredith and Tailby (Kalamazoo, Mich., 1983), p. 91.

11. See L. Petit de Julleville, *La Comédie et les Mœurs en France au moyen âge* (Paris, 1868).

12. The Introduction to Dorothy Sayers's translation of Dante's *Purgatory* contains much useful material on the medieval attitude to the Church's teaching on Purgatory; see especially pp. 54–61.

7.   A STAGE IS ALL THE WORLD

L. Petit de Julleville, *Les Mystères*, 2 vols (Paris, 1888).

——, *Répertoire du théâtre comique en France au moyen âge* (Paris, 1867).

——, *Les Comédiens en France au moyen âge* (Paris, 1868).

——, *La Comédie et les mœurs en France au moyen âge* (Paris, 1868).

Grace Frank, *The Medieval French Drama* (Oxford, 1954).

Alan Knight, *Aspects of Genre in Late Medieval French Drama* (Manchester UP, 1983). Up-to-date bibliography of non-biblical drama.

The Staging of Religious Drama in Europe in the Later Middle Ages: Texts and Documents in English Translation, ed. Peter Meredith and John Tailby, Early Drama, Art and Music Monograph Series, no. 4 (Western Michigan University, Kalamazoo, 1983). This includes many quotations from French plays and a bibliography of the religous drama.

NOTES

1. See Richard Southern, *The Seven Ages of the Theatre* (London, 1962), pp. 21–34.

2. See Peter Spufford and Wendy Wilkinson, *Interim Listing of the Exchange Rates of Medieval Europe* (University of Keele, 1977).

3. For the Lille and Saint-Omer drama references see *Staging*, ed. Meredith and Tailby.

4. It has recently been pointed out that the hitherto unstudied manuscript of French plays from the Herzog-Augusti-Bibliothek at Wolfenbüttel contains a sequence of plays from Lille designed for processional performance. The manuscript has not yet been edited. I am indebted to Professor Alan Knight for this information.

5. I am grateful to Madame Wathelet-Willem of the University of Liège for sending me a copy of the printed text of the modern version and the photographs which formed the basis of the illustration (*Le Monde et Abus*, in *Ecritures*, 78 (University of Liège, 1978), pp. 67–94).

6. See W. Tydeman, *The Theatre in the Middle Ages* (Cambridge, 1978), p. 183.

8.   INSIDE, OUTSIDE: MAN IN SOCIETY

John Fox, *A Literary History of France*, vol. 1: *The Middle Ages* (London, 1974), ch. 12–14.

M. A. Screech, *Ecstasy and the Praise of Folly* (London, 1980).

——, *Rabelais* (London, 1979). Both these books contain extensive bibliographies and many references for the period from the end of the Middle Ages and the early sixteenth century.

Janet Ferrier, *Prose Writers of the Fifteenth Century* (Manchester UP, 1953).

NOTES

1. See *Règlements sur les arts et métiers de Paris . . . connus sous le nom du Livre des Métiers d'Etienne Boileau*, ed. G. P. Depping, Collection des documents inédits sur l'histoire de France (Paris, 1837).

2. Useful bibliography for Christine de Pisan and her contemporaries is listed in the edition of the *Dictié de Jeanne d'Arc* and in the translation of *The Book of the City of Ladies* (New York, 1984).

3. Interest in the status of women in the fifteenth and sixteenth centuries is indicated by the continuing popularity of Boccaccio's book in France. It was a major source of the *Lives of Famous Women* (*Vies des Femmes célèbres*) composed by Antoine Dufour for Anne of Brittany in 1507. (The introduction to the edition of Dufour's book lists a number of other works on the same subject contemporary with it.)

4. The psychological rightness of the wife's behaviour in the context of Marie's lay distracts attention from the fact that in canon law the husband would not be free to remarry just because his wife had entered religion.

5. *The Wanderings of Felix Fabbri* occupy volumes VII–X of the Library of the Palestine Pilgrims' Text Society (rept AMS Press, New York, 1971). For general bibliography on medieval pilgrimage see Jonathan Sumption, *Pilgrimage: An Image of Medieval Religion* (London, 1975).

6. Lynette Muir, 'The Questing Beast, its Origins and Development', *Orpheus*, IV (Catania, 1957) pp. 24–32.

Appendix III: List of Modern English Translations

THE texts are arranged in sections following the chapter divisions of the book. Adaptations and retellings have not been included.

SECTION 1: ANTHOLOGIES AND SELECTIONS

The Penguin Book of French Verse, vol. I: *To the Fifteenth Century*, introduced and ed. Brian Woledge (Harmondsworth, Middx, 1961). A wide range of French texts of all kinds with prose English translation.

The Ways of Love, trans. Norma Lorre Goodrich (London, 1965). This includes extracts from Chrétien, Marie de France and *Girart de Vienne*. Also the *Romance of the History of the Grail* by Robert de Boron, the *Life of St Alexis*, the *Châtelain of Coucy* and the *Swan Knight*.

SECTION 2: 'CHANSONS DE GESTE' AND EPIC LITERATURE

The Song of Roland, trans. D. D. R. Owen (London, 1972).

The Song of Roland, trans. Dorothy L. Sayers (Harmondsworth, Middx, 1957).

William, Count of Orange: Four Old French Epics, ed. Glanville Price (London, 1975). This contains the *Crowning of Louis*, the *Waggon-Train of Nîmes*, the *Capture of Orange* and the *Song of William*.

SECTION 3: ROMANCES AND COURTLY LITERATURE

Chrétien de Troyes, *Arthurian Romances*, trans. W. W. Comfort (London, 1975). This includes *Erec*, *Cligès*, *Yvain* and *Lancelot*.

——, *Lancelot or the Knight of the Cart*, trans. W. Kibler (New York, 1981).

——, *Yvain or the Knight of the Lion*, trans. R. Cline (Athens, Georgia, 1976).

——, *Yvain, the Knight of the Lion*, trans. R. Ackerman and F. Locke (New York, 1971).

——, *Perceval: The Story of the Grail*, trans. N. Bryant (London, 1982).

——, *Perceval, or The Story of the Grail*, trans. Ruth Cline (Oxford, 1983).

——, *Erec and Enid*, trans. Carleton W. Carroll (New York, 1984).

——, *King William the Wanderer*, trans. W. G. Collingwood (New York, 1976).

Sir Gawain and the Lady of Lys, trans. Jessie L. Weston (London, 1907). This is translated from Wauchier de Danain's *Continuation of Chrétien's Perceval*.

Sir Lancelot of the Lake, trans. Lucy Allen Paton, Broadway Medieval Library (London, 1929). This includes parts of the *Prose Lancelot*, the *Quest* and the *Mort Artu*.

The High History of the Holy Grail, trans. Sebastian Evans (London, 1912). This is translated from *Perlesvaus*.

253

The Romance of Perceval in Prose, trans. Dell Skeels (Seattle, 1961). This is translated from the *Didot-Perceval*.

The Quest of the Holy Grail, trans. Pauline Matarasso (Harmondsworth, Middx, 1969). This is translated from the prose *Queste del Saint Graal*.

The Death of King Arthur, trans. James Cable (Harmondsworth, Middx, 1971). This is translated from the prose *Mort Artu*.

Beroul, *The Romance of Tristan*, trans. Alan S. Fedrick (Harmondsworth, Middx, 1970).

Thomas, *Tristran*, in Gottfried von Strassburg, *Tristan*, trans. A. T. Hatto (Harmondsworth, Middx, 1960).

Aucassin and Nicolette and Other Tales, trans. Pauline Matarasso (Harmondsworth, Middx, 1971). This includes the *Lay of the Reflection*, the *Dapple Grey Palfrey*, the *Count of Ponthieu's Daughter* and the *Châtelaine of Vergy*.

Aucassin and Nicolette and Other Medieval Romances, trans. Eugene Mason (London, 1910). This includes fifteen other stories ranging from romance to miracles of the Virgin.

Marie de France, *Medieval Fables*, trans. Jeanette Beer (Limpsfield, 1981).

Marie de France, *Lays*, trans. Eugene Mason (London, 1966). This includes also four other lays. (Originally entitled *French Medieval Romances*.)

Guillaume de Lorris and Jean de Meung, *The Romance of the Rose*, trans. Charles Dahlberg (Princeton UP, 1971).

The Comedy of Eros: Medieval French Guides to the Art of Love, trans. Norman R. Shapiro (Illinois, 1971). This includes three versions of *Ovid*, a poem on Courtesy and selections from Robert de Blois's *Advice to Women*.

SECTION 4: FABLIAUX, SATIRE AND BOURGEOIS LITERATURE

Fabliaux: several selections have been translated:

The Literary Context of Chaucer's Fabliaux, trans. Larry Benson and Theodore M. Andersson (Indianapolis and New York, 1971).

Gallic Salt, trans. Robert Harrison (University of California, 1974).

Fabliaux: Ribald Tales from the Old French, trans. Robert Hellman and Richard O'Gorman (New York, 1965).

The French Fabliau: The Berne Manuscript, trans. Raymond Eichmann and John DuVal (New York, 1984). This is the first segment of a complete translation of major *fabliau* manuscripts.

Medieval French Plays, trans. Richard Axton and John Stevens (Oxford, 1971). This includes *Le Jeu d'Adam*, *La Seinte Resureccion*, *Le Jeu de Saint Nicolas*, *Courtois d'Arras*, *Le Miracle de Théophile*, *Le Garçon et l'Aveugle*, *Le Jeu de la Feuillée* and *Le Jeu de Robin et Marion*.

Adam, trans. Lynette R. Muir (Leeds Literary and Philosophical Society, Leeds, 1970). This includes the prophet play which is omitted in *Medieval French Plays*, ed. Axton and Stevens.

Adam de la Halle: Lyrics and Melodies, trans. Deborah Hubbard Nelson (New York, 1984). This includes the music as well as the words.

Renard the Fox, trans. Patricia Terry (Cambridge, Mass., 1984).

SECTION 5: HISTORY AND GENERAL SUBJECTS

Only a few of the works in Chapter 5 have been translated, such as historical texts, but many are available in medieval English versions.

SECTION 6: RELIGIOUS LITERATURE

Miracles of the Virgin, trans. C. C. Swinton Bland, Broadway Medieval Library (London, 1928). The source used is a late Latin one but the collection includes many tales also found in French and is therefore listed here.

SECTION 7: FIFTEENTH-CENTURY DRAMA

The True Mystery of the Passion, trans. and adapted James Kirkup (London, 1962). It is translated from Greban's *Passion*. The scenes selected are all from the Holy Week section of the play.

Master Peter Pathelin, trans. Edwin Morgan (for the Medieval Players production of *Pathelin* (Glasgow, 1983).

The Pie and the Tart, trans. Jane Oakshott, in *Medieval Interludes*, ed. Neville Denny (London, 1972).

Scenes from the Fifteenth-Century Mystère du Siège d'Orléans, selected and trans. Joan Evans, text edited by P. Studer (Oxford, 1926).

SECTION 8: LITERATURE AFTER 1350 (EXCLUDING DRAMA)

Guillaume de Machaut, *The Judgement of the King of Bohemia*, trans. R. Barton Palmer (New York, 1984).

Christine de Pisan, *The Epistle of the Prison of Human Life*, trans. Josette Wisman (New York, 1984).

Christine de Pisan, *The Treasure of the City of Ladies or the Book of the Three Virtues*, trans. S. Lawson (Harmondsworth, Middx, 1985).

Christine de Pizan, *The Book of the City of Ladies*, trans. Earl Jeffrey Richards (London, 1983).

The History of Fulk Fitz-Warine, trans. Alice Kemp-Welch (King's Classics, London, 1904).

Antoine de la Sale, *Little John of Saintré*, trans. Irvine Gray, Broadway Medieval Library (London, 1931).

The Book of the Knight of the Tour Landry, modernised by G. S. Taylor from the Middle English translation (The Verona Society, London 1930).

The Goodman of Paris, trans. Eileen Power, Broadway Medieval Library (London, 1928).

François Villon, *The Poems*, trans. Galway Kinnell (Princeton UP, 1982).

Appendix IV: Bibliographical Index

The French titles of medieval works cited in the text and notes are listed here together with cross-references to the English/ short titles used. Most of the works are followed by a letter and numbers (e.g. B1234) which refer to the relevant entry in R. Bossuat, *Manuel bibliographique de la littérature française du moyen âge* (Melun, 1951, nos 1–6016; Supplément I, Paris, 1955, nos 6017–7109; Supplément II, Paris, 1961, nos 7110–8026; reprinted in one volume by Kraus, 1970). For works not in Bossuat, bibliographical references are given in the Index. No reference indicates there is no modern edition of that particular work.

To facilitate reference to Bossuat, I have generally followed his Index in the use of accents on some medieval titles and in the alphabetical ordering of authors' names; where there is an established English form of a name that has been used, otherwise the French original has been retained. Except for the medieval French translations, references to the books of the Bible and to works by Classical and patristic writers have not normally been indexed; entries are, however, included for recurrent themes, characters and genres, complementing the information provided by the Table of Contents, Appendix II and the cross-references in the body of the text.

The following abbreviations are used in the Index:

PMLA   *Publications of the Modern Language Association of America*
ZRP   *Zeitschrift für Romanische Philologie*

KING ALFRED'S COLLEGE
LIBRARY